The Gateway to Liberty:

THE CONSTITUTIONAL POWER

of

THE TENTH AMENDMENT

Archie P. Jones

AMERICAN VISION PRESS
POWDER SPRINGS, GEORGIA

The Gateway to Liberty:
The Constitutional Power of the Tenth Amendment
by Archie P. Jones

Copyright © 2010 by Archie P. Jones
Printed July 2010.

Published by:
   American Vision Press

   The American Vision, Inc.
   3150 Florence Road
   Powder Springs, Georgia 30127-5385
   www.AmericanVision.org • 1-800-628-9460

Printed in The United States of America.

Cover Design by Luis D. Lovelace
Interior Layout by Michael Minkoff, Jr.

ISBN13: 978-0-9826105-4-1

*To Jennie, who has done so much to help produce this book,
is so dedicated to the true principles of American government,
and so committed to the whole counsel of God.*

ARTICLE THE TENTH

THE POWERS NOT DELEGATED TO THE UNITED STATES BY THE CONSTITUTION OR PROHIBITED BY IT TO THE STATES, ARE RESERVED TO THE STATES RESPECTIVELY, OR TO THE PEOPLE.

CONTENTS

Preface

No amendment in our Bill of Rights is more deeply rooted in American history, politics, and government than our Tenth Amendment. Its roots are deep in the colonies' histories, in the framing and ratification of our first constitution, our Articles of Confederation, and in the framing and ratification of our Constitution and our Bill of Rights. They might be traced back to English history and the authority of self-governing entities in medieval law, and even to the form of civil government which God gave His people when they entered the Promised Land after their exodus from Egypt,[1] though that is beyond the scope of this work. It should be enough for us to know that the Tenth Amendment's protection of federalism—of each state's right to govern its own internal affairs except for those few areas of authority which the states delegated to our central government in the Constitution and those few powers which the states forbade to themselves in our fundamental law—was not an afterthought but an explicit reaffirmation of a principle that is absolutely fundamental to our constitutional system of civil government.

Without federalism there would have been no Constitution. Federalism is more than a protection of the lion's share of the states' traditional self-government. Its protection of the right of each state to govern itself is essential to liberty because it protects the people against the fallen nature of man which often produces incompetence, injustice, and tyranny in centralized government. From the facts that state governments too are run by fallen human beings and that state

---

1. E. C. Wines, *Commentaries on the Laws of the Ancient Hebrews* (Powder Springs, Georgia: American Vision, [1853] 2009), Book II, The Organic Law of the Hebrew State.

governments can and have enacted unjust laws it does not follow that centralized government is superior to federalism. By James Madison's own reckoning, federalism—"half" of our Constitution's system of separation of powers and checks and balances—provides a "double security to the rights of the people," a double security to all Americans' liberty. Because the nature of man is not changeable by man, nor by man's exercise of total or limited power through civil government, federalism is essential to the protection of liberty for future generations.

Because discerning opponents of the Constitution detected flaws in its design—defects which threatened federalism and thereby the rights and liberty of the states and all Americans—the Bill of Rights was added to our Constitution. This included the Tenth Amendment which provided explicit protection for federalism and the authority of the state governments against deceitful misinterpretation of our Constitution, usurpation of power from the states, concentration of power in our central government, and the destruction of Americans' liberty.

A Constitution intended to subvert and eventually replace federalism with centralized government would have been rejected with scorn as an enemy to the states' rights to govern themselves and to Americans' liberty.

Such a "Constitution" we now, in effect, have—thanks to more than a century and a half of deceit and force; modern man-centered philosophical, ethical, "scientific," social, political, legal, and economic thought; political opportunism; civil government-controlled education; unethical rhetoric; and the silence, cowardice, ignorance, or apostasy of the church. It is a Constitution honored only in speech, but perverted by academics and judges, circumvented by presidents, bypassed by bureaucracies, misrepresented by the news media, and ignored by Congress. Instead of restraining civil government, its clauses, perverted by politicians, have enabled our increasingly centralized, increasingly increasing government to do what the Anti-Federalist opponents of our original Constitution predicted it would do—and Federalist advocates of our Constitution's ratification denied it would do—to usurp power from the state governments, intrude the central government into every nook and cranny of state, local, and family and individual business, disestablish justice, and destroy liberty.

The causes of our predicament are complex and long-standing.
The cures extend beyond the realm of civil government and involve
deep, wide-ranging, long-range changes in a sufficient number of
Americans' thought and actions. But there are still actions we can take
if we want to reclaim the liberty which the framers and ratifiers of our
Constitution and Bill of Rights bequeathed to their posterity. One is to
recapture a knowledge of the original intentions of those great statesmen who gave us the Constitution and its great Bill of Rights. Another
is to make that knowledge the basis of our educational and political
action. A third is to take back our civil governments—local, state, and
national—and to do all that we can to ensure that our elected and appointed representatives in those governments work in terms of the
good and true intentions of the statesmen who gave us our Constitution and Bill of Rights.

No amendment is of more practical importance than our Tenth
Amendment for protecting what remains of our liberty and recover-
ing the huge percentage of liberty that previous generations, and we
ourselves, have surrendered to the Federal Leviathan. For our federal
system was and still is a system of separation of powers with checks
and balances between our national/central government and our states'
governments. Our state governments have powers which can be used
against central government usurpations. And our state and local government officials, not to mention our states' citizens, have means of
influencing the officials of our national government to obey the oaths
of office which all our elected and appointed officials take to uphold
our Constitution.

It is encouraging to see that more and more of our elected officials,
particularly at the state level, are realizing the importance of our Tenth
Amendment to the proper functioning of state government and its
function as the gateway to the preservation of our liberty. It is my hope
that this humble volume will help those who are on the front lines of
the great conflict between the advocates of arbitrary, unlimited government and limited, constitutional government; and that it will help
inform Americans of the historical, foundational, and essential importance of our Tenth Amendment to constitutional government, the rule
of law, and freedom for all Americans.

Thanks to Gary DeMar for encouraging me to write this book, for allowing various chapters of it to be published on his website, americanvision.com, and for publishing this finished product. Thanks to Brandon Vallorani for publishing several chapters on his website, *patriotdepot.com.* Thanks also to Michael Minkoff, Jr. for laboring through my prose and trying to make it comprehensible to the reader. Last, but certainly not least, thanks to my daughter Jennie, for her encouragement, her shepherding of this humble work through its various stages of growth, and her unfailing good humor.

I can think of no one else to justly blame for whatever errors are in this work than myself.

The Gateway to Liberty:

The Constitutional Power of The Tenth Amendment

1

The Liberty Amendment

No fundamental provision of the Constitution or the Bill of Rights is more neglected today—or more thoroughly violated—than the Tenth Amendment. One can see its violation in the teaching of American history and civics, legal theory, and what passes for "Constitutional Law," as well as in the everyday functioning and typical media analysis of American politics and government.

Our Constitution—as the very words of the Tenth Amendment make clear—was intended to be a document of delegated powers. The states that formed and ratified the Constitution were free and independent, having the characteristics of nations. As Raoul Berger stated after surveying the scholarly controversy about whether the nation or the states came first:

> In sum, the colonies, having severed their common allegiance to Great Britain, were sovereign and independent of each other. Lee's resolution of July 2, 1776, attests such independence, and it is confirmed by the Declaration of Independence signed on behalf of the thirteen separate States. That independence was explicitly safeguarded in the Articles of Confederation, which merely set up a "league," and it was further recognized in the peace treaty with Britain, signed on behalf of the thirteen individual states.[1]

These free and independent nations were Christian states with Christian constitutions, declarations of rights, or bills of rights, and

---

1. Raoul Berger, *Federalism: The Founders' Design* (Norman and London: University of Oklahoma Press, 1987), 47.

fundamentally Christian laws,[2] and they delegated—and manifestly intended to delegate—carefully restricted authority and powers to the central or national government created by the Constitution. By clear intention and unmistakable logic, they delegated only those powers stated in the Constitution—**and no more**. As stated in Article I, Section 10 of the Constitution, the states forbade themselves certain powers they had not already been granted, but retained all other previously established authority and powers.

The Constitution therefore is a reserved powers document. The powers which the states have neither forbidden to themselves in the Constitution nor delegated to the central government in the Constitution are "reserved to the States respectively, or to the people" that is, they are reserved to each individual state. The "people" mentioned here cannot have reference to the people of the nation as a whole, for that would mean that the reserved powers ultimately default to the central government, which would make the Tenth Amendment meaningless, unnecessary, and absurd. It is clear then that unless a state (either through its government or people) explicitly delegates certain powers to the central government *constitutionally*, these powers remain in the exclusive domain of each state's government and people.

Our neglected, abused, and violated Tenth Amendment is more than an amendment to our Constitution; it is the anchor and guarantee of federalism,[3] a fundamental principle insisted upon by the states whose representatives framed and ratified the Constitution. Our Constitution contains protections for the reserved powers of the several states imbedded within the very design of our governmental system, which has *federalism* at its core.

---

2. Archie P. Jones, *Christianity and Our State Constitutions, Declarations, and Bills of Rights, Parts I and II* (Marlborough, New Hampshire: Plymouth Rock Foundation, 1993). An excellent collection of the laws of the colonies before they became states is W. Keith Kavenagh, ed., *Foundations of Colonial America; A Documentary History*, 3 vols. (New York: The Confucian Press, [1973] 1980). Most of these laws, of course, were retained after independence.

3. "Federalism," simply, is the belief in and practice of *contractually limited government*, but it has resulted in, and become characterized by, the horizontal and vertical separation of powers between and among central/national and provincial governments with accompanying checks and balances between and among departments in those governments.

Congress, the most important branch of our central government, is composed of representatives elected from each state. The House of Representatives consists of local representatives from districts within states. The Senate consists of senators elected from each state in general. Originally, Senators were chosen by the Legislature of each state.[4] The President is elected by the votes of electors from each state: the Electoral College. The number of each state's electors is based upon the number of the state's representatives in the House of Representatives (which depends on the population of the state) and the number of United States senators a state has (an equal number for each state, for each state was originally equal as a nation and each state is considered equal, regardless of population, today). If the Electoral College cannot decide who shall be President, then the House of Representatives makes the choice, and each state, no matter how many representatives it may have, casts one, equal vote. Members of the judicial branch of our national government are appointed by the President, who is elected by votes from the states, and confirmed by the U.S. Senate, whose members are from their respective states, originally to be chosen by their respective state legislatures representing the people of their particular states.

Thus the respective states have representation in every branch of our national government, which representation should protect the states against usurpations of authority and power by the national government and shield the state's people from a tyrannical central government's encroachments on their rights and liberty. The Tenth Amendment supplements this protection by clearly limiting our central government and obligating it to honor the states' reserved powers and their right of self-government.

The Tenth Amendment protects the self-government of the people of each state by protecting the powers which the state has neither assigned to the central government nor forbidden to itself in the Constitution. It thus protects each state's authority, right, and freedom

---

4. Article I, Section 3 of the Constitution states: "The Senate of the United States shall be composed of two Senators from each State, chosen by the Legislature thereof, for six Years; and each Senator shall have one Vote." This constitutional provision was overturned with the passage of the Seventeenth Amendment.

to govern itself as its people and their representatives see fit (so long as they do not set up a non-republican form of civil government or violate the Constitution's prohibitions of certain powers to them). Our Tenth Amendment is thereby a key protector of the minority's rights and liberty, for the people of any state are but a minority of the people of the nation. It protects against abuses of power perpetrated by a national majority, a powerful minority, or a popular individual who may have seized the reins of power in the national government. The Tenth Amendment protects localism and local self-government against centralism—the theory and practice of top-down, unilateral government.

The Tenth Amendment does not represent an isolated idea in the Constitution; it is but an additional, explicit protection for federalism, and federalism is, as James Madison tells us in Federalist No. 51, an essential portion of the Constitution's system to secure the blessings of liberty. Federalism, Madison tells us, is a system of *separation of powers* and *checks and balances* between the central or national government and the state governments. This famous system was intended to protect liberty and justice by preventing the concentration of power, and consequent abuses and usurpations of power, in any one branch of the national government. The intent of federalism is to provide "a double security" to liberty. It is "double" because it supplements the separation of powers and the checks and balances of our central government with the separation of powers and checks and balances between the central government and the state governments to secure, i.e., *keep protected*, all the rights and liberties the Constitution and Bill of Rights originally intended to protect.

Federalism—not the phony "federalism" as redefined by "political scientists" and power-hungry politicians, but the separation of powers between a would-be all-powerful central government and our states—is more than a constitutional principle. Given the fallen nature of man, it is not time-bound but timeless this side of Heaven. It is essential to the protection of liberty and justice. The Tenth Amendment clearly intended to establish federalism as basic to both the interpretation of the Constitution and its application in constitutional law. That is why it has been known as the Liberty Amendment. No fundamental provision of the Constitution and the Bill of Rights needs more urgently to be restored to its rightful place in American political thought, constitutional law, and civil government, for its restoration is a necessary condition for the rekindling of justice and freedom in America.

2

Bulwark of Federalism— and of Liberty

Our Tenth Amendment was intended to be the guarantee and bulwark of the federalism inherent in the Constitution's design.[1] Some of the most basic characteristics of the Constitution, when unpacked, demonstrate that permanently delimiting the central government's powers was of preeminent importance to the framers of our Constitution.

Unlike the British constitution, our constitution was and is **a written document**. A written constitution is designed to protect justice and liberty (unless, like the constitution of the former Soviet Union, its intention is to present a false face to its citizens and other nations) because anyone can read for himself the structure of the governmental system, its various offices, how men are selected to serve in those offices and institutions, how long they may hold office, how they are to be replaced, the authority and powers of the civil government in general and of its institutions and offices, the limits on and prohibitions of authority (if any) of the civil government in general and of its offices and officials, who is to make the laws, who is to enforce laws, who is to adjudicate disputes under the law, and how the fundamental law may be changed. Without a clear knowledge of these things, those in power in civil government can claim and usurp authority and powers to which they are not entitled. By quick force or slow calculation and maneuver, they can discard the limits on their authority, increase their powers, and enable themselves to rule on the mere basis of their arbitrary will. A written constitution decreases this possibility by making the "rules for rulers" accessible to lesser magistrates and the citizenry.

---

1. The best scholarly work on federalism and what the courts have done to it is Raoul Berger, *Federalism: The Founders' Design*.

The Constitution also limits the authority of the central government and its officials by the fact that it is **a delegated-powers document**. The powers or authority which the Constitution places in the hands of the national government, in its three branches, and in the officials of those three branches are only those powers which the state governments have specifically *delegated*. These are powers which the states, or state governments—which asserted their independence in a Declaration and maintained said independence through war—rightly possessed, in principle, as equals with all other nations on earth. In our Constitution, these states, or the people of these states acting through their duly elected civil representatives, invested certain of *their* powers in the central government. They assigned only these powers to the national government and no more powers.

The Constitution is **an expressed-powers document**. The powers placed in the hands of the central government and its officials are only those stated expressly in the Constitution. The central government has—and was clearly intended to have—no more authority or powers. Expressed powers are stated powers. Powers which are *not stated* in an expressed-powers document are *not authorized* by those who have delegated powers to their civil government or its offices. If the states whose representatives framed and ratified the Constitution had intended the Constitution's central government to have other powers in addition to those stated in the Constitution they would have written those powers into the appropriate places in our Constitution. As Raoul Berger has said,

> Fearful of the greedy lust for ever more power, the Founders resorted to a written Constitution in order, Chief Justice Marshall stated, to "define and limit" the power they delegated, reflected in Jefferson's urgent admonition to bind the delegates "down from mischief by the chains of the Constitution." If it was to serve its purpose, the Constitution had to be "fixed," unalterable save by amendment, the more so because it expressed the consent of the people, who chose "to be governed,"

in the words of a prominent Founder, James Iredell, "under such and such principles. They have not chosen to be governed or promised to submit upon any other."[2]

The Constitution is also **a reserved-powers document**. The states consigned only certain powers and authority to the central government and its officials. Some other powers (stated in Article I, Section 10) the states prohibited to themselves. Yet the states retained all other powers—all powers which they had not delegated to the central government or forbidden to themselves in the Constitution. These powers are the reserved powers of the states, or state governments, or of the people of the states whose representatives established their own civil governments with their own distinctive constitutions (and in most cases also declarations of rights or bills of rights).

The Tenth Amendment was intended to be a written guarantee to each state and the people of each state that the Constitution is a delegated-powers document, an expressed-powers document, and particularly a reserved-powers document. It states explicitly that the states or the people of each state retain all of the states' reserved powers—all powers neither delegated by the states to the central government in the Constitution nor denied to the state governments in the Constitution.

Federalism is, and was intended to be, a legal and governmental arrangement in which the central or national government is authorized to exercise all powers delegated to it by the states, and the state governments are authorized to exercise all their reserved powers, i.e., all powers which they have neither assigned to the central government nor forbidden to themselves in the Constitution. These powers gave the state governments—and were manifestly intended to give the state governments—far, far more authority over the lives of the residents

---

2. *Federalism: The Founders' Design*, 10–12. Berger quotes Alpheus T. Mason's observation that "America was steeped in this distrustful philosophy long before it found embodiment in the Articles of Confederation and the Constitution" (10, n. 29). The sources of this "distrustful philosophy," of course, were the Christian doctrine of total depravity (that every aspect of man's being has been damaged by the Fall) and early Americans' knowledge of history, particularly classical history.

of each state than the central government was given over the lives of American citizens. As Madison said in Federalist No. 45:

> The powers delegated by the proposed Constitution to the federal government are few and defined. Those which are to remain in the State governments are numerous and indefinite. The former will be exercised principally on external objects, as war, peace, negotiation, and foreign commerce... The powers reserved to the several States will extend to all the objects which, in the ordinary course of affairs; concern the lives, liberties, and properties of the people, and the internal order, improvement, and prosperity of the State.

The Tenth Amendment was clearly intended to safeguard our federal system by making the governmental authority structure explicit—plainly stated for all to read and comprehend. The Tenth Amendment was meant to be a legal barrier to keep the central government within its area of authority, and it was also meant to keep the state governments within their boundaries, helping to prevent them from exercising powers which they had either forbidden to themselves in the Constitution or delegated to the central government. It was meant even more seriously, however, to prevent the central government from encroaching into the sphere of the states' reserved powers. It was meant to protect each state's right to govern its own internal affairs without interference from the national/central government. It was meant to protect the liberty of the people of each state by protecting each state against both partial and systemic intrusion by our central government.

But the Tenth Amendment was not intended merely to be a paper bulwark; it was intended to be a practical as well as a legal fortification that would encourage and enable the people and the civil governments of the several states to resist all central government usurpation as well as to legally authorize such defensive action. The Tenth Amendment put the responsibility for the defense of liberty in the hands of the people and individual states, thus to stimulate collective resistance to central government usurpation, injustice, and tyranny.

Today when we are faced with the escalating threat of a central government grown monstrous by many decades of unchecked usurpation—and by many decades of academic, journalistic, and educational justification, obfuscation, and praise of such usurpation—it is essential to recover an appreciation of the Tenth Amendment's power to preserve the justice and liberty of Americans in every state. If we are to preserve what little liberty we have left and to recover our lost liberty we must presently utilize that great bulwark which the authors and ratifiers of the Bill of Rights bequeathed to us.

3

A Bulwark Against Centralism

A key reason why our Tenth Amendment reserved to the several states all powers which they had neither assigned to the national government nor forbidden to themselves in the Constitution is that the Tenth Amendment was—and is—intended to be a bulwark against what Americans of the day called "centralism." By centralism they meant the concentration of authority and power in a central government resulting in top-down rule by the central government. "Centralism" does not have primary reference to a *form* of civil government; it is a political *philosophy* which requires authority to be concentrated in, and administered by, a central government, a governmental system in which every civil government institution is an administrative subdivision of a centralized authority structure.

The doctrine of centralism springs from fallen man's desire for power over his fellow man. It may also spring from a false religious-philosophy which requires concentration of political power in order to impose the will of a ruler, an elite, or the majority upon everyone else in society. In its modern forms, it purposes to impose some rationalistic, pseudo-scientific, or irrationalistic social, economic, and political ideal on society (e.g., to make everyone socially, economically, and politically equal; to legislate and enforce either the will of a "Leader," or "the majority," or a deputized minority, or the nation, or a favored race on the rest of society or mankind; to "solve the problems" of mankind, etc.).

Centralism vs. God's Government

Centralism is opposed to the biblical pattern of civil government— and to liberty. In the Creation Mandate (Genesis 1:26–28), God commanded our first ancestors to be fruitful and multiply and fill the earth

15

to have dominion over the earth and its creatures, under Him. The Creation Mandate has never been revoked, and is still mandatory for man. It requires that man walk in faith in God and obedience to His commandments. It requires man to be free to act to obey God's commission to man—and requires civil governments to protect that freedom under God's law. Since the Fall and God's institution of civil governments, this implies multiple civil governments for men whose extended families are spread throughout the earth.

Man's rebellion against God at the Tower of Babel was an attempt to establish a centralized, tyrannical one-world government based on the arbitrary word and law of man. God thwarted that manifestation of centralism and dispersed mankind throughout the world. Yet sinful man persisted in establishing centralized governments. Centralized government in the form of monarchy was typical in antiquity, but most ancient "pagan" aristocracies or oligarchies, democracies, and republics were centralized as well—and under none was there the degree of individual freedom which God's people had under God's law.

God freed His chosen people Israel from Egyptian centralized tyranny. Upon bringing them into the Promised Land He gave them the best form of civil government, a federal, republican form of civil government. He gave them a strong central, but not *centralized*, government so they could unite to fight against their enemies, but He also gave them largely self-governing independent jurisdictions: the tribal republics, with their own legislatures and judges, and largely self-governed cities.[1] And with that federal republic He gave them liberty and prosperity under His law—so long as they maintained faith in Him and obedience to His commandments (Leviticus 26; Deuteronomy 8; 28).

When His people turned against His rule over them, they turned to centralized government in the form of monarchy—like the heathen peoples around them. Though God warned them that their kings would become tyrants, violating His laws and abridging their liberty, they insisted upon monarchial centralism and got exactly what God had foretold (1 Samuel 8). The biblical pattern of civil government was

---

1. See E. C. Wines, *Commentaries on the Laws of the Ancient Hebrews; with An Introductory Essay on Civil Society and Government* (Philadelphia: Presbyterian Board of Publication, 1853). This book was reprinted by American Vision, Powder Springs, Georgia in 2009.

designed to maximize justice and liberty. It was tailored to maximize God's providentially created diversity of society, to keep the civil governments which affected the people closest to the people's influence, and to produce the greatest probability of keeping the people free under God's holy, just law.

Centralism in all forms opposes both the biblical form of civil government and the law of God which accompanied that form of government, so that rulers can impose their will upon all arbitrarily, whether through a rationalistic ideal, a pseudo-scientific delusion, an egalitarian dream, or an irrationalist[2] concept. Ultimately, power-hungry government desires to thumb its nose at the Ruler of the Nations.

American Federalism vs. Centralism

American federalism grew largely out of the history of the peoples of the colonies which became the free and independent states whose representatives framed our Articles of Confederation and then radically modified that document to make it our Constitution. But American federalism also grew out of American religion and culture. The people of those states were overwhelmingly Protestant Christians greatly influenced by the Protestant Reformation's emphasis on the Bible as the only infallible rule of faith and practice and Calvinism's application of the Bible and Christian versions of "natural law" to ethics, government, and law.[3] Their states were Christian states with Christian constitutions, declarations of rights or bills of rights, and laws. Their civil governments,

---

2. Irrationalism is the denial that there is any rational Being, and therefore any rationally-known laws or principles in terms of whom or which reality can be comprehended and man can have objective, universally valid ethical standards. Modern man-centered thought has "progressed" from rationalism to irrationalism, or irrationality. See C. Gregg Singer, *From Rationalism to Irrationality: The Decline of the Western Mind from the Renaissance to the Present* (Phillipsburg, New Jersey: Presbyterian and Reformed Publishing Co., 1979). An "irrationalist concept" is an idea or pseudo-imperative based upon and derived from irrationalist thought—as in National Socialism, fascism, Marxism, Communism, historicism, Existentialism, individualistic and collectivistic Social Darwinism, Pragmatism, atheism, and evolutionist environmentalism.

3. Supporting the Protestant Reformation and Calvinism, of course, were centuries of Christian ethical, legal, and political thought.

constitutions, and declarations were designed (though not necessarily well-designed) to secure liberty and justice to themselves and their posterity. Their governments were republican both because of their people's histories and because of their people's religion and cultures. They demanded that the new Constitution protect and preserve the authority of those largely independent republican governments—against centralism—for religious and cultural reasons as well as for diverse reasons of individual and collective self-interest and their varied traditions of state self-government.

The Framers and Ratifiers[4] of our Constitution and our Bill of Rights, not yet having seen the horrors of modern man-centered political rationalism and irrationalism, and focusing their attention on the particular form and powers of our civil government, were more concerned with men's desire for power than with men's politico-religious philosophies—what Gary North calls power religions. (That was one of their shortcomings as political thinkers.) But their opposition to centralism gave our Constitution federalism, and federalism gave us—and still gives us—a bulwark against centralism and a means of opposing both power religions and power-hungry politicians.

---

4. Throughout this work the popular term "Founders" or "Founding Fathers" is avoided because many of these statesmen, particularly in the South, saw themselves as seeking to frame a constitution of civil government for an already-established society with a deep-rooted governmental and legal tradition, not as founding something new. They sought to preserve in and through the Union formed by the Constitution an existing order, not to create something wholly new. The terms "Framers" and "Ratifiers," or "Framers and Ratifiers," are used to emphasize the reality that our Constitution was framed by one group of men but had to be ratified by other groups of men—state by state—without whose assent we would have had no constitution. Though it may be strange, and somewhat odd, to the reader to repeatedly encounter the phrase "Framers and Ratifiers," this writer has used that phrase consistently to make the point that the intentions behind our Constitution include the dynamics of the ratification debates and politics, as well as the opinions of those participants in the ratification debates who either advocated, opposed, or were undecided concerning the proposed Constitution.

4

A Double Security to the Rights of the People

The framers of our Constitution had a biblical understanding—well buttressed by their knowledge of history—of the fallen nature of man. They were not deceived by Locke's opinions that man's mind is a "blank slate" at birth and man a mere product of the influences of his environment. Nor were they gullible enough to believe Rousseau and the Romantic notion that man is naturally good. Hence—unlike our "liberals," Marxists, and other kindred spirits—they did not want a constitution with no limits on the power of civil government, nor one which could rightly be "reinterpreted" to allow a supposed group of "wise men" in power to exercise total power in order to transform or perfect our society.

Although there are many written indications of the Framers' realistic comprehension of the fallen nature of all men, including civil government officials, perhaps James Madison said it best in Federalist No. 51:

> ...what is government itself, but the greatest of all reflections on human nature? If men were angels, no government would be necessary. If angels were to govern men, neither external nor internal controls on government would be necessary. In framing a government which is to be administered by men over men, the great difficulty lies in this: you must first enable the government to control the governed; and in the next place oblige it to control itself.

Upon the foundation of this true view of man they gave themselves, and intended to give their posterity, a constitution which would create the greatest probability of preserving and protecting the people's rights and liberty—not only against foreign powers but also against the internal machinations of fallen civil government officials.

The Framers desired to protect the rights and liberties of both the majority and the minority. As Federalist No. 10 makes so clear, both majorities and minorities can easily and naturally become "factions," that factions can take many forms, and that factions violate the common good and others' rights, threaten justice, menace liberty, and imperil popular government itself.

That is why they gave us a constitutional system with carefully allotted—and judiciously limited—powers, a system deliberately shaped to represent and protect both majorities and minorities against each other. Thus, as Paul Eidelberg has explained in *The Philosophy of the American Constitution* and *A Discourse on Statesmanship: The Design and Transformation of the American Polity*, the Framers gave us neither an oligarchy nor a democracy but a mixed regime (classically the best practical form of civil government), a civil government having democratic, aristocratic (or at worst oligarchic), and monarchial attributes to take advantage of the best features of each of the basic forms of civil government: to protect justice and liberty for all the people— both majorities and minorities. Thus the House of Representatives was given democratic characteristics; the Senate was designed to be somewhat aristocratic; the judiciary was meant to be very aristocratic; and the Presidency was given certain monarchial features.

The Framers divided the basic functions of civil government—legislative, executive, and judicial— among the three branches of our central government because they knew what temptations to the abuse of power come upon men who have too much power. Their biblical heritage taught them the superiority of republican government with diverse governmental institutions, and history taught them the value of divisions of authority and power among governmental institutions, not just on paper, but in reality.

They sought particularly to protect against a gradual concentration of powers in the hands of any one branch of government. To do this they designed our government's three branches to keep each other "in their proper places." They sought to give each department a will of its own, and so to make the members of each "have as little agency as possible in the appointment of the others." Beyond this they tried to give those of each department "the necessary constitutional means and personal motives to resist encroachments of the others," making ambition counteract ambition, and connecting "the interest of the man" with "the constitutional rights of the place" so that "the private interest of every individual may be a sentinel over the public rights."

They knew that it is impossible to give each branch of government an equal power of self-defense, but sought to give each department partial control over the others. Since in republican governments the legislature "necessarily predominates," they divided our national legislature into two "houses," giving each "different modes of election and different principles of action": the House being more democratic (but only *more* democratic, not thoroughly democratic), the Senate more aristocratic (but not thoroughly aristocratic). They strengthened the executive by giving the President a veto over legislation passed by both houses but kept the President from having too much power by giving Congress the ability to override a president's veto.

The separation of powers applied mainly to the legislature and the executive. The federal judiciary (intended to be "the least dangerous branch" because it was the least powerful branch of the national government) were partly exempted because of the particular qualifications required of judges and because of the essentially lifetime tenure of the judges. Yet they gave Congress checks on federal judges in Article III of the Constitution, which gives Congress the authority, for example, to limit the appellate jurisdiction of the federal courts.

The complex system of separation of powers in our national or central government was the Constitution's first functional security to liberty, to the rights of the people. But it was only the first. The Framers were well aware that the people of each state were minorities too, and that they needed—and demanded—protection against a faction gaining control of the national government. They designed our governmental system to protect the rights and liberty of the people of the states. A fundamental part of that design was federalism. The preservation of the states made the American Union "a confederate republic," a "compound republic," a republic of republics, each of which had its own system of separation of powers and accompanying checks and balances among its branches of government.

The Framers intended federalism to work for liberty in two basic ways. The "extended republic" of the United States, by including many republics and far more territory, would tend to make it harder for potential majority factions to work together to oppress minorities. As Madison explained in Federalist No. 51,

> In the compound republic of America, the power sur-
> rendered by the people is first divided between two
> distinct governments, and then the portion allotted to
> each subdivided among distinct and separate depart-
> ments. Hence a double security arises to the rights
> of the people. The different governments will control
> each other, at the same time that each will be con-
> trolled by itself.

The influence of federalism on the central government gave some protection to the states, for the states are represented according to their population in the House of Representatives, and the states' leg-islatures originally controlled the election of U. S. senators and the states are equally represented as states in the Senate. And the Sen-ate—originally elected by the states' legislatures—has the power to block the President's nominees to the federal courts and the various departments of the executive branch of our national government. The states' representation in both houses of Congress, the most important and powerful branch of our central government, of course, enables the respective states to influence the laws of the nation and to protect themselves.

Even this sketch of our constitutional system makes it clear that federalism was, and was intended to be, absolutely fundamental and essential to the Framers' reasoned and biblically legitimate desire to *institutionally* secure the blessings of liberty to themselves and their posterity—who we are—by designing our system of government to protect against the political manifestations of the sinful nature of man.

5

A Guarantee of the Covenant Between
The States and The Central Government

The Tenth Amendment is a guarantee of the covenant between the states whose representatives framed and ratified the Constitution and the new central government created by the Constitution. The Constitution is the covenant which contains that solemn agreement.

The agreement between the several states and the new central government created by the Constitution was really much more than a "deal" (or set of deals), as it has sometimes been called. For those civil governments were governments which considered themselves under God's authority, subject to His providential blessings or chastisements for their faithful obedience or unfaithful disobedience to His eternal standards of rightness and justice. Really, the Constitution was a compact between Christian states—which had Christian constitutions, declarations, and laws—and the new Christian central government which they had authorized with the Constitution, for the Constitution was a Christian document. In that compact the states agreed to abide by the terms of the Constitution and the officials of the new central government, by taking their oaths of office, also agreed to abide by the terms of the Constitution.

As Madison says in Federalist 39, the foundation on which the Constitution was established was "the assent and ratification of the people of America...not as individuals composing one entire nation, but as composing the distinct and independent States to which they respectively belong. It is to be the assent and ratification of the several States, derived from the supreme authority in each State,—the authority of the people themselves." And "Each State, in ratifying the Constitution, is considered as a sovereign body, independent of all others, and only to be bound by its own voluntary act."

That covenant was also a covenant among the states, for every state which originally ratified the Constitution and joined the Union understood the Constitution's intended meaning and went through an official deliberative process to consider the characteristics of the Constitution to determine whether or not it would join the other states—nations which had declared and won their independence from Britain—in Union under the Constitution. Each state ratified the Constitution as a state, not as an administrative subdivision of America as a whole, nor as a mere percentage of the populace of America. Each state ratified with a full knowledge of its authority as a state, of the powers which it and its sister nations agreed to forbid to themselves, the powers which it and its sister states agreed to delegate to the central government, and the powers which it and its sister states agreed to reserve to themselves respectively. In ratifying our Constitution each state agreed with each other state to abide by the terms of the covenant which united them.

Without that "deal" between—and among—the several states and the new, stronger central government which the Constitution created there would have been no Constitution. Without that agreement there would have been no means of the people of the several states and of the Union to enjoy the results of the improvements which the new Constitution had made on the design of the Articles of Confederation. For although the sentiment of nationalism was so strong and awareness of the weakness of their state was so acute that some of the representatives of the smaller states were willing to speak of surrendering the "sovereignty" (authority over its own affairs) of their state to secure a national government strong enough to protect them, such views were rejected by most of the framers and enactors of our Constitution. Hence the Constitution incorporated diverse protections for the authority of the states to govern themselves in most things, and diverse means by which the states could prevent or resist encroachments on their authority by the central government.

The nature of the agreement among the states and between the states and the central or national government in our Constitution is at least the following:

1. The central/national government is limited—very limited—in its authority and powers.

2. The central government has only the authority, only those powers, delegated to it by the states in the Constitution.

3. Although the central/national government has certain authority and powers over constitutionally specified areas of national concern, the central government does not have authority or powers over everything which may be said to be of national concern or importance, for the states have only delegated certain powers to the central government. As Madison explained in Federalist 39, "...the proposed government cannot be deemed a national one; since its jurisdiction extends to certain enumerated objects only, and leaves to the several States a residuary and inviolable sovereignty over all other objects."

4. The central government is not the sole determiner of its own authority, for the state governments and the people of those states have the right and duty to determine the meaning of the Constitution, the nature and extent of the central government's authority and powers, and the nature and extent of the powers of their respective state's government.

5. The state governments are somewhat limited in their authority and powers. They are limited in two ways. First, they have delegated some of their authority or powers—the powers of nations equal in principle to the authority and powers of any and all nations on earth, for they were free and independent nations after they won their independence from Great Britain—to the new central government which their representatives framed and ratified with the Constitution which replaced the Articles of Confederation. Second, they have forbidden themselves certain other powers—as stated in the Constitution.

6. Although the state governments have denied them-
    selves certain powers in the Constitution and as-
    signed to the central government certain other pow-
    ers in that document, the state governments retain
    all other powers of "sovereign" states or nations: all
    other powers of self-governing nations.

7. The authority and powers retained by the several
    states, by the civil government of each state or the
    people of each state, are—and should be—far greater
    than those of the central government in the degree
    to which the states' governments touch the lives of
    the people of their respective states. For the states
    have only delegated certain powers over interna-
    tional relations and specific national concerns to the
    central government—and have retained nearly all
    other powers over their own domestic affairs.

8. Thus each state is to be, and remain, a self-governing
    entity controlling its own internal affairs. Humanly
    speaking, concerning its own internal affairs, each
    state is under the authority of its own people and con-
    stitution, and is to be governed by its own republican
    government in accordance with its own constitution,
    bill of rights or declaration of rights, and laws.

9. The central government may only interfere with the
    legislative, executive, and judicial action of a state in
    the areas permitted by the Constitution. The central
    government may not interfere with the legislative,
    executive, and judicial action of any state in any area
    not permitted by the Constitution.

10. The Constitution of the United States does not speak
    clearly about who has the ultimate authority to inter-
    pret the meaning of the Constitution. It does not say
    that the officials or institutions of the central govern-
    ment have greater authority or a greater duty than
    the officials or institutions of the state governments

in interpreting the meaning of the Constitution. In fact, the Constitution requires the officials of the states' governments—and ultimately the people of the states—to interpret the meaning of the Constitution in order to make the Constitution's system of separation of powers and checks and balances work. For federalism, as Madison tells us in Federalist 51, is a system of separation of powers and checks and balances between the states and the central government that gives us "a double security to the rights of the people." Thus the people of the several states and their elected representatives have a constitutional duty to interpret the Constitution in order to protect their own rights and liberty against injustice or tyranny emanating from the central government.

These things can be seen by (1) a careful reading of the Constitution, (2) the debates over the ratification of the Constitution, (3) the discussions of the relationship between the central government and the state governments in *The Federalist*, (4) "Publius's" (the pen name of the authors of *The Federalist*) repeated designation of the Constitution's form of government as a "confederate republic," not simply a republic, and (5) the attitudes of early Americans and their representatives toward their states, their states' rights or authority, and the Union.

The purpose of the Tenth Amendment was to guarantee the preservation of the terms of the compact among the states—and among the peoples of the states—and the compact between the states and the central government by making the basic terms of that twofold covenant specific.

Attempts to weaken, undermine, circumvent, or effectively nullify the Tenth Amendment have been and are attempts to destroy the original compact among the states whose representatives formed the Union and the original covenant between the peoples of the several states and the people of the Union. They also have been and are efforts to destroy the covenant between the states and the central government in order to augment the authority of the central government through the usurpation of each state's authority and power. These attempts are efforts to destroy the advantages of federalism, the liberty and the rights of the people of the States and of the Union which the Tenth Amendment was intended to protect.

6

The Tenth Amendment and The War for Independence

Our Tenth Amendment developed naturally from our War for Independence. As Robert Allen Rutland noted, "the American Revolution had its seeds in the Puritan Revolt of English forbears, with the avowed goal of giving citizens the freedoms won a century earlier in the mother country."[1] Our "Revolution," or War for Independence, did not spring from "Enlightenment" rationalism, but from Christianity.[2] Unlike the French Revolution and the modern revolutions which have followed in the train of that gory humanistic upheaval, it was not an attempt to overthrow the old religious, legal and social order or to give the people of the colonies something new, but rather to give them "that which they had formerly possessed."[3]

What the people of the colonies had formerly possessed were their God-given, long-held, legal rights, their individual liberty, and their corporate liberty to govern themselves as independent political units. What the people of the colonies sought was the restoration of their God-given, providentially-established and inherited legal rights and liberty and the restoration or continuation of their respective colonies'

---

1. Robert Allen Rutland, *The Birth of the Bill of Rights 1776-1791* (New York: Collier Books, 1962), p. 13.

2. Archie P. Jones, "The Christian Roots of the War for Independence," *The Journal of Christian Reconstruction* 3:1 (Summer 1976), 6–51.

3. *The Birth of the Bill of Rights,* p. 13. On this point see also Rousas John Rushdoony, "The Myth of an American Enlightenment," *The Journal of Christian Reconstruction,* Vol. III, No. 1 (Summer, 1976), 69-73; J. Murray Murdoch, "1776: Revolution or War for Independence?", *The Journal of Christian Reconstruction,* Vol. III, No.1 (Summer, 1976), 74-88; and Gary North, "The Declaration as a Conservative Document," *The Journal of Christian Reconstruction,* Vol. III, No. 1 (Summer, 1976), 94-115.

ability to govern themselves as independent states. What their "Unanimous Declaration...," better known as the Declaration of Independence, claimed for them was:

> ...That these United Colonies are, and of Right ought to be Free and Independent States; that they are Absolved from all Allegiance to the British Crown, and that all political connection between them and the State of Great Britain, is and ought to be totally dissolved; and that as Free and Independent States, they have full Power to levy War, conclude Peace, contract Alliances, establish Commerce, and to do all other Acts and Things which Independent States may of right do.

Contrary to Lincoln's crafty claim in the Gettysburg Address, they did not seek to bring forth, nor did the success of their arms bring forth, "a new nation." Obviously, by the plain words of their Declaration they sought to bring forth, and did bring forth, thirteen new nations: the states whose representatives signed the Declaration—and signed it not as unconnected individuals but grouped together as representatives of their respective states. In the ultimate paragraph of the Declaration they forthrightly claimed for their respective states all the authority, all the powers to which any state or nation has a moral right.

From the outset of the long military struggle[4] by which they won their independence the people of our thirteen original states planned, organized, and conducted their resistance to British misrule as individual states. Yes, they did share information and coordinate efforts by committees of correspondence between and among states. And yes, they did form a Continental Congress to give themselves a more or less united government. And yes, that Continental Congress did establish, equip, and oversee a Continental Army. But the colonies' initial political and diplomatic resistance was through their own colonial governments, and their initial military resistance was by means of their respective colonies' militias. The

---

4. Actually it was only a comparatively long military struggle. The Dutch fought for nearly 80 years to gain their independence from Spain, and the Spanish fought for nearly 800 years to gain their independence from the Moors.

colonies' militias continued to be a vital part of their resistance through-out the war. At the beginning of the war the colonies' or states' militias outnumbered their troops in the Continental Army. In 1776 and 1777 their forces were about equal to the Continentals. From 1778 on, with some ups and downs, the Continentals outnumbered the states' militias.[5]

The militias pre-existed the war, of course. They had fought in previous conflicts: King Philip's War, the French and Indian Wars, and various Indian raids. In the South, especially in the Carolinas and Georgia, the system of mounted patrols to protect against slave uprisings gave the militia of these states a trained force of mounted musketeers.[6] The militia was sometimes divided into specialized units; Boston's militia included cadets, grenadiers, infantry, and artillery units.[7] In New England some of the militia units were amphibious. New England's famous Minutemen were a special organization within the states' militias.[8] Though the training, discipline, and effectiveness of the militia units varied widely and were generally inferior to what that of the Continental troops came to be, they progressed from disparate modes of drill and diverse weapons to fairly standardized drill and weapons, and improved their combat effectiveness.[9] Localism characterized the outlook of many militia members: they wanted to serve with men from their own locality.[10] When the colonies converted their local militias into armies, these were made the armies of their respective states.[11] At the state level, a similar *esprit de corps* generated by state solidarity prevailed, which is not surprising, for Americans' chief attachment then, and for long thereafter, was to their respective states.

---

5.   Edward E. Hale, "The Naval History of the American Revolution," in Justin Windsor, ed., *The American Revolution: A Narrative, Critical and Bibliographical History* (New York: Land's End Press, 1972), 588.

6.   Bruce Lancaster, *From Lexington to Liberty: The Story of the American Revolution* (Garden City, New York: Doubleday & Company, Inc., 1955), 74-75.

7.   Ibid., 59–60; 72-78.

8.   Ibid., 77; 70–80.

9.   Ibid., 87.

10.   Ibid., 121.

11.   Lancaster, *From Lexington to Liberty*, 122-123.

The militia did not like holding positions against possible attacks. They were far more responsive to actual attacks on their localities or states, and the more immediate and greater the danger the more quickly they responded and the greater the number of them who mustered for duty.[12] The militia had the chief duty of defending their states against external and internal threats. They converged quickly where the British or the Tories threatened, provided the first line of defense in all the states, harassed the invaders or raiders, raided the Tories and defended against Tory raids, defended the new state governments, suppressed the Tories, shielded Washington's army from the British forces, and were a main source of manpower for the Continental army.[13] Militia units answered to local, state, and Continental officers. The state governments had an important part in the war. They were supreme over their state militia, and Washington was careful to work through the state governments when he needed troops.[14]

Even under the Articles of Confederation, the central government had authority only to declare war and negotiate peace, not the authority to impose taxes on the states to finance the war. Congress could only *request* money from the states, it could not *require* money from them. Scheer and Rankin have summarized well the primacy of the states in the conduct of the war:

> Everywhere the states were neglecting the needs of the Continental Army in favor of those of their own militia, and the Congress could not force them to meet their army quotas. States maintained their own armies, navies, and boards of war. They competed with each other for materiel and raided each other for manpower...Each state issued letters of marque and reprisal to privateers.[15]

---

12. Mark V. Kwasny, *Washington's Partisan War, 1775-1783* (Kent, Ohio & London: The Kent State University Press, 1996), 185-186.

13. Ibid., 329-332.

14. Ibid., 333.

15. George F. Scheer and Hugh F. Rankin, *Rebels and Redcoats* (New York: World Publishing, 1972), 355-356.

In 1778 the states were told to provide clothing, arms, and ammunition to their own troops in the Continental Army.[16] Such attitudes and policies grew out of and fostered state-centered localism: they were inimical to the centralization of governmental authority.

Although the necessity of defending their states against raids and invasions led national and state leaders to work closely together throughout the war, fear of a regular, standing army—a manifestation of state-centered localism—continued throughout the war and the revolutionary period.[17] Each state's respective traditions concerning a national army grew out of their citizens' military service during the war and contributed to the states' fear of an excessively powerful national government—and a desire to be able to protect themselves against any such government. This quite rational fear—in light of human nature and history—is manifest in the Articles of Confederation, our first constitution, as well as in the federalism of our current Constitution, which exhibits the justified fear the Anti-Federalists had of an oppressive central government.

Our Tenth Amendment was a product of the colonial, and eventually state, militia traditions developed before and during our War for Independence, but it also gained impetus from a rational, experience-based fear of a tyrannical national government exercising menacingly powerful military capabilities (the States had recently gained a costly independence from just such a power). Our Tenth Amendment was meant to help protect the rights of the several states to govern themselves, free from unconstitutional intrusion and usurpation by the national government. It was meant to help the states protect themselves politically. It was also meant to help the states protect themselves militarily, if,—God forbid!—it ever came to that. It would accomplish this by clearly stating the separation of powers which is the essence of federalism; by affirming the limited-powers, expressed-powers nature of the central government; by emphasizing the states' retention of their reserved powers; and by implying the right of the states to act in defense of those powers if the central government should threaten them. Our states fought a war to gain their independence. They

16. Ibid., 356.
17. Kwasny, 335.

framed our Articles of Confederation to help retain their independence. They framed and ratified our Constitution to retain the great majority of their independence in our federal system. They ratified our Bill of Rights and its Tenth Amendment to both protect that measure of independence and to remind future Americans of the importance of preserving it.

7

The Tenth Amendment and Early State Constitutions

Our early state constitutions were our first constitutions. They were the fundamental laws of their states, in most states replacing the colonial charters. (Connecticut retained its colonial charter as its constitution until 1818; Rhode Island, until 1842.) They grew out of more than 140 years of their separate histories which gave them distinctly different, deeply rooted cultural and governmental traditions. They were products of the collective world-views and values, the histories and corporate identities of the people of each of our states which were striving to win their independence, or had won their independence, from Great Britain.

These state constitutions established and defined the institutions of civil government for each state. They defined the powers of civil government for their respective states, and placed legal limits on the authority and powers of civil government's institutions, offices, and officials. Through these means and the formation of declarations of rights or bills of rights they placed legal limits on the kinds of laws each state government (and its legal "creatures," the local governments) could enact.

These constitutions were based upon the colonial charters which they replaced and on the colonists' understanding and valuation of the English Constitution and its principle of the right of resistance against violations of that Constitution.[1] As Willi Paul Adams, the leading authority on our early state constitutions said,

---

1. M.E. Bradford, *Original Intentions: On the Making and Ratification of the United States Constitution* (Athens and London: The University of Georgia Press, 1993), p. 26.

> The central role played by British constitutionalism
> in justifying colonial resistance was carried over into
> American thinking when the colonies began writing
> their own in 1776. The basic premise of the colonists'
> argument was the political order created in 1688 [the
> Glorious Revolution], though formulated only in
> statutes [which appealed to other statutes, petitions,
> rulings, and charters], could not be changed, even
> by a majority decision in Parliament approved by the
> Crown. This English Constitution, the colonists ar-
> gued, was a permanent code to which the stewards of
> government power—the King and Parliament—were
> subject and that they had no authority to alter.[2]

These early American constitutions, with their declarations or
bills of rights, were Christian documents—some more manifestly so
than others. They honored God, recognizing His existence and stating (some more fully than others) certain truths about His nature:
Almighty, Creator, Lord, Governor of the Universe, Savior, Inspirer
of the Scriptures of the Old and New Testaments, and the like. These
are Christian affirmations, not products of eighteenth-century Deism,
much less of "religious neutrality." Many of these declarations implied
that the people of the given state were in a covenantal relationship
with God: in their recognition of Him as the "Governor of the Universe," the "Great Legislator of the Universe," and their recognition of
His divine providence. This covenantal relationship is particularly clear
in their numerous statements—reminiscent of Deuteronomy 8, 28, and
Leviticus 26—of the necessity of "religion," Christianity, to the preservation of virtue in the people and of the necessity of virtue for the
preservation of liberty. They spoke of "rights," "natural rights," and "the
law of nature," but the context of these statements made it clear that
these rights, and that law, are from God (as in the Declaration of Independence's phrase, "the laws of nature and of nature's God"). Some

---

2. Willi Paul Adams, *The First American Constitutions: Republican Ideology and the Making of the State Constitutions in the Revolutionary Era* (Chapel Hill: University of North Carolina Press, 1980), p. 18, quoted in Bradford,
Original Intentions, p. 26.

constitutions had Christian oaths or affirmations—of belief in Christianity, Trinitarian Christianity, or Protestant Christianity—which holders of public office were required to make.

To one degree or another, these constitutions, bills of rights and declarations of rights were based on a Christian view of the nature of man. They saw man as having been created by God, as the Declaration of Independence states (not as having "evolved"!); thus they saw man as being valuable (and far more important than animals). They saw man as being responsible, under God, for his actions: not as a naturally "neutral," much less "naturally good," product determined by his environment. They saw man as having certain inherent, God-given rights, liberties, and duties. Given the overwhelming predominance of Christianity in these states (contrary to the myth that America of the day was dominated by "Enlightenment" rationalism)—in religion, education, law, legal thought, legal education, and political thought—it is easy to see that such "rights" were based on biblical ethical thought. The right to life was based on God's prohibition of murder (with no pietistic, humanistic, antinomian prohibitions of capital punishment for those whom God's law deems worthy of death). The God-given right to liberty meant freedom within the boundaries of Christian morality: they did not conflate liberty and license. The right to religious freedom or the freedom of worship meant the freedom to worship God within the boundaries of Christian morality (not an unbounded freedom of men to engage in all manner of sins under the guise of "religious worship"). The right to property was based on God's prohibition of covetousness, adultery, and theft.

Consistent with the Bible's teaching that all men are fallen in sin, these governmental documents were founded on a realistic distrust of the nature of all men, even government officials, not upon a confidence in human nature. Consistent with Romans 13 (which teaches that the civil government is a ministry of God to protect those who do good and punish, and so restrain, those who do evil—and which indicates that God's ministry of civil government must abide by God's law's definitions of good and evil), these constitutions and their bills or declarations of rights saw the purpose of civil government, under God, to protect men's God-given rights against both the private and the gov-

ernmental actions of men. Denying the neutrality or goodness of man
and rather believing in his sinfulness, they made written constitutions,
supported with bills of rights or declarations of rights, to limit the authority and powers of the rulers of civil government and the authority of
"great men," minorities, or majorities in control of the machinery of civil
government. They designed republican (representative) governments so
that the people of their states could influence their civil governments,
but they made these limited governments. These men were not pietistic:
they did not separate Christianity from civil government, nor did they
advocate absolute submission of the people to civil government or mere
passive obedience to rulers. They designed systems of separation of
powers, with checks and balances between and among the legislative,
executive, and judicial branches of their governments to prevent these
institutions and officials from usurping power and violating the people's
rights and liberty. Their constitutions, declarations of rights, and bills of
rights implied (because they were products of each colony's resistance
to British tyranny as well as of a long tradition of Christian political and
legal thought easily traceable back through the Protestant Reformation
to the medieval period), and in some cases explicitly stated, the right of
resistance against arbitrary, unjust laws and tyranny.

And, consistent with biblical teaching, they did not rely on the
design of their constitutions alone, or on their delineated rights.
Rather, they taught that the preservation of liberty depends on the
preservation of virtue among the people, which in turn depends on the
continuing influence of "religion," meaning Christianity, on the people.
They talked of "free government," but they meant by it a civil government which protects the freedom and honors the rights of the people,
not a civil government free to do whatever its rulers think best. They
taught that "free government" cannot be maintained if the people are
not virtuous, and that "religion" is the foundation of that necessary
virtue, and so of freedom.

These states' constitutions, declarations, and/or bills of rights
were not mere works of necessity, but the products of long-standing
cultural legacies, histories, and cherished ways of life. They were, by
the language of the Declaration of Independence, the constitutions,
declarations, and bills of rights of **nations**, of separate and equal

peoples which had won their stations as equals to the other nations of the earth. The people of each of these states wanted to preserve and protect not only their individual liberty but also their corporate identities as sovereign states, their beliefs and values, their ways of life. They were willing to give up, at least for the foreseeable future, a small portion—a very small portion—of their state's authority in order to better protect their individual liberty and their state's corporate identity via the Articles of Confederation.

When the government of the Articles did not work well, they were willing to delegate a little more authority and power to the new governmental system established by the Constitution—but only *a very little more* authority and power. Not enough to threaten their own state's (or, in principle, any other state's) corporate identity or its right to govern itself. Nor enough to threaten their states' protection of their people's individual liberty. For the Constitution's federal system of civil government was intended to be consistent with the states' constitutions, bills of rights, and/or declarations of rights: not to threaten them, nor the corporate identities, nor the ways of life they were framed to protect.

That is why, when thoughtful opponents of the Constitution—and judicious men who were neither opponents nor advocates of its ratification—raised legitimate questions about the efficacy of the Constitution to preserve and protect individual liberty, justice, and the rights or powers of the states to govern themselves and preserve their ways of life, so many states' legislatures or ratification conventions proposed amendments to the Constitution protecting the reserved powers of the states. Eight states' proposed some 210 amendments, or about 100, leaving out the duplications.[3] They saw many threats to the reserved powers of the states, and to the liberty of their people. That is why what became our Tenth Amendment was so easily added to the Constitution: "The powers not delegated to the United States by the Constitution or prohibited by it to the States, are reserved to the States respectively, or to the people."

---

3. Jeffrey St. John, *Forge of Union, Anvil of Liberty: A Correspondent's Report on the First Federal Elections, the First Federal Congress, and the Bill of Rights* (Ottawa, Illinois: Jameson Books, Inc., 1992), p. 82.

8

The Tenth Amendment and
The Articles of Confederation

Our first constitution was "The Articles of Confederation," so it should be known as *our* Articles of Confederation. Although it was abandoned in favor of the Constitution because of its weaknesses, it contained principles which the vast majority of Americans wanted in the Constitution. When enough Americans and their statesmen saw that the defects of the Constitution would or could be used to usurp authority and powers from the state governments and create a centralized government which would violate these principles, Americans added what became the Tenth Amendment to our Constitution to protect these principles.

Our Articles of Confederation were framed during the early years of our struggle for independence. On June 12, 1776, even before the signing of the Declaration of Independence, the Continental Congress appointed a committee (significantly, one man from each colony) to draft a plan of confederation. From July through mid-November Congress debated the draft and greatly revised the Articles. The major issues in the debates in Congress all focused on the states: the representation of the states in Congress (the colonies were fighting to gain their independence as states); the basis for taxation of the states; and the control of the western lands claimed by various states. The fundamental issue, however, was whether "sovereignty" (ultimate human political authority: none wanted to claim absolute power for civil government) would be located in the central government or in each state government. After much debate in Congress, it was decided that "sovereignty" would remain in the state governments—*not* the central government. In mid-November of 1777 Congress finally sent the final version of the Articles of Confederation to the states for consideration.

However, the Articles were not ratified by all the states until March 1, 1781—three years and four months later.

Ratification took so long because many people feared that the central government proposed by the Articles, Congress (the civil government framed by the Articles had no executive or judicial branches), would have or usurp too much power. They worried about taxation of the states. They noted a division of interests between the Northern and Southern states, and Southerners, noting Northern animosity against the Southern states and a desire of those states to dominate their Southern neighbors, argued that the sovereignty of their states would be destroyed by the Northern states. Southerners were also concerned about the apportionment of troops among the states—and between the Northern and Southern states. Southerners and Northerners said the Articles gave Congress too much authority over the "sovereignty" of the states; and that there was a danger of "loose construction" (changing the intended meaning) of the Articles' terms by future Congresses.

The form of government in our Articles of Confederation was, as the name indicates, a confederacy—a union of states for mutual support or action. Article III said that

> The said states hereby severally enter into a firm league of friendship...for their common defence, the security of their Liberties, and their mutual and general welfare, binding themselves to assist each other, against all force offered to, or attacks made upon them, or any of them, on account of religion, sovereignty, trade, or any other pretence whatever.

Most of the authority and power in the civil government established by the Articles was in each state government. Each state retained its sovereignty and every power not expressly delegated to the central government. The central government (Congress) had only those powers which were expressly delegated to it by the states. Article II said, "Each state retains its sovereignty, freedom, and independence, and every Power, Jurisdiction, and right, which is not by this confederation expressly delegated to the United States, in Congress assembled"—a concept strikingly similar to the central idea of what would become our Tenth

Amendment. The central government was weak in comparison to the state governments, or to any state government.

The states were fairly well protected in the Articles' government. Each state had from two to seven representatives in Congress, but had only one vote. Every state, regardless of size, population, or wealth, was equal. Nine states out of thirteen had to agree in order to pass a law. Article V gave the state legislatures a check against the central government by requiring that the delegates of the states to Congress be chosen in a way determined by each respective state legislature (just as U.S. senators were originally to be chosen under our Constitution). Each state could also recall any or all of its delegates, and replace him or them for the rest of the year: a further check of the state legislature on Congress. Article XIII, moreover, gave each state legislature a veto on any proposed change in the Articles by requiring the agreement of **every state's legislature** to any proposed change.

The principles of the Articles which the overwhelming majority of Americans insisted on protecting by an amendment were: the right of the American people to be many at the same time they were one; the right of the people of each state to maintain their own corporate ways; the authority of each state's people and their state government over their own internal affairs; and the protection of individual liberty against centralized government and its virtually inevitable tyranny.

Our Articles of Confederation was replaced by the Constitution because its central government was too weak. It had no power to tax; the most it could do was request money from the states. It did not have enough power over foreign commerce and had no power over interstate commerce. It had no power to raise an army; all it could do was request troops from the states. It had no executive—law-enforcing—branch of government. It had no judicial branch of government, so it had no means of settling disputes over national laws. Its requirements made the enactment of laws too difficult. And the Articles were too hard to amend since they required unanimous consent of the states to any amendment.

Though these defects were remedied in the Constitution, Americans were dedicated to the right of each state to govern its own internal affairs which they knew protected individual liberty by limiting the power of the national government. This led the framers of the Constitution to exercise great care in designing the structure, powers, and limits of the new governmental system established by the Constitution. These principles also mandated that federalism—the separation of powers between the central government and the states' governments, with constitutional means by which the states can check central government injustice and tyranny—would be fundamental to the Constitution.

Yet the Constitution had its own defects, as the Anti-Federalist criticisms made clear. Concern about the consequences of these defects—usurpation of power from the states; centralization of power in the national government; concentration of power in Congress, the President, and/or the Supreme Court; and unjust, even tyrannical rule by the central government or its institutions—led to insistence on the addition of a bill of rights to the Constitution. And concern by the respective states for the preservation of federalism—and of the states' authority over their own internal affairs, and of liberty—ensured that what became our Tenth Amendment was to be an integral part of the Bill of Rights.

9

Ratification of The Constitution

Humanly speaking, the authority of our Constitution is not based on the authority of the people of the nation or the Union but upon the authority of the people of the respective states. The famous Senator Daniel Webster to the contrary notwithstanding, the Preamble's opening phrase, "We the people of the United States..." did not mean, and was not intended to mean, the people of the United States as a united whole—as Federalist advocates of ratification of the Constitution had to admit again and again during the various states' debates on ratification of the Constitution.[1]

The evidence on this is quite clear despite the fact that it is seldom taught in our educational establishments. Our War for Independence was fought to achieve the independence of the thirteen colonies—not of "a new nation," as Lincoln, who sought to recast our nation based on a particular reading of the Declaration, claimed. Our Declaration of Independence manifestly proclaimed the independence not of "a new nation" but of those thirteen "free and independent" states. The Articles of Confederation, our first constitution, was framed by representatives of those thirteen states, then ratified by the legislatures of those same states. The Articles united those states under a national legislature but in a confederation which, by definition and design, left each state free to govern itself. Our Constitution was framed by representatives of those thirteen independent states—who voted as states, one vote per state, regardless of the size, wealth, or population of the state, not as individual representatives, nor as a national major-

---

1. This is why it is important to read and study the debates in the state ratification conventions—and a chief reason why they are neither read nor studied in our colleges and universities.

ity constituted of the majority of the representatives present in the Philadelphia Convention. The finished Constitution was sent not to an election of the people of the whole United States but to the individual states for ratification. Without being ratified, of course, the Constitution could not have had the authority to function as law, much less as our fundamental law.

The Constitution was ratified by those states as states, each of which designated a special session of legislature or a special state ratification convention wherein delegates, chosen by the people from the various districts of the state, discussed and debated the document and its various provisions, and then voted to ratify the Constitution or not. As Madison said in Federalist No. 39, "ratification is to be given by the people, not as individuals composing one entire nation, but as composing the distinct and independent States to which they respectively belong." And, "Each State, in ratifying the Constitution, is considered as a sovereign body, independent of all others, and only to be bound by its own voluntary act."

Moreover, it is important to note that the predominant intention of those who framed and ratified our Constitution was, as it had been in fighting for the independence of the states and in establishing the Articles of Confederation, to preserve the states' and their citizens' legal heritage of limited government and local self-government derived from the English constitution. They planned to accomplish this through a carefully designed system of civil government with diverse kinds of representation for the people of the states, thus preserving each respective states' forms of government; deliberately complex, inefficient institutions and processes of making, enforcing, and adjudicating laws; and limitations on the authority of the central government first and foremost, but also of the states' governments—so that they would have the greatest probability of preserving their traditional liberty, diversity, and state individuality. Their intention was not to create a new concept of civil government, a civil government that would function to pursue abstract principles foreign to Americans' English political and legal heritage (before King George III and Parliament violated that heritage), or a new content of fundamental law.[2] The intent was to preserve the state-sovereign status quo, not to pursue abstract, rationalistically-conceived ideas via the power of the national government created by our Constitution.

The people of the nation, as such, had no part in either framing or ratifying the Constitution, but gave approval *through* their state representatives. The states created our central government; our central government did not create the states.

The process of ratification by the states, as Madison noted, made each state which ratified the Constitution the party to a covenant or compact. That compact was a covenant among the respective states and their peoples, not between the peoples of the several states and the people of the whole nation.[3] The fundamental law established by our Constitution did not obliterate the authority of the civil governments of the states which formed the Union. Nor did the Constitution give the central government established by that document the authority to meddle with the corporate identities of the peoples of the states. The Constitution was plainly not intended to do either. As Madison said in Federalist No. 39, although the *operation* of the powers which the central government does have is national, the *extent* of its powers is not. In the extent of its powers "the proposed government cannot be deemed a *national* one; since its jurisdiction extends to certain enumerated objects only, and leaves to the several States a residuary and inviolable sovereignty over all other objects."

The states' documents stating their ratification of the Constitution provide powerful testimony to their intention to keep the central gov-

2. Bradford, *Original Intentions*, demonstrates this by examining the background and processes of the making and ratification of our Constitution, the biographical evidence of the influence of religion on the Framers, and the intentions behind the Reconstruction Amendments.

3. As indicated above, inasmuch as officials of the new central government created by that compact among the states or the people of the states were and are required to swear an oath (or make an affirmation) to support our Constitution, the compact among the states also created a compact between the states (or their people) and the officials of our central government. Both officials of the states' governments and officials of the central government bind themselves to that compact in swearing to support our Constitution.

ernment within its constitutional bounds, retain their own non-delegated powers, and reserve their right to defend their people's inherited ways and liberty against central government injustice or tyranny. At least three of the states—Virginia, New York, and Rhode Island—made it clear in their ratification documents that they had the right to secede from the Union or to take back the powers which they had delegated to the central government whenever those powers were perverted by the central government, or whenever it should become "necessary to their happiness"—just as all the states had done against the British king's and Parliament's violations of the colonies' and colonists' legal rights under the British constitution. Those states ratification documents also guarded against central government officials' self-interested misconstruction of the Constitution's wording to imply that Congress is entitled to any powers not stated in the Constitution.

Virginia declared (1788):

> We the Delegates of the People of Virginia duly elected
> in pursuance of a recommendation from the General
> Assembly and now met in Convention having fully
> and freely investigated the proceedings of the Federal
> Convention and being prepared as well as the most
> mature deliberation hath enabled us to decide thereon
> Do in the name and in behalf of the People of Virginia
> declare and make known that the powers granted un-
> der the Constitution being derived from the People
> of the United States may be resumed [i.e., taken back]
> by them whensoever the same shall be perverted to
> their injury or oppression and that every power not
> granted thereby remains with them and at their will:
> that therefore no right or any denomination can be
> cancelled abridged restrained or modified by the Con-
> gress by the Senate or House of Representatives acting
> in any Capacity by the President or any Department or
> Officer of the United States except in those instances
> in which power is given by the Constitution for those
> purposes...

New York's ratification instrument (1787) declared:

> We the Delegates of the People of the State of New
> York, duly elected and Met in Convention, having
> maturely considered the Constitution for the United
> States of America... Do declare and make known.
>
> That all Power is originally vested in and conse-
> quently derived from the People, and that Government
> is instituted by them for their common Interest Pro-
> tection and Security.
>
> That the enjoyment of Life, Liberty and the pursuit
> of Happiness are essential rights which every Govern-
> ment is instituted by them for their common Interest
> Protection and Security.
>
> That the Powers of Government may be reassumed
> by the People, whensoever it shall become necessary
> to their Happiness; that every Power, Jurisdiction and
> right, which is not by the said Constitution clearly del-
> egated to the Congress of the United States, or the de-
> partments of the Government thereof, remains to the
> people of the several States, or to their respective State
> Governments to whom they may have granted the
> same; And that those Clauses in the said Constitution,
> which declare, that Congress shall not have or exercise
> certain Powers, do not imply that Congress is entitled
> to any Powers not given by the said Constitution; but
> such Clauses are to be construed either as exceptions
> to certain specified Powers, or as inserted merely for
> greater Caution.

Rhode Island's 1787 response to the Constitution proclaimed:

> We the Delegates of the People of the State of Rhode-Is-
> land, and Providence Plantations, duly elected and met
> in Convention, having maturely considered the Consti-
> tution for the United States of America... and having
> also seriously and deliberately considered the present
> situation of this State, do declare and make known

1ˢᵗ That there are certain natural rights, of which men when they form a social compact, cannot deprive or divest their posterity, among which are the enjoyment of Life and Liberty, with the means of acquiring, possessing and protecting Property, and pursuing and obtaining happiness and safety.

2ⁿᵈ That all power is naturally vested in, and consequently derived from the People; that magistrates therefore are their trustees and agents, and at all times amenable to them.

3ʳᵈ That the powers of government may be reassumed by the people, whensoever it shall become necessary to their happiness:—That the rights of the States respectively, to nominate and appoint all State Officers, and every other power, jurisdiction and right, which is not by the said constitution clearly delegated to the Congress of the United States or to the departments of government thereof, remain to the people of the several states, or their respective State Governments to whom they may have granted the same; and that those clauses in the said constitution which declare that Congress shall not have or exercise certain powers, do not imply, that Congress is entitled to any powers not given by the said constitution, but such clauses are to be construed as exceptions to certain specified powers, or as inserted merely for greater caution.

And the first amendment proposed by the Rhode Island delegates, an obvious precursor of our Tenth Amendment, stated:

The United States shall guarantee to each State its sovereignty, freedom and independence, and every power, jurisdiction and right, which is not by this constitution expressly delegated to the United States.

Some other states' ratification documents made it clear that each state retained all powers which it had not explicitly delegated to the central/national government and that these powers remained with each state—as our Tenth Amendment later made explicit. South Carolina proclaimed (1788):

> This Convention doth also declare that no Section or paragraph of the said Constitution warrants a construction [i.e., interpretation] that the states do not retain every power not expressly relinquished by them and vested in the General Government of the Union.

New Hampshire (1788) declared:

> ...The Convention do therefore recommend that the following alterations & provisions be introduced into the said Constitution—First That it be Explicitly declared that all Powers not expressly & particularly Delegated by the aforesaid Constitution are reserved to the several States to be, by them Exercised.

North Carolina (1788) expressed the same views at greater length and more forcefully:

> Resolved, That a Declaration of Rights, asserting and securing from encroachment the great Principles of civil and religious Liberty, and the unalienable Rights of the People, together with Amendments to the most ambiguous and exceptional Parts of the said Constitution of Government, ought to be laid before Congress, and the Convention of the States that shall or may be called for the purpose of Amending the said Constitution, for their consideration, previous to the Ratification of the Constitution aforesaid, on the part of the State of North Carolina.

DECLARATION OF RIGHTS

1st That there are certain natural rights of which men, when they form a social compact, cannot deprive or divest their posterity, among which are the enjoyment of life, and liberty, with the means of acquiring, possessing, and protecting property, and pursuing and obtaining happiness and safety.

2nd That all power is naturally vested in, and consequently derived from the people; that magistrates therefore are their trustees, and agents, and at all times amenable to them.

3rd That Government ought to be instituted for the common benefit, protection and security of the people; and that the doctrine of non-resistance against arbitrary power and oppression is absurd, slavish, and destructive to the good and happiness of mankind.

AMENDMENTS TO THE CONSTITUTION

I. That each state in the union shall, respectively, retain every power, jurisdiction and right, which is not by this constitution delegated to the Congress of the United States, or to the departments of the Federal Government.

XVIII. That those clauses which declare that Congress shall not exercise certain powers, be not interpreted in any manner whatsoever to extend the powers of Congress; but that they be construed either as making exceptions to the specified powers where this shall be the case, or otherwise, as inserted merely for greater caution.

These states' manifest intention was to protect their reserved powers—each state's authority to govern itself—as much as to limit the powers of the central government. Inseparably linked to these ideas was the desire to prevent the officials of the national government from misconstruing the Constitution to the detriment of the powers of the states and of liberty.

This, of course, is the essential idea of the Tenth Amendment: protection of the powers which the states had neither delegated to the national government nor forbidden to themselves in the Constitution. Their intent was to prevent both the usurpation of these powers by the central government and the denial of these powers to the states by the central government. The power of this concept explains why what became the Tenth Amendment was added to our Constitution. **The people of the states whose representatives framed and ratified the Constitution insisted that the authority of their states to govern their own internal affairs, and the powers necessary to accomplish that end, remain in the hands of their respective state governments.**

Thus the ratification of our Constitution clarifies both the principles of what became our Tenth Amendment and the intensity with which Americans embraced the principles of that great amendment.

10

The Principles of Compact, and the Laws of Nature and of Nature's God

Our Constitution was based on a compact (or covenant) among the thirteen new states which had declared their independence in our Declaration of Independence; framed, then ratified the Articles of Confederation; then, being dissatisfied with the Articles, framed, then ratified our Constitution after much debate. The Constitution was a continuation of the compact among the states whose representatives had framed, debated about, and then ratified the Articles of Confederation.

That original compact among the newly independent states of America gave them a fundamental law titled "Articles of Confederation and Perpetual Union between the States of...," which we call the Articles of Confederation. Not only did that document, which was formally agreed to by the states, claim that their union was "perpetual," but also its terms required that every state agree to any change in the fundamental law set forth in the Articles.

Because so many people in so many states were dissatisfied with the functioning of their mutual system of civil government under the Articles, the Philadelphia Convention was established to revise the Articles of Confederation. But because so many of the states' representatives sent to Philadelphia were convinced that the Articles was so radically defective that it needed to be scrapped altogether and replaced by a new governmental system, the states' representatives at the convention deliberately abandoned their original purpose and adopted a new purpose. They abandoned the Articles and designed a new system of civil government and fundamental law. They made the Philadelphia Convention the Constitutional Convention and presented their states with a new, architectonically designed system of civil government and fundamental law, the Constitution of the United States.

That Constitution, framed by representatives of the states who voted as states, not as individuals, had to be ratified by the states of the Confederation in order to become authoritative and exist as their fundamental law. But unlike the Articles of Confederation it had to be ratified by only nine of the thirteen states which were parties to the compact of the Articles. Since the Constitution represented a huge change in the Articles, ratification of the Constitution meant a change, an amendment of the Articles. So states' ratification of the Constitution, once nine of them did it, established the compact which made the Constitution the law of the land—but violated the compact of the Articles of Confederation.

Were the states then justified in violating the compact of the Articles to make themselves parties to the compact of the Constitution? Upon what basis could a state, or some states, abandon the compact of the Articles and join that of the Constitution without the unanimous consent of the states which were parties to the compact of the Articles?

In Federalist No. 43 James Madison dealt with this problem, asking, "On what principle the Confederation, which stands in the solemn form of a compact among the States, can be superseded without the unanimous consent of the parties to it?" He states that this question

> is answered at once by recurring to the absolute necessity of the case; to the great principle of self-preservation; to the transcendent law of nature and of nature's God, which declares that the safety and happiness of society are the objects at which all political institutions aim, and to which all such institutions must be sacrificed.

The transcendent law of nature and of nature's God teaches the great principle of self-preservation, or the happiness and safety of society, said Madison. Since self-preservation is the purpose which all political institutions seek to achieve, a society or state is justified in leaving a union or compact which it has joined if that union or compact fails to achieve, or works against, the happiness and safety of that society. Since the system of civil government established by the Articles failed to achieve the happiness and safety of a state, or even threatened its self-preservation, that state is justified in seceding from the compact which formed the union under the Articles in order to better secure its own self-preservation, happiness, and safety.

Madison found another answer "in the principles of the compact itself":

> It has been heretofore noted among the defects of
> the Confederation, that in many of the States it had
> received no higher sanction than a mere legislative
> ratification. The principle of reciprocality [reciprocity]
> seems to require that its obligation to the other States
> should be reduced to the same standard. A compact
> between independent sovereigns, founded on ordinary
> acts of legislative authority, can pretend to no higher
> validity than a league or treaty between the parties. It
> is an established doctrine on the subject of treaties,
> that all the articles are mutually conditions of each
> other; that a breach of any one article is a breach of the
> whole treaty; and that a breach, committed by either of
> the parties, absolves the others, and authorizes them,
> if they please, to pronounce the compact violated and
> void.

Since the principle of reciprocity is a fundamental principle of justice, Madison's distinction between the "ordinary" and the "extraordinary" acts of a legislature in forming a compact is unnecessary. For no act of a legislature can justify the party to a compact in violating the terms of that compact—nor can it bind another party or parties to that compact to remain in that violated compact if they choose to leave it.

The states that left the compact of the Articles for the compact of the Constitution were well aware of these principles, and either presupposed them or made them explicit in their Constitutional ratification documents. Virginia's ratification instrument declared "that the powers granted under the Constitution being derived from the People of the United States may be resumed by them whensoever the same shall be perverted to their injury or oppression..." New York declared "that the Powers of Government may be reassumed by the People, whensoever it shall become necessary to their Happiness..." Rhode Island declared "that the powers of government may be reassumed by the people, whensoever it shall become necessary to their happiness..."

The states, therefore, framed and ratified the compact of the new Constitution to give themselves and their people a system of civil government and law which would be much more likely than that of the Articles to secure their self-preservation, safety, happiness, and liberty—along with their continued right to govern their own internal affairs. This desire to maintain state "sovereignty" was, again, implicit in every state's ratification of the Constitution, but it was made explicit by some of the states. Rhode Island declared that every "power, jurisdiction and right, which is not by the said [C]onstitution clearly delegated to the Congress of the United States or to the departments of the government thereof, remain to the people of the several states, or their respective State Governments to whom they may have granted the same...." New York declared "that every Power, Jurisdiction and right, which is not by the said Constitution clearly delegated to the Congress of the United States, or the departments of the Government thereof, remains to the People of the several States, or to their respective State Governments to whom they may have granted the same...." Virginia declared that "every power not granted [by the state in the Constitution] remains with [the people of the individual United States] and at their will: that therefore no right or any denomination can be cancelled or abridged[,] restrained or modified by the Congress[,] by the Senate or House of Representatives acting in any Capacity[,] by the President or any Department or Officer of the United States except in those instances in which power is given by the Constitution for those purposes..."

These convictions and the purposes which undergirded them—the principles of compact, the laws of nature and of nature's God, and the desire of the people of each state to govern itself—are obviously those which drove the states to insist on the addition of the Tenth Amendment to our Constitution: "The powers not delegated to the United States by the Constitution or prohibited by it to the States, are reserved to the States respectively, or to the people." Our Tenth Amendment thus stands on a deeper, broader, firmer foundation than the will of the people of the states who insisted upon its addition to our Constitution; it stood, and therefore still stands, on law-principles of universal validity, undiminished by the passing of time.

11

The Tenth Amendment and Interposition

The doctrine of interposition is based on the biblical truth that the powers that be, the rulers of civil government, are ordained by God and are His ministers (see Romans 13:1-10 for this and the discussion which follows). As God's ministers they are to serve Him—not anyone else. They are to serve Him by protecting and giving praise to those who do good, and by punishing, and therefore restraining, those who do evil. As God's ministers they must follow, obey, and apply *His* standard of what is good and what is evil. They do not have authority to originate or employ any other definition of good and evil but God's, for God, not man, is the measure of all things.

All the rulers of civil government—no matter what their level or scope of authority—are ordained by God to be His ministers. Romans 13:8-10 makes it unmistakably clear (if we missed the clear implication of Romans 13:1-7) that God's law defines good and evil, and that the rulers or officials of civil government—no matter what their level of authority—are to function in terms of God's law, serving God rather than men. All rulers of civil government have a duty to God to protect those under their authority against those who do evil—**all** those who do evil.

Since all rulers or officials of civil government are men, they are therefore sinners who are tempted to do evil and subjects of God's authority over them. No civil ruler, from the highest ranking king to the lowest village magistrate, is justified in doing evil or in legislating, executing, or adjudicating a law (or system of laws) which is evil or which harms those who do good. A high-ranking official is not exempt by way of his great stature, nor is a low-ranking official exempt because of his relative insignificance. Since "lesser civil magistrates," or lower-ranking civil government officials are God's ministers too, they have a duty as God's servants to protect those under their authority from evil laws, policies, decisions, etc. enacted, decreed, or promulgated by higher-ranking civil government officials; they may not cooperate with the law-breaking of their superiors.

The doctrine of interposition holds that the lower-ranking civil government officials must place themselves "between"[1] any and all higher-ranking civil government official(s) who may be attempting to enforce an evil law, policy, decision, etc. and the people under the lower-ranking civil government official's authority. It is the duty of the lesser as well as the greater civil government officials to serve God by protecting the people under their authority against injustice and tyranny (evil) from all sources. For lower-ranking civil government officials, this means protecting the people under their authority against evil laws, policies, etc. mandated by the king or any higher-ranking civil government officials or institutions. Thus the lower-ranking civil government officials have an inescapable duty to use their civil government authority to render null (either by outright resistance or passive non-enforcement) any unjust ordinances set forth by higher-ranking civil government officials.

The framers and ratifiers of our Constitution certainly believed in the doctrine of interposition. They had used it in resisting the tyrannical rule of King George III in Parliament, and in declaring and winning the independence of their states. They had presupposed it and in effect designed it into our first constitution, the Articles of Confederation by making each state sovereign over its own internal affairs and protecting it against usurpation by Congress. They presupposed it in enabling the states to break away from the Articles of Confederation in order to ratify the Constitution—as no less an authority than James Madison argued in Federalist No. 43—maintaining that such action was based on principles prior to all forms of civil government, the principles of justice in the law of compacts, principles of the very "laws of nature and of Nature's God."

---

1. The word "interposition" or "interpose" has its origin in the Latin *interponere* meaning "to set between."

Our Constitution presupposed the validity of interposition. The framers and ratifiers of our Constitution intentionally gave us a system of separation of powers with accompanying checks and balances to give us a means of resisting injustice and tyranny emanating from the central government. That system was designed to use the self-interest of civil government officials to protect justice and liberty against the effects of faction and evil ambition. That system of separation of powers and checks and balances gave the states certain means of internal resistance to the central government's factional domination. These include: a written constitution, selection of senators from their respective states, equal representation of states as states in the Senate (regardless of population, wealth, or any other criteria), election of U.S. senators by their respective state legislatures (a protection foolishly but intentionally destroyed by the "progressive" 17th Amendment in 1913), and even selection of members from the House of Representatives from districts in their respective states (rather than, say, from larger regions of the country or nationally).

That system of separation of powers with accompanying checks and balances included more than the famous division of powers in our national/central government. As Madison stated so clearly in Federalist No. 51, it included a separation of powers between the central government and the state governments:

> In the compound republic of America, the power surrendered by the people is first divided between two distinct governments, and then the portion allotted to each subdivided among distinct and separate departments. Hence a double security arises to the rights of the people. The different governments will control each other, at the same time that each will be controlled by itself.

The federal system of America—our double security to the rights of the people—was based on a realistic understanding of human nature, e.g., man's love of power, which would lead the officials of the state governments to resist attempts by central government officials and institutions to usurp state governments' authority and powers. As Hamilton noted in Federalist No. 28:

> It may safely be received as an axiom in our political system, that the State governments will, in all possible contingencies, afford complete security against invasions of the public liberty by the national authority. Projects of usurpation cannot be masked under pretences so likely to escape the penetration of select bodies of men, as of the people at large. The [states'] legislatures will have better means of information. They can discover the danger at a distance; and possessing all the organs of civil power, and the confidence of the people, they can at once adopt a regular plan of opposition, in which they can combine all the resources of the community. They can readily communicate with each other in the different States, and unite their common forces for the protection of their common liberty.

Note that Hamilton was speaking in this commonly neglected number of *The Federalist* (and, reflecting on its content and argument, we do not find it difficult to know why it is commonly neglected) of the exercise of what he called "that original right of self-defence which is paramount to all positive forms of government" which is the last resource "if the representatives of the people betray their constituents..." Consistent with biblical teaching on resistance to tyranny, Hamilton made resort to arms the last stage in resistance. Our federal system gave us various political means of defense which the states and their people were to use before the ultimate resort to arms. These were collectively a system of constitutional interposition by which the states could cooperate to thwart central government tyranny—a means of avoiding, if possible, the ultimate right of interposition by force of arms.

But that federal system of separation of powers, as Hamilton noted in Federalist No. 28, is also based on the understanding of the people and their dedication to the preservation of their own liberty:

> The obstacles to usurpation and the facilities of resistance increase with the increased extent of the state, provided the citizens understand their rights and are disposed to defend them....in a confederacy the people,

without exaggeration, may be said to be entirely the
masters of their own fate. Power being almost always
the rival of power, the general government will at all
times stand ready to check the usurpations of the state
governments, and these will have the same disposition
towards the general government. The people, by throw-
ing themselves into either scale, will infallibly make it
preponderate. If their rights are invaded by either, they
can make use of the other as the instrument of redress.

Do enough Americans today understand our rights? Are enough
Americans disposed to defend our liberty? Do enough understand
the constitutional means of using the powers of the states to defend
and recover our liberty? Our Tenth Amendment's statement that the
powers not delegated by the people of the states to the central government are retained by the people of the states respectively was meant to
make Americans understand our rights and those of our states. It was
meant to protect our constitutional system of interposition, and so to
motivate us to defend our liberty before we let conditions become so
dire that we urge our states to resort to our ultimate defense against
centralized tyranny.

12

The Tenth Amendment and Nullification

The principle of nullification is essential to federalism, for without it, the state governments are largely defenseless against power-hungry, unscrupulous central government encroachments and usurpations. Nullification laws are laws enacted by a state legislature declaring unconstitutional "federal" (central government) laws to be without authority in the state and rendering such laws inoperative in that state. Without the right of nullification, a state has only the influence it can exert through its elected representatives in the central government to restrain and oppose central government usurpation of the state's powers and authority.

Nullification is a form of interposition: it is a means by which the state's civil government officials can protect the lives, persons, property, and liberty of the people of their state against unconstitutional laws and actions emanating from the "federal" or central government. By extension, if other states are persuaded to join in enacting and enforcing similar legislation, nullification protects the liberty and wellbeing of the people of the whole United States against unjust and unconstitutional laws promulgated by the central government. As a form of interposition, nullification is more than a right of a state's civil government: it is a moral duty of a state's civil government and its officials to protect the moral and constitutional liberty of that state's people against injustice and illegality emanating from the central government.

Nullification is constitutional. Our Constitution does not state that the central government or any of its offices or institutions is the final interpreter of the constitutionality of any law. The Constitution does not state that **any** institution of our complex federal system is the final interpreter of constitutionality. Our Constitution gives every official in our governmental system the responsibility of interpreting the constitutionality of every law enacted and enforced by every governmental jurisdiction in our system. Local governments and officials are not authorized by our Constitution to violate the Constitution—quite the contrary! Similarly, state governments and officials are not authorized by our Constitution to violate the Constitution, but are required to uphold it. And the national or central government and its officials are not authorized by our Constitution to violate the Constitution. They, too, must swear an oath (or make an affirmation) that they will uphold the Constitution. All and each of these officials must understand the meaning of our Constitution in order to distinguish between what is constitutional and what is not. All and each must do this in order to uphold the Constitution, which they swear or affirm they will do when they take their oath of office.

It is important to note that our Constitution implies that "we the people of the United States" have a duty to know the meaning of our Constitution and its various provisions. After all, it is "we the people of the United States" who elect, directly or indirectly, all the officials who make, enforce, and/or adjudicate the laws of our various civil governments. We do not have to take an oath (or make an affirmation) to do this, but the ultimate responsibility for the people whom we choose to run our civil governments is ours. They are all *our* representatives—at the local, state, and/or national level. If we elect representatives who do not *respect* or *understand* our Constitution, we cannot realistically expect them to *obey* our Constitution. If we elect representatives who have a religious-philosophy, world-and-life view, or system of ethics (or pseudo-ethics!) which permits or encourages them to use deceit and/or force to accomplish their ideological goals, we cannot realistically expect them to obey the terms of our Constitution. If even we do not understand our Constitution, we cannot realistically expect to elect representatives who will continue to honor and obey our Constitution. If *we* do not care about our Constitution, how can we expect those who represent us to care? Though all of our elected representatives in civil government are responsible to uphold the Constitution, the ultimate responsibility for upholding the Constitution is ours.

The most important institution of civil government for protecting our liberty in the complex system of civil government bequeathed to us in our Constitution is the government of each state. The central or national government is, of course, important, partly because its power can deter or defeat foreign aggressors, and partly because its design was intended to attract and get men of higher intellectual and moral character to make and enforce our national laws, and thereby to give us (believe it or not!) wiser, more just, more farsighted laws. But partly also because the central government was designed with a system of separation of powers and accompanying checks and balances to protect liberty and justice by preventing any one branch of our national government from usurping and accumulating power at the expense of the other two branches of our central government. However, as Madison said so famously and well in Federalist No. 51, separation of powers in our national government is only half of the story of the design of our system of civil government for protecting justice and liberty. The system of separation of powers between our national and state governments is the other half of our Constitution's design for protecting justice and liberty.

As noted before, this "double security to the rights of the people" necessarily means the rights of the people of the several states. Our original states' representatives who framed and ratified our Constitution intended our Constitution's federal system to protect the liberty of the people of their states as well as that of the people of the nation. They left the great majority of governmental powers in the hands of the state governments because they saw that as necessary to the ratification of the Constitution but also because they understood that it is good that the people of each state be free to govern their own internal affairs. Obviously, they intended the civil government which most affected the lives of Americans to be the state government,[1] not the national government.

---

1. Actually, as R. J. Rushdoony pointed out in *The Nature of the American System* (Fairfax, Virginia: Thoburn Press, [1965], 1978), they intended local government, preeminently the county government, to be what it already was, the civil government which most affected the lives of Americans. Local government is, however, legally a creature of the state government. This, of course, only emphasizes more strongly the point that the framers and ratifiers of our Constitution did not want the central government to be—or become— the most influential American government.

Advocates of the centralization of American governmental power like to appeal to the "Supremacy Clause" (Article VI, Paragraph 2). But the Supremacy Clause does not make any and every law enacted by Congress, much less every executive order of the President or decision by the Supreme Court or any other Federal Court—not to mention the regulations concocted by a federal bureaucracy!—the supreme law of the land. It only makes laws made "in pursuance" of the Constitution the supreme law of the land. Laws not made in pursuance of the Constitution cannot—logically or constitutionally, or morally—be the supreme law of the land.

So the states are not bound by any constitutional (or moral) authority to obey such laws. And if they are not bound to obey such laws they must be authorized to resist such laws: to nullify such laws. Moreover, according to the plain meaning of the Supremacy Clause the states are certainly justified in opposing, resisting, and nullifying such unconstitutional laws. Without being authorized and able to take such actions, the states would be powerless to resist usurpation of their powers, centralization of power, and arbitrary rule by our central government. Without our states being authorized to take such actions, our federalism would be the mere "paper barrier"—a totally ineffective device for securing liberty—which Madison complained against in Federalist No. 51.

Nullification, therefore, is obviously constitutional. If nullification were not constitutional, the Constitution would have created a centralized government, not a federal one, for the state governments would not be justified in doing anything to oppose unconstitutional "federal" laws.

13

The Tenth Amendment and The Bill of Rights

Our Bill of Rights was created because of widespread fear that the Constitution which was in the process of being ratified by the states was a threat to liberty and justice against the people of the several states as well as against the people of the Union that document would form. The arguments against the Constitution should be familiar, though they are often overlooked in our celebration of the Constitution's excellence. Basically, the Anti-Federalist opponents of the Constitution argued that too much power was given to the central or national government in general and to its three branches in particular. Congress, the Presidency, and the Federal Judiciary all had powers which could, and sooner or later would, threaten liberty in general and the freedom of the people of each state to govern itself in particular. The Constitution was too loosely worded and contained insufficient restrictions on the power and actions of central government officials and institutions. Human nature being what it is—fallen, hence power-hungry—men would take advantage of those loosely worded clauses to escape the Constitution's inadequate limits on their power. The possessors of these federal government offices would do what fallen men have done throughout history—abuse their power, create opportunities to usurp power from other branches of the central government and especially from the state governments, abuse *that* ill-gotten power, and, sooner or later create a tyrannical government. As we shall see,[1] and as we are seeing today, the fears that the Constitution would threaten justice and liberty were justified.

In virtually every state, there was widespread popular support for amending the Constitution with a bill of rights to protect justice,

---

1. Chapters 14-20.

liberty, and the authority of the states against abuses of power by the
new national government. It is clear that very many Americans either
supported the Anti-Federalist position entirely or at least disbelieved
that the Constitution could secure their rights. This insecurity was
expressed before, during, and after the states' ratification conventions. State ratification conventions or legislatures produced lists of
proposed amendments to the Constitution. Federalist supporters of
ratification of the Constitution agreed to work for the addition of a
bill of rights to the Constitution—after it was ratified. When the First
Congress met in 1789, honorable Federalist congressmen and senators
worked with Anti-Federalist congressmen and senators to distill a list
of amendments to be considered for adoption by the states as a bill of
rights for our Constitution. Our Bill of Rights was adopted to protect
the rights of the people of the states against the central government.

All of the amendments adopted by the states' legislatures acted
against the central government, to restrain or prohibit its powers.
None acted against the state governments.

The First Amendment prohibited Congress, not the state governments, from making any law having the effect of creating a national established church,[2] from interfering with the free exercise of "religion"
(that is, Christianity or religions which conform to Christian ethics);
from abridging freedom of speech or of the press, or from abridging
the right of the people to assemble peaceably to ask the government to
redress grievances.

The Second Amendment prohibited the national government from
infringing the right of the people to keep and bear arms, and made
clear that this provision could not be infringed because "a well regulated Militia" is necessary to the security of a "free State." In America at
the time of the Bill of Rights the militia was neither a private organization nor the equivalent of a standing, regular armed force. The militia

---

2. Not to "separate church and state" in the sense of separating Christi-
anity or "religion" from civil government, law, and public life! Contrary to
ACLU-type propaganda, the evidence for this is overwhelming and has long
been available to scholars, though it has been neglected by propagandists. See
B. F. Morris, *The Christian Life and Character of the Civil Institutions of the
United States* (Powder Springs, Georgia: The American Vision, [1864] 2007).

was a part-time force of citizen-soldiers who were not enlisted in any branch of the national military.[3] Membership in the militia was compulsory and was required of all able-bodied men—not including clergymen, most city and state officials, physicians, and full-time policemen and firemen—between the ages of eighteen and forty-five. Each militiaman was subject to call by the governor of his state, according to rules established by his state's legislature. Each was registered locally according to his company, battalion, regiment, and brigade.[4]

The militiamen used and were required to have their own personal weapons, ammunition, and equipment, and to participate in military exercises on certain dates.[5] These weapons were their property and they kept them in their own homes. They did not have to go to the equivalent of an armory to have small arms weapons and ammunition issued to them: that would have made the militia an ineffective ready-response force. The Second Amendment protects an individual right of self-defense which is connected to the public purpose of defending the liberty of the people of each state.

Robert B. Weaver has given us a good basic definition of this purpose:

> The Militia is the armed force of a State organized to support the State government in the fulfillment of its duties concerning the State's internal affairs and for the protection of the people and the government of the State against any outside force, including any Federal government forces which may seek to abuse the peace or the rights of the people.[6]

By "the State," of course, Weaver means not civil government as such but any and every state which formed (and forms) our federal Union. The militia was first and foremost a military force of its par-

---

3. Tom Parent, *The Constitutional Militia and the Second Amendment* (Privately Published, 1988), p. 5.

4. Ibid.

5. Ibid.

6. *Birth of Our Nation and Foundation of Our Republic: The Declaration of Independence [and] the Constitution of the United States of America* (DeLand, Florida: Patriotic Education, Inc., 1974), p. 56.

ticular state for the defense of the rights, persons, property, and liberty of the people of that state.

The Third through Eighth Amendments protect against common abuses of power by civil governments:

The Third Amendment protects against the quartering of military personnel in anyone's house during peacetime and, subject to laws enacted by Congress, in war.

The Fourth Amendment protects "the right of the people to be secure in their persons, papers, and effects, against unreasonable searches and seizures."

The Fifth Amendment protects the right of indictment by a grand jury for serious crimes; the right against double jeopardy; the right against self-incrimination; the right of due process of law; and the right of just compensation for private property taken for public use.

The Sixth Amendment protects the right to a speedy, public trial by an impartial jury of the state and district in which the crime is committed; the right to be informed of the nature of the accusation against oneself; the right to confront witnesses against oneself; the right to a compulsory process to get witnesses in one's favor; and the right to the assistance of a lawyer for one's defense in criminal cases.

The Seventh Amendment protects the right of trial by jury in suits at common law, and the right to have all facts tried by a jury protected in any re-examination of them by the rules of the common law.

The Eighth Amendment protects against excessive bail, excessive fines, and cruel and unusual punishments.

The Ninth Amendment is a "catch-all" to include all individual rights not stated in the previous eight amendments. It was framed in answer to arguments such as that of Alexander Hamilton in Federalist No. 84, that since it would be virtually impossible in a bill of rights to state all the legal rights of Americans, there should be no bill of rights added to our Constitution because the omission of any rights would be construed as a denial that Americans have such rights. The language of the Ninth Amendment answers Hamilton's criticism and protects Americans' rights against misconstruction: "The enumeration in the Constitution, of certain rights, shall not be construed to deny or disparage others retained by the people." Note that the misconstruction that the Ninth Amendment is concerned with is that by national government officials—for is speaks directly of the Constitution which created the national government—not state government officials. Each state government, of course, would be under the provisions and restrictions of its own constitution and declaration or bill of rights. As with the previous eight amendments, this amendment is meant to provide legal protection against the central government.

Amendments I-VIII were against potential abuses of power and violation of rights by the central government, not the state governments. The Ninth Amendment was a catch-all to protect all unstated rights against the central government. The Tenth Amendment protected the right of the states to govern their own internal affairs. It protected the authority of the state governments against central government usurpation.

In protecting the authority of each state to govern itself, the Tenth Amendment protects the power of each state to defend its powers against central government usurpation. The Second Amendment protects the chief ultimate means of each state's defending its powers against central government usurpation: the right of the people to keep and bear arms. The Tenth Amendment therefore protects the power of the states to check, balance, and resist violations of the people's rights which are protected "on paper" by the first nine amendments. This resistance can and should be political and governmental. It can be by a single state, a group of states, or all the states. In the last resort it can be military, as Hamilton makes clear in Federalist No. 28.

Just as Pennsylvania is said to be the keystone of our federal arch, our Tenth Amendment is the gateway of the defensive structure formed by our Bill of Rights. It is the gateway to the Bill of Rights because it reaffirms the crucial nature of the right of each state to govern its internal affairs free from central government intervention and interference. It confirms the fundamental nature of federalism to our system of civil government and to liberty. It also, more importantly, as Madison argued in Federalist No. 51, reminds us that the state governments were and should be a key to the functioning of our complex system of separation of powers and checks and balances. Moreover, it reminds everyone, as Alexander Hamilton argued in Federalist No. 28, that the state governments and the citizen-soldiers of their militias, exercising their Second Amendment rights, are the ultimate means and the last resort by which the people of the states can defend their liberty and rights against a tyrannical central government.

14

The Tenth Amendment and The Federal Judiciary

We have the Tenth Amendment, at least in part, because of Anti-Federalist criticisms of the Constitution's provisions respecting the federal courts in general and the U.S. Supreme Court in particular.

The Anti-Federalists warned that the Supreme Court had been given too much power and would craftily abuse that power to usurp more power. Congress, with the exclusive constitutional authority to make laws, was intended to be the most important and powerful of the central government's three branches: before a law can be enforced or adjudicated, it must be made. But the Supreme Court, Anti-Federalists argued, could use its power to declare acts of Congress unconstitutional, thus redefining—and in effect changing—the Constitution. It could thus increase its own power over that of Congress, thereby usurping power of Congress and making itself the most powerful branch of the central government. It could also usurp power from the state governments, thus making the governmental system increasingly centralized and placing itself atop the national government's authority structure.

George Mason, a Framer of the Constitution and chief author of the Virginia Bill of Rights who opposed the finished Constitution, said in the Virginia Ratification Convention,

> When we consider the nature of these [federal] courts, we must conclude that their effect and operation will be utterly to destroy the state governments: for they will be the judges of how far their laws will operate. They are to modify their own courts, and you can make no state law to counteract them. The discrimination between their judicial power, and that of the

states, exists, therefore, but in name... The principle itself goes to the destruction of the legislation of the states, whether or not it was intended... There are many gentlemen in the United States who think it right that we should have one great national, consolidated government, and that it was better to bring it about slowly and imperceptibly rather than all at once.[1]

Robert Yates of New York, another framer of the Constitution who ended up opposing it, wrote a series of prescient letters, significantly signed "Brutus,"[2] and published in a New York newspaper, against ratification of the Constitution. In the eleventh letter he said that those who are to be given the judicial power under the Constitution

...are to be placed in a situation altogether unprec-
edented in a free country. They are to be rendered
totally independent, both of the people and the legislature, both with respect to their offices and salaries.
No errors they may commit can be corrected by any
power above them, if any such power there be, nor can
they be removed from office for making ever so many
erroneous adjudications....
    This part of the plan is so modeled, as to authorize
the courts, not only to carry into execution the powers
expressly given, but where these are wanting or am-
biguously expressed, to supply what is wanting by their
own decisions.[3]

He explained further:

They will give the sense of every article of the constitution, that may from time to time come before them.

---

1. Cecelia M. Kenyon, ed., *The Antifederalists* (Indianapolis: The Bobbs-Merrill Co., 1966), 265.

2. Marcus Junius Brutus (c.85-42B.C.) was one of the conspirators who murdered Julius Caesar because Caesar had overthrown the Roman Republic and made himself a tyrant.

3. Robert Yates, *The Letters of "Brutus,"* No. XI, in Kenyon, 335.

> And in their decisions they will not confine themselves
> to any fixed or established rules, but will determine,
> according to what appears to them, the reason and
> spirit of the constitution. The opinions of the supreme
> court, whatever they may be, will have the force of law;
> because there is no power provided in the constitution,
> that can correct their errors, or control their adjudica-
> tions. From this court there is no appeal.[4]

He maintained that the federal judges would favor the national government and "will give such an explanation of the constitution, as will favour an extension of its jurisdiction" for several reasons. First, most of the Constitution's articles which convey important powers to the national government "are conceived in general and indefinite terms, which are either equivocal, ambiguous, or which require long definitions to unfold the extent of their meaning"[5] and the court will use these vague clauses to justify the expansion of the national government's authority. Second, as men in an institution endowed with power, they will want both to keep and to increase the power of their institution. Yates reasoned,

> this of itself will operate strongly upon the courts to
> give such a meaning to the constitution in all cases
> where it can possibly be done, as will enlarge the
> sphere of their own authority. Every extension of the
> power of the general legislature, as well as of the judi-
> cial powers, will increase the powers of the courts; and
> the dignity and importance of the judges, will be in
> proportion to the extent and magnitude of the powers
> they exercise.[6]

Yates explained the process more fully in No. 12 (which required a two-part essay): "in their adjudications they may establish certain principles, which being received by the legislature, will enlarge the sphere

---

4. Ibid., 338.
5. Ibid., 339.
6. Ibid., 340.

of their power beyond all bounds."[7] Since the Supreme Court, he reasoned, "has the power, in the last resort, to determine all questions that may arise in the course of legal discussion, on the meaning and construction [explanation] of the constitution" "the court must and will assume certain principles, from which they will reason, in forming their decisions. These principles, whatever they may be, when they become fixed, by a course of decisions, will be adopted by the legislature, and will be the rule by which they will explain their own powers."[8] They will use the vaguely worded clauses of the Preamble—such as to provide for the general welfare, to establish justice, to form a more perfect union, to ensure domestic tranquility—and the Necessary and Proper Clause (Article I, Section 8) to develop "very liberal" principles of constitutional interpretation. By these principles they would "extend the powers of the [central] government to every case, and reduce the state legislatures to nothing..."[9]

Yates concluded that the powers granted in the Constitution to the federal judiciary "will operate to a total subversion of the state judiciaries, if not to the legislative authority of the states."[10] And reiterated: "The judicial power will operate to effect, in the most certain, but yet silent and imperceptible manner, what is evidently the tendency of the constitution: ...an entire subversion of the legislative, executive, and judicial powers of the individual states."[11]

The Federalists replied that the Court does not have too much power and will not usurp power from the other branches of the national government or from the states. The Constitution makes the Supreme Court the least powerful, and therefore the least dangerous branch of the national government, said Hamilton, in Federalist No. 78. The Federalists argued that the Constitution's carefully designed system of separation of powers with its studiously crafted system of checks and balances will keep the federal courts in general and the Supreme Court in particular in bounds. Congress has the authority (in

7. No. XII, in Kenyon, 343.
8. Ibid.
9. Ibid., 347.
10. Kenyon, 336.
11. Ibid., 339.

Article III) to rein in the federal courts and the Supreme Court, and so will prevent it from usurping power.

Mason, Yates, and other great Anti-Federalists lost the argument over the Constitution's ratification. Yet they were right and the Federalists were wrong about what the federal courts and the Supreme Court would do in the long run for the power of the central government and the power of the Supreme Court, as well as what injury they would wreak against both the people's liberties and the unhindered exercise of each state's self-government.

Though they were unable to prevent ratification of the Constitution, the arguments of Anti-Federalists sufficiently unsettled enough Americans that an amendment was added to the Constitution to protect the powers of the several states against central government usurpation in general and even against subtle, calculated usurpation and self-aggrandizement by the Supreme Court. That amendment, of course, is our Tenth Amendment, which explicitly denies the usurpation of power from the state governments by the central government, and implicitly forbids similar actions by subtle Supreme Court "justices."

15

Against Subversive Legal Philosophies

The Anti-Federalists were wiser than the Federalists in their understanding of the fallen nature of man. They more clearly understood man's love of power, and therefore feared that the central government would attempt to usurp more power, even to the destruction of the American people's liberty. Consequently, they more accurately foretold what violence federal judges, particularly those on the Supreme Court, would do to the Constitution's system of limited government, separation of powers, checks and balances, and federalism.

The Anti-Federalists predicted that the federal courts and especially the judges of the Supreme Court would use their power to decide cases to explain the "sense" of every part of the Constitution that came before them. In doing so, Robert Yates predicted, "they will not confine themselves to any fixed or established rules, but will determine, according to what appears to them, the reason and spirit of the [C]onstitution."[1] They reasoned that the federal courts would expand the power of the central government (to increase their own power) by exploiting the Constitution's vague wording, especially in those articles which convey important powers to the central government. And they would use these vaguely worded clauses to establish "very liberal" (a prescient term, is it not?) principles of constitutional interpretation. The principles or rules which the courts' decisions would establish would then become accepted by Congress, which would explain its own powers by the principles the courts have created, thereby legitimizing the courts' expansions of central government power and simultaneously withdrawing power from the states' legislatures and courts.[2]

---

1. Robert Yates, *The Letters of "Brutus"*, No. XI, in Cecelia M. Kenyon, ed., *The Antifederalists* (Indianapolis: The Bobbs-Merrill Co., 1966), 335.

2. Ibid., 343, 347.

The Anti-Federalists understood and predicted what would become known as "loose construction." "Strict construction" limits the application of the words of a document to the cases clearly described by those words. Loose, or "liberal" construction interprets the meaning of the words of a document in such a way as to more effectively achieve the interpreter's purpose.[3] Anti-Federalists understood judicial restraint—self-restraint which leaves the making of laws to the legislature—and predicted that the federal courts and the Supreme Court would not exercise it but would instead usurp legislative power from Congress which would then usurp power from state legislatures, which were intended to have far more authority over the lives of the American people than was Congress.

Our Tenth Amendment, which declares that the powers not delegated by the states to the central government in the Constitution nor forbidden to the states by the Constitution are reserved to the states, was enacted to protect against loose construction and the federal courts' lack of judicial restraint.

What the Anti-Federalists did not understand, or did not make explicit, was the extent to which man's fallen nature—his rebellion against God and His law—would lead modern thinkers to concoct legal philosophies which would justify such loose construction, wild judicial abandon, and ever-greater usurpations of power and assaults on Americans' liberty. Three of the most influential and destructive of these bodies of thought are Legal Positivism, evolutionism, and "Non-Interpretivism."

Nineteenth century man-centered thought gave us Legal Positivism, which continues to be foundational to the thinking of most judges and to the philosophy of law taught in pre-law courses in colleges and in most law schools. Legal positivism holds that there are no God-given ethical laws which can be known by man; that there are no universally true, knowable ethical principles; hence there is no objective content to "justice." Legal Positivism considers a law just if it is enacted

---

3. William Safire, *Safire's Political Dictionary: An Enlarged, Up-to-Date Edition of The New Language of Politics* (New York: Ballantine Books, 1978), 699.

according to a given regime's prescribed process and if said regime has the power to enforce the law.[4] This reduces law to a matter of the successful use of power and deceit by civil government officials—including judges. Thus if judges can deceive others into accepting their decisions as law the judges' decisions are "just." This makes the meaning of a constitution what the judges say it is—or what they can deceive others into believing it is—which makes a constitution meaningless, replaces the rule of law with the arbitrary rule of men, and justifies judges in doing whatever they can get away with. At least in their own minds, this justifies American judges in doing whatever they can to expand the powers of the central government, usurp powers from the states, and destroy our freedom.

Nineteenth century man-centered thought also gave us evolutionism, which latter-nineteenth century legal thinkers applied to law and twentieth and twenty-first century judges have used to rewrite our Constitution. Basically, if evolutionism were true (it isn't), then the Bible would be false and there would and could be no universally valid ethical laws by which man should live his individual or collective life. Neither the Bible nor any theories of "natural law" could provide us with universally valid ethical principles for law.

Law, then, would have to "evolve" in accordance with... what? Not any objective standard, though various pseudo-standards have been claimed by men (e.g., the knowledge of an elite of some kind; the will of a Leader; the will of the rulers; the will of "the people"; the supposed demands or "needs," or "spirit" of the time, the supposed findings of the "social sciences"). Among other things, evolutionary theories of

---

4. Strictly speaking, Legal Positivism is the application to legal philosophy and law of the nineteenth-century body of pseudo-scientific thought founded by Auguste Comte and known as "Positivism." Positivism held that the only way that man can have certain knowledge is through empiricism, the evidence from the physical world that he derives from his senses, the "scientific method." Comte was ignorant of the insoluble problems with such a man-centered theory of knowledge, but he did note that the scientific method, since it deals only with physical things, cannot give man a knowledge of ethical or moral principles because they are not physical things. Hence the application of Positivism to law makes it impossible (according to positivistic assumptions) for law to be founded on ethics or morality.

law allow judges to "reinterpret" the law to "adapt" it to the time—or to provide judicial justifications for presidential or legislative usurpations of power and violations of the intentions behind the Constitution, amendments, and/or laws. It is from such origins that we get the notion that the judges (and their fellow usurpers) must constantly "reinterpret" the Constitution because it is "a living document."

What they have actually done is murder our Constitution and its provisions' intended meanings in order to make it "alive" to the desires of today's judges, politicians, and left wing intellectuals. And (because of the nature of the leftism dominant among intellectuals and judges) this just happens to necessitate the concentration of power in the central government, further usurpation of power from our states' governments, the removal of limits on civil government's power, and the use of the civil government's power to coercively intervene in virtually every area of our lives in order to accomplish impossible, destructive goals which collectively violate justice and destroy our liberty. All of this is done, of course, in the name of the Constitution, by radical "reinterpretations" (carefully calculated changes in the meaning) of the Constitution—by loose construction to the nth power and the infinite restraint of judicial restraint.

Non-Interpretivism, a product of audacious twentieth-century legal Luddites, goes far beyond loose construction. Non-Interpretivism holds that judges have no responsibility to even attempt to interpret the Constitution. (Some non-interpretivists argue that we cannot know the framers' intentions for our Constitution's provisions—a ridiculous and dishonest claim in light of the fact that we have volumes and volumes of the debates in the Constitutional Convention and the states' ratification conventions, and the writings of the Federalists explaining and defending the Constitution and its provisions against Anti-Federalists' criticisms.) Instead, it maintains, a judge's responsibility is to make rulings on the basis of his own views of the world and of life—and to call the result "constitutional."[5] Such a legal philosophy brazenly reduces the Constitution to a nullity. It scraps the Constitution's own plainly-stated means of changing the Constitution and makes the judges totally arbitrary rulers unbound by anything other

---

5. See Gary L. McDowell, *The Constitution and Contemporary Constitutional Theory* (Cumberland, Virginia: Center for Judicial Studies, 1985).

than the practical limits of their ability to deceive the American people and our elected representatives in the other two branches of the central government—and the increasingly impotent state governments.

Such subversive legal philosophies ignore, obscure, or deny constitutional scholar Charles Warren's dictum, a statement as *consistent* with the concept of constitutionalism and as congruent with the intended interpretation of our Constitution as these legal philosophies are *inconsistent* with both: "However the [Supreme] Court may interpret the Constitution, it is still the Constitution which is the law, and not the decision of the [Supreme] Court."[6] And they are not only contrary to, but also a million miles from George Washington's statement, in his Farewell Address, that until our Constitution is "changed by an explicit and authentic act of the whole people, [it] is sacredly obligatory on all."[7]

Such legal philosophies—along with "sociological jurisprudence" (making rulings on the basis of supposed sociological data rather than upon the intent or wording of the law) and intellectually popular "moral" beliefs rather than the intent of the Constitution and its amendments—have led Federal and U.S. Supreme Court judges to falsify constitutional history, to formulate deceitful legal arguments and rationales to mask the political agendas upon which their decisions are really based, and to engage in what some legal scholars have rightly termed "bald-faced judicial imperialism."[8] It has also led the U.S. Supreme Court into bizarre, illogical reversals of its own recent decisions, brazen rewriting of the unmistakable intent of laws enacted by Congress, court-ordered policies such as forced school bussing which injure innocent parties, and manifest violations of republicanism, federalism, and individual liberty.[9]

Although the authors of the Tenth Amendment did not foresee the development of such subversive legal philosophies—though they did

---

6. Quoted in Berger, 5.

7. Quoted in Berger, 11, n. 32.

8. Thomas E. Woods Jr. and Kevin R. C. Gutzman, *Who Killed the Constitution?: The Fate of American Liberty from World War I to George W. Bush* (New York: Crown Forum, 2008), 41-54.

9. Woods and Gutzman, 55-69.

foresee power-hungry man's ingenious capacity to circumvent restrictions on his power—our Tenth Amendment still gives us an important means of resisting the judges (and others) who serve them. For these perverse legal philosophies are at bottom Machiavellian philosophies of the pragmatic use of power and deceit, and power and deceit can be resisted and overcome. Deceit can be overcome by the dissemination of truth and the refutation of deceit's lies and fallacious arguments. Abusive power can be overcome by truth, resistance, and righteously used power.

The Tenth Amendment is still right there in our Constitution. It still says that the states retain all powers which they have neither forbidden to themselves in the Constitution nor delegated to the national government in the Constitution. The fact that it was added after the ratification of the Constitution (not to mention the legislative history of the Tenth Amendment!) indicates that it was added to check against the misinterpretation of clauses in the Constitution. And this helps us to use it to protect ourselves (and our fellow Americans) against all deceitful attempts, by courts or by others, to usurp powers from the state governments, augment the central government, deprive us of our liberty, and (whether they intend it or not) injure innocent people in the process.

The Tenth Amendment means that each state government still rightly has all powers which it has not delegated to the central government in the Constitution and/or has not forbidden to itself in the Constitution. Each state government can enact laws, pass resolutions, and inform and lead the public in its state—and thereby influence people in the other states of the Union. Each state still has representatives in the central government who have been elected by its people: its members of the House of Representatives and the Senate. Thus the states still have an internal means of checking usurpations and tyranny by the central government. Article I, Section 8 and Article III, Section 1 give Congress the authority to "constitute tribunals inferior to the Supreme Court," and in constituting those lower federal tribunals Congress can limit their authority explicitly. Article III of the Constitution gives Congress important authority over the federal courts.[10] Article III, Section 1 states that federal judges, including Supreme Court judges, "shall hold their offices during good behaviour..." Judicial legislation, courts acting as constitutional conventions in continuous session, deceitful rationales formulated by judges, and the enactment of judicial policies which injure innocent people do not constitute good behavior. Article I, Section 2 gives the House of Representatives the sole power of impeachment. Impeachment by the House of Representatives and removal from office by the Senate are at least basic constitutional actions which the representatives of the people of the states should apply to federal and Supreme Court judicial usurpers and tyrants. Article III, Section 2, Paragraph 2 gives Congress the authority to regulate and make exceptions to the appellate jurisdiction of the Supreme Court, thereby limiting the damage judicial imperialists, usurpers, and tyrants of that court can do. From the fact that this has not been done, or seldom been done, it does not follow that it cannot be done—nor that is should not be done. The state governments can work together against such usurpations and tyranny even to push for amendments to the Constitution, if necessary. They can work to protect and reclaim their powers—and our liberty.

But the Tenth Amendment cannot be used for such important ends if there are not enough Americans who know its meaning and significance. And, more importantly, if there are not enough Americans who are militantly dedicated to using it as the Anti-Federalists and others who gave it to us intended it to be used: as the gateway of our liberty.

---

10. This authority is discussed and defended very ably by Ralph Rossum, *Congressional Control of the Judiciary: The Article III Option* (Cumberland, Virginia: Center for Judicial Studies, 1988).

16

The Tenth Amendment and The Presidency

Our Tenth Amendment was framed to protect the reserved powers of the state governments, and it was certainly framed with a cautious and somewhat fearful eye on the American presidency. Anti-Federalists agreed that the presidency was a dangerous institution. It was *too powerful*, especially with the President's power as commander-in-chief, and *too little circumscribed by constitutional limitations*, especially with no bill of rights to protect Americans' rights and liberty. They saw it as an institution tending strongly toward monarchy, and despotic monarchy at that.

"Philadelphiensis" (probably Benjamin Workman, a tutor at the University of Pennsylvania[1]) declared that "the *president general* will be a *king* to all intents and purposes, and one of the most dangerous kind too; a king elected to command a standing army" and a tyrant.[2] He pictured the president as "a *military king*, with a *standing army devoted to his will*", working with a legislative quorum of the "well born" "to have an uncontrolled power over our lives, our liberty, and property, in all cases whatsoever."[3] He saw the president's power over the militia as one which would be used to squelch the liberty of the common citizen soldier under the president's command.[4] If the president were an ambitious man, he would use the veto to control the legislature and shape the laws to fit his will; if he were not an ambitious man, then he would be the minion of the aristocrats, servicing their will rather than

---

1. Cecelia M. Kenyon, ed., *The Antifederalists* (Indianapolis: Bobbs-Merrill, 1966), 69-70.
2. "Letter IX" (1788), in Kenyon, 72, 73.
3. Ibid., 72.
4. Ibid., 73.

the public good, particularly with no bill of rights to protect the people and their liberty.[5] He said that the president, "who is to be our *king* after this government is established, is vested with powers exceeding those of the most *despotic monarch* we know of in modern times"— "an *elective king*" with a standing army.[6]

The great Patrick Henry, in the Virginia Ratification Convention (1788), said, "Your President may easily become king."[7] And warned

> If your American chief be a man of ambition and abili-
> ties, how easy is it for him to render himself absolute!
> The army is in his hands, and if he be a man of address,
> it will be attached to him, and it will be the subject of
> long meditation with him to seize the first auspicious
> moment to accomplish his design... If we make a king,
> we may prescribe the rules by which he shall rule his
> people, and interpose such checks as shall prevent him
> from infringing them; but the President, in the field, at
> the head of his army, can prescribe the terms on which
> he shall reign master, so far that it will puzzle any Amer-
> ican ever to get his neck from under the galling yoke.[8]

Henry said the President would use the army to "beat down every opposition"; that the militia (drawn by the President from the respective states) would "leave you and assist in making him king, and fight against you; and what have you to oppose this force? What will then become of you and your rights? Will not absolute despotism ensue?"[9]

George Clinton, the New York statesman, in the fourth of "The Letters of Cato" (1787), cited Montesquieu on republics against the President's great powers and long tenure. He saw these as a temptation to the President's ambition and a threat to Americans' liberty.[10] Using the great French political philosopher's warning, Clinton said of the President,

---

5. Ibid., 74.
6. Ibid., 77.
7. Ibid., 257.
8. Ibid., 257-258.
9. Ibid., 258.
10. Ibid., 303.

> ...his eminent magisterial situation will attach many
> adherents to him, and he will be surrounded by ex-
> pectants and courtiers, his power of nomination and
> influence on all appointments, the strong posts in each
> state comprised within his superintendence, and gar-
> risoned by troops under his direction, his control over
> the army, militia, and navy, the unrestrained power of
> granting pardons for treason, which may be used to
> screen from punishment those whom he had secretly
> instigated to commit the crime, and thereby prevent
> a discovery of his own guilt, his duration in office for
> four years: these, and various other principles evident-
> ly prove the truth of the position, that if the president
> is possessed of ambition, he has power and time suf-
> ficient to ruin his country.[11]

The President, "possessing the powers of a monarch," would be surrounded by courtiers like a monarch—courtiers whose character is ambitious but idle, base but prideful, avaricious but lazy, averse to truth and perfidious, flattering, treasonous, adulating people of fortune and power, and above all perpetually ridiculing virtue.[12] Clinton asked, "...wherein does this president, invested with his powers and prerogatives, essentially differ from the king of Great Britain[?]..."[13] The exercise of such powers, Clinton reasoned, would tend "either to the establishment of a vile and arbitrary aristocracy or monarchy."[14]

In his fifth letter (1787), Clinton warned that Americans could not count on either the presumption that American rulers would govern well or the belief that the opinions and morals of the American people "are capable to resist and prevent an extension of prerogative or oppression..." He warned that

> ...you must recollect that opinion and manners [mor-
> als] are mutable, and may not always be a permanent

---

11. Ibid., 304.
12. Ibid., 304-305.
13. Ibid., 305.
14. Ibid., 306.

obstruction against the encroachments of government; that the progress of a commercial society begets luxury, the parent of inequality, the foe to virtue, and the enemy to restraint; and that ambition and voluptuousness, aided by flattery, will teach magistrates where limits are not explicitly fixed to have separate and distinct interests from the people; besides, it will not be denied that government assimilates the manners [morals] and opinions of the community to it. Therefore a general presumption that rulers will govern well is not a sufficient security.[15]

And he predicted that "...your posterity will find that great power connected with ambition, luxury, and flattery, will as readily produce a Caesar, Caligula, Nero and Domitian in America, as the same causes did in the Roman Empire."[16]

If the President would be an ambitious man who would be surrounded by a corrupt, flattering court and make himself a despotic king, or descend to the immoral depth of a Caligula or a Nero, the presidency was a dangerous institution, and certainly not a model for Americans. A presidency with such inherent temptations to our chief executive, such dangerous powers and innate threats to Americans' liberty was also a threat to the states' powers, self-government, and inherited ways, for an ambitious president would surely usurp power from the states and seek to subordinate all things to his will. Such a presidency was a threat to the liberty of the people of the states.

These analyses and warnings of the Anti-Federalists, which resonate so powerfully today, after the growth of the "imperial presidency" and particularly under the administration of a president who recognizes virtually no constitutional limits on his actions and has expressed a desire for an internal police force equal in power to our army, were an important part of the case made by thoughtful opponents of ratification of the Constitution. These warnings are an important part of the reason why we have the Bill of Rights—and why the Tenth Amend-

---

15. Ibid., 309.

16. Ibid.

ment, protecting the reserved powers of the states and thus protecting Americans against centralized tyranny, was an essential component of our Bill of Rights.

17

Versus "Constitutional Dictatorship"

Along the main lines of their concerns about the Presidency, the Anti-Federalists were right. The Presidency was too powerful, too little restrained by constitutional limitations, too vulnerable to abuse by a man ambitious of great power—especially in conjunction with his party having controlling majorities in both houses of Congress. The Constitution's failure in this regard left an "ambitious" President too much temptation to seize—or create—a crisis or emergency in order to augment his own power. And the aggregate of that presidential power, we who have seen the destructive effects of modern man-centered ideologies can add, made the American governmental system too vulnerable to presidents motivated by the dream of using unlimited power to achieve the purposes of a man-centered ideology such as "democracy,"[1] progressivism, liberalism, or some other variety of socialism.

The power of the Presidency, and Americans' tolerance of that power, have grown tremendously—partly by presidents' designs, partly by the opportunities for usurpation provided by historic crises, partly

---

1. "Democracy" is, properly speaking, a form of popular government ruled directly by the majority. Republican government is another—better—form of popular government which is based on rule by representatives chosen by the majority, or by various groups within the territory of a republic. Almost all (all but one, James Wilson) of the framers of our Constitution wanted a republic, not a democracy—for good reasons drawn from biblical teaching and human experience. "Democracy" as an ideology glorifies "democracy" in the abstract, ignores the distinction between democratic and republican civil governments, assumes that everyone is "equal" (contrary to biblical teaching, human experience, and empirical evidence), glorifies the majority will, supposes that the "democratic process" necessarily produces a good result. Proponents of democracy worship equality and make an undefined "equality" the touchstone of all that is deemed good in society, civil government, and economic life.

through bipartisan factionalism, and partly by our elected officials' (presidents and others) dereliction of duty. Presidential power has also grown partly because of the perversion of our educational system[2] and the consequent constitutional ignorance of the American people.[3]

The growth of presidential power began with Lincoln, of course, and his use of the crisis of the "Civil War," partly provoked by his own actions,[4] to incline our governmental system away from the intentions of the Constitution's Framers and Ratifiers and toward a more democratic system based on national majority will,[5] a process by which he radically changed the Union from a federal to a centralized one. Lincoln violated the Constitution royally during his term of office, claiming the war powers of the Presidency to justify his actions. So extensively did he violate the Constitution that Clinton Rossiter included Lincoln's actions in his study, *Constitutional Dictatorship—Crisis Government in the Modern Democracies.*[6] M.E. Bradford thus summarized **some** of Lincoln's unconstitutional actions:

> Lincoln began his tenure as dictator when between
> April 12 and July 4 of 1861, without interference from

---

2. If space permitted, at least three facets of this would have to be discussed: (1) the abandonment of Christian education by Christians; (2) the widespread adoption of "free public education" and the perversion of that education under the influence of the main currents of modern man-centered philosophical, educational, and political thought; and (3) the perversion of American higher education under the same influences.

3. This is certainly an incomplete list, to which would have to be added at least: the failure of the church, the crafty influence of the arts of publicity and propaganda, the seductive lure of socialistic "programs," the leftist dominance of the mass media, and many Americans' larcenous hearts.

4. Particularly his insistence on continuing the tariff, the longest-debated political issue in the years prior to the "Civil War," which the South saw as legalized theft benefitting Northern manufacturing interests at its expense, and his insistence on garrisoning and reinforcing the Federal troops in U.S. military installations such as Fort Sumter, located in Southern states.

5. So say Lincoln's ablest defenders.

6. (Princeton University Press, 1948). Rossiter approved of Lincoln's actions, though he knew that they were unconstitutional and thought that constitutions should provide for systematic violation of their limitations on civil government in times of crisis.

Congress, he summoned militia, spent millions, sus-
pended law, authorized recruiting, decreed a blockade,
defied the Supreme Court, and pledged the nation's
credit. In the following months and years he created
units of government not known to the Constitution and
officers to rule over them in "conquered" sections of the
South, seized property throughout both sections, arrest-
ed upwards of 20,000 of his political enemies and confined them without trial in a Northern "Gulag," closed
over 300 newspapers critical of his policy, imported an
army of foreign mercenaries (of perhaps 500,000 men),
interrupted the assembly of duly elected legislatures and
employed the Federal hosts to secure his own reelection—in a contest where about 38,000 votes, if shifted,
might have produced an armistice and a negotiated
peace under a President McClellan. To the same end he
created a state in West Virginia, arguing of this blatant
violation of the explicit provisions of the Constitution
that it was "expedient."[7]

Lincoln's presidential rhetoric, Bradford noted, was even worse, for it
justified the attempt to achieve vaguely defined, high-sounding ends by
unconstitutional means.[8] The combination of Lincoln's rhetoric with his
concentrations of power in the national government and the Presidency,
Gottfried Dietze noted, turned our governmental system away from freedom:

---

7. M.E. Bradford, "The Lincoln Legacy: A Long View," *Modern Age*, Volume 24, Number 4 (Fall, 1980), 359.

8. M.E. Bradford, *A Better Guide Than Reason: Studies in the American
Revolution* (La Salle, Illinois: Sherwood Sugden & Co., 1979), 29-57 and
185-203; "Dividing the House: The Gnosticism of Lincoln's Rhetoric," *Modern
Age*, 23 (1979), 10-24; "The Lincoln Legacy: A Long View," *Modern Age*, 24
(1980), 355-363; M.E. Bradford, *The Reactionary Imperative; Essays Literary
and Political* (Peru, Illinois: Sherwood Sugden & Co., 1990), "Against Lincoln:
A Speech at Gettysburg," 221-226. As Woods and Gutzman, 43-69, note,
such an attitude was also responsible for the U.S. Supreme Court's deliberate
perversion of the meaning of the 14th Amendment in order to achieve a social
and political result which it thought was "just" but knew was unconstitutional.

> Lincoln's administration…opened the way for the de-
> velopment of an omnipotent national executive who
> as a spokesman for the people might consider himself
> entitled to do whatever he felt was good for the Na-
> tion, irrespective of the interests and rights of states,
> Congress, the judiciary, and the individual.[9]

Clearly Lincoln centralized the formerly Federal Union, radically increased the powers of the Presidency, and established a precedent for jettisoning the Constitution's restraints on executive power in the name of a national "emergency." Even assuming, as does Rossiter, that Lincoln intended his dictatorship to be temporary, the Constitution has no provision allowing even for temporary dictatorship. The kinds of things Lincoln did were what the Anti-Federalists had feared and predicted.

Lincoln's example paved the way for later presidents to use real or alleged "crises" or "emergencies" as opportunities to disregard or throw off the Constitution's restraints on the central government in general and the Presidency in particular. (This helps us understand President Obama's deliberate likening of himself to Lincoln before his inaugura-tion.) Woodrow Wilson, who was an influential political scientist as well as a powerful politician, sought to make our central government into a majority-rule, socialistic democracy. As a political scientist he criticized the Constitution's deliberately complex, purposely inefficient system (it was intended to protect property and liberty and maximize justice, not to be efficient in enacting restraints on people's freedom) and advocated a democratic government like the British parliamentary system. As an orator he attacked free enterprise and the wealthy, and laid the founda-tion for the establishment of a socialistic (tax-funded) "welfare state." As President, Wilson used the "crisis" of World War I to establish unconsti-tutional, dictatorial controls over American economic life and thought.[10] These controls included a propaganda campaign to convince the Ameri-

---

9. *America's Political Dilemma: From Limited to Unlimited Democracy* (Baltimore: Johns Hopkins Press, 1968), 58, quoted in Bradford, "The Lincoln Legacy: A Long View," 362.

10. See Paul Eidelberg, *A Discourse on Statesmanship; The Design and Transformation of the American Polity* (Urbana: University of Illinois Press, 1974).

can people to support the war, the conscription of millions of Americans into the armed forces, and a successful effort to criminalize opposing views and suppress the freedom of speech of those who opposed the war "to make the world safe for democracy."[11]

A most insidious means of expanding presidential power invented by Wilson (in 1916) was the issuing of presidential "executive orders," through which the President essentially issues commands (legislates) for the federal bureaucratic agencies. Subsequent presidents used executive orders, which have the force of law and require a two-thirds vote of Congress to nullify, to build a massive, unpublicized program of controls—an unconstitutional, unlimited, bureaucratic state—over American life. Presidential executive orders have used the possibility of an undefined national "emergency"—which could be a peacetime condition—to claim virtually unlimited powers to control Americans' lives, property, and activities.[12] In such an undefined but presidentially-declared "emergency," said Sen. Mathias of Maryland in 1975,

> ...the President may: seize property; organize and control the means of production; seize commodities; assign military forces abroad; institute martial law; seize and control all transportation and communication; regulate the operation of private enterprise; restrict travel; and, in a plethora of particular ways, control the lives of all American citizens.[13]

Franklin Delano Roosevelt used the crisis of the Great Depression (which his actions and policies helped deepen and prolong) to attack free enterprise and the wealthy, establish central government controls over economic life and debase our money to fiat currency, and estab-

---

11. Woods and Gutzman, 5-20. Woods and Gutzman, 6-7, 21, note that President Jefferson would have argued that the Sedition Act of 1918 violated both the First Amendment's protection of freedom of speech and the Tenth Amendment because the states never delegated a power to criminalize speech to the federal government.

12. Gary North, *Government by Emergency* (Fort Worth: American Bureau of Economic Research, 1983), ix-xi, 99-110.

13. Quoted in North, 103.

lish a socialistic "welfare state"—all in blatant violation of the intentions behind and principles of our Constitution. He used the crisis or "emergency" of World War II (or our participation in it—chiefly as a result of his policies) to increase central government and presidential controls over Americans' lives and American economic life, partly by creating federal regulatory bureaucracies and partly by creating central government "entitlement" programs by which to "transfer" wealth and property from one group of citizens to others. And he used his multi-term presidency (which may have continued if not for his death) to recast the U.S. Supreme Court, which was formerly protecting the original intent of the Constitution, into a self-consciously Constitution-subverting ("reinterpreting", i.e., amending) institution.

With the partial exception of Ronald Reagan, subsequent presidents—Republican as well as Democrat—have followed in Lincoln's, Wilson's, and Roosevelt's footsteps. President Truman seized America's (actually Americans') steel mills during the "crisis" or "emergency" of the Korean War although he had neither constitutional nor statutory authority to do so.[14] In doing so, Truman followed the two major false arguments premeditated by the Republican Roosevelt (Theodore) in the early 20th century: (1) that "the president is the unique representative of the American people"[15] and (2) that the president's power

---

14. Woods and Gutzman, 23-29.

15. Ibid., 31. This argument is false for several reasons. First, our Constitution contains several kinds of representation of the American people: the representatives which the people of each state elect to their state's government; the representatives which the people of the states elect to the U.S. House of Representatives; the representatives which the state legislatures, then (after the ratification of the 17th Amendment in 1913) the people of each state elect to the U.S. Senate; the President, who is elected by the representatives of the people via the Electoral College, not the direct vote of the national majority; and the federal and U.S. Supreme Court judges, who are appointed by the President with the consent of the U.S. Senate. The Constitution neither states nor implies that any of these kinds of representation is any higher than any other. Second, our Constitution is based on a separation of powers which does not give the President **any** legislative authority, much less any authority to in effect amend our Constitution by doing what the document does not authorize him to do. Third, the debates in the Constitutional Convention and particularly those in the states' ratification conventions (and, for that matter,

is absolute unless some provision of the Constitution expressly denies authority to him.[16] Lyndon Johnson's "Great Society" programs made our government even more socialistic and more unconstitutional, further undermined federalism, and made us less free. The Obama administration, though shocking in its usurpations, speed of attack, advancement of socialism, and incursions on what remains of our liberty, does not represent a radical break with the intentions of some of our previous presidents.

Presidents have not done this alone. They have been helped governmentally by congressional majorities and U.S. Supreme Court decisions.[17] Intellectually they have been aided by the mainstream of collectivistic social, political, and legal thinkers—and many socialist or interventionist economists. Politically they have been helped by writers of textbooks, professors and teachers, publicists, political consultants, and propagandists who have attacked the authors of our Constitution, praised presidents who have violated the Constitution, and popularized, apologized, and propagandized for left-wing politicians who have wanted to violate the Constitution.

Today the Presidency is an imperial presidency[18] defined by the legacy of the great violators of the Constitution. The President is more

---

the writings of the Constitution's advocates) make it clear that the Framers and Ratifiers of the Constitution intended the President's power to be limited, not unlimited, even in "crisis" situations and "emergencies."

16. Woods and Gutzman, 32. This argument is so bald-facedly unconstitutional (for at least the reasons stated before) that a President should be impeached for even using it: for it is nothing less than a deceitful rationale for usurpation of power, the transformation (or deformation!) of the presidency into an office of virtually unlimited power, and a manifest threat to Americans' liberty. It is therefore among the "high crimes and misdemeanors" for which a president should be impeached. It is also a vindication of the Anti-Federalists' wisdom.

17. Ibid., 32-37, note that virtually none of the U.S. Supreme Court judges who considered Truman's seizure of the steel mills had a truly constitutional view of the President's powers.

18. "Liberal" historian Arthur M. Schlesinger, Jr.'s book *The Imperial Presidency*, as many have noted, was correct about the modern American presidency but his book was a work of opportunistic hypocrisy, since Schlesinger had spent his academic career praising presidents who usurped power to the

than ever, as the Anti-Federalists predicted, surrounded by ambitious, base, prideful, avaricious, perfidious courtiers who ridicule virtue, covet power, and, we must add, are too often motivated by the evil doctrines of one variety or another of modern socialistic ideology. If he is a leftist he is supported by an army of willing accomplices in our news media. Our current President, backed by sympathetic Democrat majorities in both houses of Congress, is eager to abandon all constitutional limitations in order to exercise arbitrary, virtually unlimited power to achieve his ideological and political ends. But whoever the President is, he has thousands of executive orders—those decreed by previous presidents (Republicans and Democrats) and his own—available to enable him to rule arbitrarily, for Congress has not checked these usurpations of power. Moreover, the President has hundreds of special laws which he can use during a "declared national emergency," which he can declare without initial congressional approval. By these "emergency" laws the President has virtually unlimited, arbitrary powers to rule the nation and control the lives of Americans without being limited by our Constitution's normal processes. Truly, these presidentially-decreed "laws" are a "blueprint for tyranny."[19]

Things are both worse than and not necessarily so bad as the Anti-Federalists predicted. The situation is dire, but the basic structure of our once federal system still exists and functions, within limits. And the Tenth Amendment is still there—in the Constitution—with the potential to be read, understood, and acted upon. Our presidents—and the Congresses which were supposed to restrain them—have acted upon their lust for power (and their desire for wealth and personal advancement) to establish their visions perverted by man-centered ideologies. Far too many of our state governments' officials have failed to act to defend the principles of the Tenth Amendment because they also have been motivated by a lust for positions of power in the national government, or by the utopian dreams of modern political and economic ideologies, and/or by covetousness to receive their share of Federal money stolen from Americans.

---

presidency and was, in typical "liberal" fashion, only opposed to "imperial" presidential power when it was in Republican hands.

19. North, 99-125,

But we the people of our respective states still have the means of influencing our countrymen. We still have the means of influencing our state's government's officials—and our state's representatives in national government—to understand the superiority of our original federal system to that of our contemporary centralized, bureaucratic, arbitrary, unconstitutional leviathan; to reassert and recapture the constitutional powers of the states to govern themselves; to oppose arbitrary, unconstitutional presidential absolutism; and to recover our lost and endangered liberty.

18

The Tenth Amendment and Congress

In the debates over the ratification of our Constitution, Congress did not escape the Anti-Federalists' discerning criticism. They feared and distrusted it.[1] William Lancaster, in the North Carolina Ratification Convention, said that too much power had been entrusted to Congress without enough restraints on their power.[2] Patrick Henry said in the Virginia Ratification Convention that "liberty has been destroyed most often...by the tyranny of rulers," and that he feared that too much power had been put into the hands of Congress.[3]

The Anti-Federalists wanted to limit Congress's power to tax. Lancaster was "apprehensive that the power of taxation is unlimited."[4] All Anti-Federalists wanted to limit Congress's power of direct taxation to cases in which a state did not pay its fair share according to the census.[5] The Pennsylvania Minority opposed internal taxation, holding that it would "effect the destruction of the State governments, and produce one consolidated [centralized] government."[6] They opposed Congress's power of direct taxation (of individuals) on two counts. First, they opposed the capitation or poll tax: "...Congress...is expressly vested with the authority of laying a capitation or poll tax upon every person to any amount." They attacked this tax as a favorite of despotic

---

1. Cecelia M. Kenyon, ed., *The Antifederalists* (Indianapolis: The Bobbs-Merrill Co., 1966), 422.

2. Ibid., 416.

3. Ibid., 243.

4. Ibid., 415.

5. Ibid., 422.

6. *The Address and Reasons of Dissent of the Minority of the Convention of the State of Pennsylvania to their Constituents* (1787), in Kenyon, 54.

governments, oppressive in its nature, and unequal in its operation.[7] Second, they attacked direct taxation as antithetical to liberty and beyond the power of the state governments to control or moderate:

> The power of direct taxation will further apply to every individual, as Congress may tax land, cattle, trades, occupations, etc., to any amount, and every object of internal taxation is of that nature that however oppressive, the people will have but this alternative, either to pay the tax or let their property be taken, for all resistance will be vain. The standing army and select militia would enforce the collection.[8]

Anti-Federalists saw Congress's taxation power as a direct threat to the authority and power of the state governments, and thus as a threat to both the states and liberty. They said that Congress would use the "General Welfare Clause" (Article I, Section 8) to "construe every purpose for which the State legislatures now lay taxes, ... and thereby seize upon every object of revenue" from the states, as "Centinel" put it.[9] Combined with the "Supremacy Clause" (Article VI), this would "absorb the state legislatures and judicatories."[10]

The Anti-Federalists wanted the diverse interests of Americans to be protected. They argued that the "extended republic" advocated by the Federalists was so big that these diverse interests could not be adequately represented in Congress. That is one reason why they favored a much larger sphere of self-government by the "small republics" of the state governments.

These discerning critics feared that the members of Congress would use their great, vaguely stated powers and opportunity to win reelection, effectively becoming a hereditary aristocracy. George Mason said, "This government will commence in a moderate aristocracy; it is at present impossible to foresee whether it will, in its operation, produce a

---

7. Ibid., 54.

8. Ibid., 54.

9. Ibid., 9. "Centinel," says Kenyon (9), was probably Samuel Bryan, one of the authors of the Pennsylvania Constitution of 1776.

10. Ibid., 10.

monarchy, or a corrupt oppressive aristocracy; it will most probably vibrate some years between the two, and then terminate in the one or the other."[11] The Pennsylvania Minority saw aristocracy as arising from the mode of election and tenure of the states' representatives in Congress: "From the mode of their election and appointment they will consist of the lordly and high minded; of men who will have no congenial feelings with the people, but a perfect indifference for, and contempt of them; they will consist of those harpies of power that prey upon the very vitals, that riot on the miseries of the community."[12]

Anti-Federalists sought to prevent such an eventuality. Hence the fourth amendment proposed by Virginia denied that any set of men are entitled to "separate or exclusive public emoluments or privileges from the community" except for public services, and denied that either such emoluments or any public office can be hereditary. And Virginia's fifth proposed amendment advocated that members of the legislature and the executive "be restrained from oppression by feeling and participating in the public burdens" by reducing them "to a private station," returning them "into the mass of the people" via term limits.[13]

These discerning critics of the Constitution saw a grave threat in the "Supremacy Clause" (Article VI), which makes treaties (negotiated by the President and ratified by the Senate) the supreme law of the land. Luther Martin of Maryland (another framer of the Constitution who refused to sign it) said of the changed version of the clause,

> ...it is now worse than useless, for being so altered as
> to render the treaties and laws made under the general
> government superior to our [Maryland's] constitution,
> if the system is adopted it will amount to a total and
> unconditional surrender to that [central] government,
> by the citizens of this state, of every right and privilege
> secured to them by our [state's] constitution, and an ex-
> press compact and stipulation with the general govern-

---

11. *Objections to the Proposed Federal Constitution*, in Kenyon, 195.

12. Ibid., 55-56.

13. Ibid., 428.

ment that it may, at its discretion, make laws in direct violation of those rights.[14]

The thirteenth proposition of the minority of the delegates to the Pennsylvania Ratification Convention sought to protect Americans' rights against this:

> That no treaty which shall be directly opposed to the existing laws of the United States in Congress assembled, shall be valid until such laws shall be repealed or made conformable to such treaty; neither shall any treaties be valid which are in contradiction to the Constitution of the United States, or the constitution[s] of the several States."[15]

These prescient statesmen saw the Constitution's defects regarding Congress as a huge threat to Americans' liberty and to the state governments which then protected their citizens' liberty. As the insightful Robert Yates put it in his *Letters of Brutus*, No. VI, the question between the advocates and opponents of ratification of the Constitution was "whether or not this system is so formed as either directly to annihilate the state governments, or that in its operation it will certainly effect it."[16] Anti-Federalists thought the Constitution's design and the powers it gave the central government would eventually result in this disastrous end.

Therefore they wanted a better system of separation of powers and checks and balances,[17] with more numerous, more effective checks and balances,[18] and more clearly stated limits on the Congressional majorities' discretionary authority.[19] Thus "Agrippa" (James Winthrop?), who provided a list of declared conditions which Massachusetts should insist

---

14. *A Letter, Number II, To the Citizens of Maryland* (1788), in Kenyon, 164.

15. *The Address and Reasons of Dissent of the Minority of the Convention of the State of Pennsylvania to their Constituents* (1787), in Kenyon, 37-38.

16. Ibid., 324.

17. Ibid., lxxvi-lxxxiii.

18. Ibid., lxxvi.

19. Ibid., lxxv.

on before it would ratify the Constitution, stated his 11th condition: "No powers shall be exercised by Congress or the president but such as are expressly given by this constitution and not excepted by this declaration…"[20] Thus Anti-Federalists insisted on the addition of a bill of rights to the Constitution, as Virginia put it, "asserting and securing from encroachment the essential and unalienable rights of the people."[21]

Anti-Federalists thought Congress would use its power to make the central government oppress the states and their people, and that the Constitution did not leave the states enough power to enable them to effectively resist such oppression. They were not naïve. They did not trust the fact that the members of Congress would be Americans to protect them against the temptations that come with the power of the sword. Nor did they place any confidence in the fact that the members of Congress would be elected by the people of their own states and districts. They did not believe Americans were exceptions to the doctrine of Original Sin, nor that a well-designed form of civil government could eliminate human sinfulness. They knew the temptation to abuse governmental power had been almost inescapable throughout history. They knew and said that virtue is essential to protect and preserve the rights and liberty of a people, but they also knew that virtue sometimes manifests itself in sustained forceful action. Thus Patrick Henry said, "My great objection to this government is, that it does not leave us the means of defending our rights, or of waging war against tyrants… Have we the means of resisting disciplined armies, when our only defence, the militia, is put into the hands of Congress?"[22] Hence the third of Virginia's proposed amendments to the Constitution included a statement (similar to that of the Maryland Constitution's bill of rights) "that the doctrine of non-resistance against arbitrary power and oppression is absurd, slavish, and destructive to the good and happiness of mankind."[23]

All Anti-Federalists sought to obtain an explicit declaration in the Constitution that the powers which the states had not delegated to the

20. Ibid., 156.
21. Ibid. 428.
22. Ibid., 243.
23. Ibid., 428.

national government are reserved to the states—but, as Kenyon notes, they did not use language indicating that these powers are reserved to the states "or to the people," as the Tenth Amendment was to put it.[24] They sought to protect the powers of the state governments against federal usurpation via Congressional legislation (as well as by presidential action and judicial chicanery) so that the states could govern their own territories—but also so that the state governments could use their remaining powers to resist central government tyranny if it became necessary.

That is why, under Patrick Henry's influence, the very first amendment which Virginia's Ratification Convention proposed to the Constitution was "That each state in the Union shall respectively retain every power, jurisdiction, and right, which is not by this Constitution delegated to the Congress of the United States, or to the departments of the federal government."[25] That is why, sharing the knowledge, views and concerns of Patrick Henry and his Virginia colleagues, the Anti-Federalists used their considerable influence to help craft what became our Tenth Amendment: "The powers not delegated to the United States by the Constitution or prohibited by it to the States, are reserved to the States respectively, or to the people."

---

24. Ibid., 422. Of course, the Tenth Amendment's "or to the people" wording meant "to the people of each respective state," for if these words had been meant to refer to "the people of the United States" such wording would have made the Tenth Amendment meaningless since it would have given the national majority a means of negating the reserved powers of the states—and of the people of each state.

25. Ibid., 431.

19

A Check to Restrain Congress

The Anti-Federalists were right about the U.S. Supreme Court and the Federal Courts. They were right about the Presidency. They were right about Congress, too. The Constitution does not *adequately hedge* Congressional powers—giving Congress more power than the Bible would justify, and far too much latitude to exercise arbitrary judgment—but the Constitution also fails to *clearly define* those given powers with great enough precision.

Congress's power to tax—via direct taxes on individuals and internal taxes on the people in their respective states—is unlimited but should have been limited. If the Framers had followed the Bible carefully and applied a strict interpretation of I Samuel 8, they would have limited the total tax burden by all levels of our civil governments (state, local and national) to less than ten percent (what God demands), and would have divided that taxing power among our three levels of civil government. This would have greatly reduced the taxing power of Congress and correspondingly increased the Constitution's protection of Americans' freedom.

Congress's unlimited power to tax is a threat to the state governments because the more Congress takes the less is left for the state governments to use for their purposes. The people can also more easily resist taxation from the state government due to its closer proximity to the people of a state than the central government is to all Americans. And, as the Anti-Federalists complained, the Constitution left the state governments no direct power to resist or modify central government taxation.[1] Beyond the limited biblical level of taxation (for God is the infallible Authority on taxation), it is true, as Chief Justice

---

1. Cecelia M. Kenyon, *The Antifederalists*, 54.

111

John Marshall later said, that the power to tax is the power to destroy. Congress's unlimited power to tax is a power to destroy both the states' governments and Americans' liberty.

The "Supremacy Clause" (Article VI, Paragraph 2) certainly was a dangerous provision to include in the Constitution, for it mandates that not only laws made pursuant to the Constitution but also "all treaties made...under the authority of the United States, shall be the supreme law of the land; and the judges in every State shall be bound thereby, any thing in the Constitution or laws of any State to the contrary notwithstanding." As the Anti-Federalists warned, this clause gives the President, who negotiates treaties, and the Senate, which ratifies treaties, the means to destroy the constitutions and bills of rights of the states, but also the rights and liberty of the people of the several states, as well as Americans' rights under the Constitution itself. We are seeing the upshot of this today with such internationalist abominations as the United Nations Convention on the Rights of the Child, whereby the central government can ratify treaties that destroy the rights of American parents to discipline and correct their children, give them a Christian or other religious education, and exercise parental authority over their own children. With internationalist documents like the United Nations "Climate Change" treaty, an American President, with Senate approval, could sign away our national sovereignty, our control over how much Americans are taxed, and the remainder of our liberty. As Maryland statesman, framer of the Constitution and Anti-Federalist Luther Martin said, the Supremacy Clause "renders the treaties and laws made under the general government superior to our constitution, if the system is adopted it will amount to a total and unconditional surrender to that government, by the citizens of this state, of every right and privilege secured to them by our constitution, and an express compact and stipulation with the general government that it may, at its discretion, make laws in direct violation of those rights."[2]

As Virginia statesman, Framer, and Anti-Federalist George Mason said, this could have been avoided "by proper distinctions with respect to treaties, and requiring the assent of the House of Representatives,

---

2. Ibid., 164.

where it could be done with safety."[3] Or, clearer yet, the thirteenth proposition of the minority of the delegates to the Pennsylvania Ratification Convention should have been made to replace the dangerous portion of Article VI: "That no treaty which shall be directly opposed to the existing laws of the United States in Congress assembled, shall be valid until such laws shall be repealed or made conformable to such treaty; neither shall any treaties be valid which are in contradiction to the Constitution of the United States, or the constitution[s] of the several States."[4] Or the suggestion by "Agrippa" (James Winthrop?) in his 18th "Letter To the Massachusetts Convention," that "Nothing in this constitution shall deprive a citizen of any state of the benefit of the bill of rights established by the constitution of the state in which he shall reside..."[5] should have been added to the Constitution. Since these things were not done, the "Supremacy Clause" is a threat to the states and to our rights and liberty.

But these clauses are not the only threat to Americans' rights and liberty—the biggest threat is the dominant attitude of Congress. Congress has long rejected the idea that its authority and powers are limited at all, much less limited to those powers plainly stated in our Constitution. It rejects the idea that the Commerce Clause (Article I, Section 8) denies Congress the power to construct (or finance the construction of) roads, bridges, canals and the like. It rejects the idea that the General Welfare Clause (Article I, Section 8) and the Necessary and Proper Clause (also Article I, Section 8) deny Congress the authority to do whatever it wants to do.[6] As Woods and Gutzman note,

---

3. Ibid, 194. Actually, Mason was half-right about this. Proper distinctions with respect to treaties would be useful, but as we know by the recent conduct of the House majority party and by the conduct of other House majorities, though the House might provide additional protection, but it could just as easily support unconstitutional decisions advocated by the Senate.

4. *The Address and Reasons of Dissent of the Minority of the Convention of the State of Pennsylvania to their Constituents* [1787] in Kenyon, 37, 38.

5. Ibid., 157.

6. James Madison and the Framers and Ratifiers of our Constitution rejected all notions of the right of Congress to evade our Constitution's limitations on Congress's power by deliberately misconstruing the meanings and intentions of these much-abused clauses, as Woods and Gutzman, 71-79

the change came in the twentieth century and can be illustrated by the fact that

> early in the century it seemed obvious to those who
> championed prohibition of alcoholic beverages that
> the federal government could impose this novel policy
> on all the states only through a constitutional amend-
> ment, and so the Eighteenth Amendment was adopted
> and ratified. Yet when various other products were
> banned later in the century, Congress felt perfectly at
> liberty to ban them without any amendment empow-
> ering it to do so.[7]

What constitutional limits does Congress now recognize upon its powers? Spending bills, which are supposed to originate in the House, sometimes originate in the Senate—without provoking any complaint from the House. Laws sometimes originate in the Executive branch, which is not authorized to make laws at all. Congress establishes un-elected federal bureaucracies which create myriads of minute regulations which have the force of law, enforce those unconstitutional regulations, adjudicate disputes concerning those regulations, and enforce those regulations within the boundaries of the states—all without constitutional authorization. Congress enacts laws which—through strings (or *chains* called "federal mandates") attached to "federal government money" made available to the states—require state governments to act as administrative subdivisions of the central government in plain violation of the Constitution. Congress enacts laws which have no basis in constitutional powers delegated by the states or which are based on powers invented by the Supreme Court but not found in the Constitution.

Congress, or the majority in Congress, recognizes no moral limits on its power to tax. By deceitful craft, it creates hidden and/or mis-leadingly-labeled taxes, and it restrains its taxation only upon the basis of current political necessity. The Anti-Federalists warned us about this too.

---

explain.

7. Woods and Gutzman, 79.

As the Anti-Federalists insisted, the Constitution needs a better system of separation of powers and accompanying checks and balances,[8] more numerous and effective institutional checks and balances to enforce the limitations written into the Constitution,[9] and more clearly stated limits on congressional majorities' authority. As Kenyon has said, "These men wanted everything down in black and white, with no latitude of discretion or interpretation left to their representatives in Congress."[10] And, "They wanted explicitness that would confine the discretion of congressional majorities within narrow boundaries."[11] How wise they were!

They especially feared collusion between the President and the Senate, particularly because of the Senate's part in appointment and treaty-ratification: they feared that this would produce "some form of joint Presidential-Senatorial tyranny," says Kenyon.[12] They thought that the longer terms of office and modes of election of our national legislators would result in something like a hereditary aristocracy. Their remedies for these ills were a constitutional provision requiring our lawmakers and other officials to share the same burdens as the rest of Americans, to be subject to the restrictions of the laws they impose on us (unlike our present Congress, which does not want to abandon its own private-enterprise-based "health-care" arrangement for the immoral, unconstitutional abomination they are seeking to impose on us); term limits for the Senate and the President,[13] and the power of recall by the state legislatures—to protect against senatorial abuse of power and to protect the states' sovereignty against the "federal" government.[14]

Anti-Federalists also warned against a standing army and Congress's control over the militia. The Pennsylvania Minority declared, in terms that should give us pause today:

---

8. Kenyon, lxxvi-lxxxiii.
9. Ibid., lxxv, lxxvi.
10. Ibid.
11. Ibid.
12. Kenyon, lxxxi; see also Kenyon, lxxx-lxxxi.
13. Ibid., lxxxiii.
14. Ibid.., lxxxv.

> A standing army in the hands of a government placed
> so independent of the people, may be made a fatal
> instrument to overturn the public liberties; it may be
> employed to enforce the collection of the most oppres-
> sive taxes, and to carry into execution the most arbi-
> trary measures. An ambitious man who may have the
> army at his devotion, may step up into the throne, and
> seize upon absolute power.
>
> The absolute unqualified command that Congress
> have over the militia may be made instrumental to
> the destruction of all liberty, both public and private;
> whether of a personal, civil or religious nature.[15]

As remedies for this, they stated the right of resistance against tyranny and the ability of the states to resist tyranny. "Agrippa" listed as
the sixth condition for Massachusetts's ratification of the Constitution
that "Each state shall have the command of its own militia."[16]

Despite the fact that they were right about these things, the Anti-
Federalists did not succeed in persuading enough other Americans
to incorporate these sage suggestions into the Constitution. Yet their
labors were not totally defeated, for they did succeed in giving us what
became our Tenth Amendment.

Our Tenth Amendment tells us that each state has powers which
are not stated in the Constitution, all the powers of any nation—minus
the powers which the state has delegated to the central government
in the Constitution or which they forbade to themselves in the Constitution. As Edward Albertson noted, "The Tenth Amendment says,
in effect, that the government of the United States has no power that
has not been set forth in the Constitution."[17] Thus the Tenth Amendment tells us that the states have a perfect moral and legal right to
exercise their powers regardless of the will of our central government.
In conjunction with the rest of the Constitution (and with plenty of

---

15. *The Address and Reasons of Dissent of the Minority of the Convention of
the State of Pennsylvania to their Constituents* (1787), in Kenyon, 157.

16. Ibid., 156.

17. *The Sabotage of the Tenth Amendment* (Los Angeles: Citizens' Legal
Defense Alliance, 1975), 16.

primary source support from the words of the Federalist supporters of ratification of our Constitution), it tells us that each state has a far greater scope of authority over its citizens than our national government does. It tells us that the powers of our central government—and of Congress—are limited. Thus the Tenth Amendment tells us that when Congress acts beyond its limited authority and trespasses on the authority of a state, Congress is violating the Constitution.

The Tenth Amendment gives each state an obvious constitutional and legal basis for resisting the encroachments and usurpations of the central government and of Congress. It should also give the officials of the state's governmental institutions motivation for asserting and protecting their legal authority and rights against congressional usurpation. And it should give each state's representatives in our national government a moral as well as a legal interest in working to protect their particular state's legal authority and rights—and thus to protect the legal authority and rights of all states, and the rights and liberty of the people against all intended usurpations by Presidents and Congresses and Supreme Courts.

20

Oaths of Office and Americans' Liberty

At the time of the framing and ratification of our Constitution and its Bill of Rights it was a settled principle of English and American law that an oath is a solemn declaration made before God. Though it is made in the presence of men, an oath has significance that transcends both the men who witness it and mankind.

Oaths of office are expressly stipulated and/or clearly implied in our Constitution for those who are to exercise public office under the Constitution. Article VI of the Constitution states:

> The senators and representatives before mentioned [Article I], and the members of the several State legislatures, and all executive and judicial officers, both of the United States and of the several States, shall be bound by oath or affirmation to support this Constitution....

An "affirmation" is essentially the same thing as an "oath" but was called by a different name to accommodate the minority of Christians who believed that the Bible forbids taking an "oath." But whether it is called an oath or an affirmation, the Constitution requires all legislative, executive, and judicial officers of our central government and our states' governments to give their word binding themselves before God and man to support our Constitution.

Though Article VI forbids a religious test be requisite for federal office, all officials who swear an oath to uphold the Constitution are swearing an oath to uphold a Christian Constitution which—despite much propaganda to the contrary—does manifestly recognize, in Article VII, the Lordship of Christ, implicitly affirming (among other things) that He is God; that He rules history; that He is in authority over these United States; that we have a covenantal relationship to Him; and that He will enforce that covenant by His providential rule of our history, blessing us if we have faith in Him and obey His commandments, but cursing us if we depart from faith in Him and consequently depart from obedience to His commandments.

Article II, Section 1 of our Constitution requires the President to make the document's most elaborate and detailed oath or affirmation before he begins to execute the duties of his office:

> I do solemnly swear (or affirm) that I will faithfully execute the office of President of the United States, and will, to the best of my ability, preserve, protect, and defend the Constitution of the United States.

It makes sense that the President's oath be more explicit and detailed, for he is our chief executive who must enforce the laws of the United States. And he is "commander-in-chief of the army and navy of the United States; and of the militia of the several States, when called into actual service of the United States" (Article II, Section 2). As such he both has crucially important duties and constitutes a great potential threat to American's liberty—as Anti-Federalist critics of the Constitution noted.(See Chapters 16 and 17.) His oath of office requires him to "preserve, protect, and defend the Constitution of the United States." It directs his attention, and ours, to the fact that he is under law: he is subservient to our Constitution, not over it. He is duty-bound before God and man to keep the Constitution from harm or deterioration, to act to guard it from injury, and to exert himself against those—all those—who would threaten it. His duty to "preserve, protect, and defend the Constitution" is explicitly not a license, and certainly not a duty, to undermine, neglect, and attack the Constitution, nor to countenance anything of the kind.

Though the oaths or affirmations required of members of Congress, of federal judges (including Supreme Court "justices"), and of all state legislative, executive, and judicial officers are implicitly shorter and simpler than the President's oath of office, they do not contradict his, nor do they constitute lesser moral obligations to God, to the Constitution, and to the people whom they represent. Similarly, their duty to "support this Constitution" does not constitute a duty to undermine, erode, attack, or overthrow the Constitution. Nor a duty or license to twist, redefine, or "transform" the Constitution—either overtly or deceitfully. Our Constitution, after all, explicitly stipulates the only means of changing its meaning and terms, clearly stated in Article V.

By making the Tenth Amendment part of our Constitution, our early statesmen established federalism as a key part of our constitutional system of fundamental law. When central and state government officials, from all branches of their respective governments, take their oaths (or affirmations) of office, they solemnly swear before God and man to support (or preserve, protect, and defend) the whole Constitution and every part of it—including federalism and the Tenth Amendment. Therefore, quite obviously, every American civil government official at every level is required to support, not undermine, the Constitution and any provision, part, or amendment of it, including the Tenth Amendment.

Federalism is absolutely fundamental to the Constitution. The Tenth Amendment was added to our Constitution to make it crystal clear to all our civil government officials—at every level and in every American civil government—that the powers which the states have neither delegated to the central government nor forbidden to themselves in our Constitution remain firmly and inseparably in the hands of the individual state governments or of the people of each respective state.

Therefore, no government official is to do anything to usurp any authority or power from the state governments. If any power is transferred (delegated) from the states' governments to the central government it must be done by the Constitution's own stated processes for changing the Constitution set forth quite clearly in Article V of the Constitution. Our Tenth Amendment imposes an inescapable moral and political duty on all American civil government officials to oppose, thwart, and defeat any and all attempts to "transfer" any power from the states' civil governments by any unconstitutional means.

Because an oath is by definition a declaration made before God, and because an oath required by our Constitution is an oath made before Jesus Christ, whom our Constitution recognizes as being in authority over our nation, our states, and our historical circumstances, Christ, God, is the ultimate Enforcer of the oaths of office required by our Constitution.

But humanly speaking we American citizens are the ultimate human guardians of that power. We are the ultimate protectors and enforcers of the Tenth Amendment. It is our duty before God and man to support our Constitution and to ensure that our directly and indirectly elected representatives support the Constitution, including all its amendments. If those elected or appointed representatives at any level do not support our Constitution, if indeed they alter it in meaning or effect with any method other than those in Article V, then they have violated their oaths of office and forfeited their authority to serve as our civil government officials. Then it is our duty before God and man to remove them from office and replace them, through the Constitution's own mechanisms, with representatives who will be true to what they swear to do, under God and before us, the people whose states and nation they represent and whose Constitution—with its included purposes of justice and securing the blessings of liberty to ourselves and our posterity—they swear to support.

21

Freedom, Diversity, and Liberty

Even at the time of the framing and ratification of the Constitution and the Bill of Rights to improve the Union established by the Articles of Confederation, the American states covered a great extent of territory and collectively included a significant amount of diversity.[1] There was geographic diversity between the New England States, the Middle States, and the Southern States, and even *within* most states between the coastal, the piedmont, and the upland regions of the state, or other geographical areas peculiar to the state. The diversity of land and waterways in each region or state lent itself to diverse needs and uses, and so contributed to a diversity of economies and economic interests. Although the free people of the Union were generally Anglo-Saxon, Christian and Protestant,[2] there was ethnic diversity, religious

---

1. This is not an exercise in praising "diversity" as such, but in praising limited diversity of the type historically embodied in and intended by our constitutional order. "Diversity" as such is certainly not necessarily good: intellectually, morally, socially, or politically. "Diversity" has worked against moral conduct toward others, peace, social order, life, justice, and liberty in the Balkans and elsewhere. Including more headhunters and cannibals in American society would increase our "diversity," but would not improve American society in any way. "Divide and conquer," or "Divide and rule," illustrates the fallacy of uncritical praise of diversity. Praise of "diversity" as though it were inherently good is a mantra of secular humanists, intellectual and moral relativists, "multiculturalists" and others who apparently either have not thought much about the consequences of their own ideas or seek to subvert and "transform" our religious, social, economic, and political order and replace it with a secularist tyranny which denies in practice the very pseudo-principle which they preach.

2. An exception to this is Maryland, which was established as a Roman Catholic colony.

diversity (overwhelmingly within Christianity), and cultural diversity from region to region, state to state, and community to community within each state, and there was further variance of culture between the East and the West (the frontier) of each state. All these diversities produced *political* differences between or among regions, within states, and within localities and communities.

Americans had achieved a measure of unity (but only a measure) in their struggle for independence from Britain. Yet the success of their war for independence had made them many, for the Declaration of Independence had proclaimed the independence not of "a new nation"[3] but of thirteen free and independent states. They had sought a limited measure of political unity under the Articles of Confederation, but this unity chiefly served for defensive purposes and protected the diversity among the states and their localities by preserving the authority of each state to govern its own affairs. Via the Constitution they sought a greater unity but not an all-encompassing, nor an all-absorbing one. They sought to remain many while they became—for certain national purposes specified in the Constitution—one.

Each of the "many" states which delegated certain of its powers to the national government via the Constitution remained free to govern its own internal affairs except for the powers which it had denied to itself in Article I, Section 9 of the Constitution. Each state contained its own unity and diversity: unity of territory, unity of civil government via its state government, broad unity of Christian culture, unity of historical experience; diversity of geography, diversity of settlement, diversity of economic interest, diversity of ethnic makeup, diversity of religious belief (overwhelmingly) within Christianity, diversity of local civil governments.

The people of each state remained a more or less diverse society with a common history more or less distinct from that of the people of every other state and a similarly distinct political history of the manner in which it had sought to deal with its circumstances and difficulties. The vast majority of people in each of these societies valued their distinct history, way of life, and political bearing more than they

---

3. Contrary to Lincoln's deliberate formulation in the Gettysburg Address.

valued the history, ways and means of the people of the society of any other state. They wanted to continue to govern their own affairs without the interference of the people of any other society or state—and certainly without the interference of the peoples of the majority of the states of the Union.

Anti-Federalist critics of the Constitution argued that a national republic encompassing the territory of all the states could not adequately represent all the diverse interests of the peoples of those states. The people of these diverse states were willing to *learn* from other societies and their civil governments and laws, but they did not want to be *ruled* by them. The people of each state wanted to be and remain free to have their own society develop on its own, and they wanted to govern their own common affairs by means of *their* constitution, civil governments (state and local), and laws. They did not want an excessively powerful national or central government trying to dictate to them how they should run the affairs of their state. They wanted to be free to govern themselves, free to continue to be diverse, free to deal with their own problems in their own way. One of the meanings of liberty is, after all, "the sum of rights and exemptions possessed in common by the people of a community, state, etc."[4]

That is why the states insisted on **at most** a *federal* form of civil government for the nation. Not until they believed and knew that the framers of our Constitution had given them, and intended to give them, a federal form of central government, did their representatives ratify the Constitution. But many—all Anti-Federalists and many who were neither for nor against ratification of the Constitution—doubted that the Constitution's form of government would remain federal in perpetuity. Federalists wanted to render the public mind more favorable to the Constitution, and thus wanted to remove such doubts. That is why the states' representatives in the First Congress framed what became our Tenth Amendment and why the respective state legislatures eventually (over the course of two years) ratified it. Most Americans, of all states, wanted to be sure that the liberty of the people of their particular state, as well

---

4. Jean L. McKechnie, ed., *Webster's New Twentieth Century Dictionary of the English Language; Unabridged*, Second Edition (Cleveland: The World Publishing Co., 1971), 1042.

as the liberty of the people of each other state, to govern themselves free from central government interference would *remain* fundamental to the governmental system established by the Constitution.

Our states today are at least as diverse, in some ways more diverse, than were the states which founded our Union. The people of each state still want to govern themselves as they see fit, free from the interference of other states and, to a large degree, free from the interference of the national government. (Some, a distinct minority, want the central government to intervene in most, many, or all things; some want the central government to intervene in a few things; some want the central government to intervene in a few things but resent the economic and social costs of such interference; and some, a substantial minority, want to be free from central government interference altogether.)

The people of each state still have a moral right, and a constitutional right to govern themselves. Our Tenth Amendment still guarantees federalism and the liberty of each state to govern itself free from unconstitutional "federal" interference, dictation, or coercive "mandates." What is needed is the sustained political will to uphold, defend, and protect the principles of the Tenth Amendment by electing representatives who will do the same.

22

Freedom vs. Centralization

Unlike God's law (which is supremely authoritative, just, and universally applicable), the laws enacted and enforced by men, even when they are based on God's law, are confronted by the diversity of the conditions of God's world and the diversity of the circumstances of life in particular parts of God's world at a given time and era.

This is why central government economic planning is inferior to a free market. Economic planners face an insuperable problem of acquiring and managing more relevant economic data than can be effectively assessed in time to be useful for making policy, which problem does not concern men acting in a free market economy which is regulated by the voluntary exchanges of goods and services between and among individuals who are continually evaluating their own economic interests in response to the ever-changing circumstances of their lives.

But the problem of knowledge affects more than central *economic* planning; it also comes to bear when a central government enacts uniform laws for a diverse territory and people. As "Agrippa" (Massachusetts statesman James Winthrop?)[1] said when questioning the wisdom of the framers of the Constitution in creating what he (correctly) believed was too much power in Congress,

> As in every extensive empire, local laws are necessary to
> suit the different interests, no single legislature is adequate
> to the business. All human capacities are limited to a nar-
> row space, and as no individual is capable of practicing a
> great variety of trades, no single legislature is capable of
> managing all the variety of national and state concerns.[2]

---

1. Kenyon, 131.
2. "The Letters of 'Agrippa,'" No. XVIII (February 5, 1788), in Kenyon, 154.

National lawmakers cannot know all the diverse circumstances which face the individuals who live in all the different communities throughout their entire country. The more extensive and diverse the country, the greater this problem is for the central government's legislators. Local circumstances differ, and local officials are, of all civil government officials, the most likely to know the circumstances which confront the people of their respective communities or districts. It makes no sense for a large country's rulers to attempt to exercise centralized legislative control over the people of the country. Moreover, the same is true even within a state. The division of a state into counties with their own civil governments, and cities and towns with their own civil governments, allows the people of these areas to deal more realistically and efficiently with their own local circumstances and issues.

God's law is true, good, valid, and applicable in all times and places because it is given by the one true, holy, righteous, omnipotent, omnipresent, omniscient God. God's law is applicable in all circumstances because God, who governs all circumstances and knows all things, has given it to man. Man is not only fallen in sin and so in natural rebellion against God and His law, but also finite. Man's knowledge is necessarily and inescapably limited. He is not omnipresent and cannot become so, no matter how abundant or advanced his technology. He is not omniscient and cannot become so, no matter how sophisticated his technology—or inflated his ego. And no matter how powerful his technology he cannot become omnipotent. Man cannot overcome his finitude. Thus man cannot replace God's law with an equal, much less a superior, man-made law or set of laws. Man's attempts to replace God's law with man-made laws are exercises in futility, self-delusion, and self-imposed disaster—partly because God judges man's governmental actions in history, and partly because of the "natural" consequences of the defects of man's laws.

Man can know that his law is just if it conforms to God's law. Beyond that, man's law may be just insofar as it is based on knowledge of the true circumstances for which he is legislating (assuming that his laws do not contravene God's word and law). But man's law must be unjust and unwise insofar as it is based on man's ignorance of the circumstances for which he legislates.

The framers of our Constitution knew these things, and designed our Constitution accordingly, giving us a federal, not a centralized republic. Federalism works against centrally-mandated ignorance and injustice by allowing each state to govern its own internal affairs. Federalism was a practical necessity, given Americans' loyalty to their respective states, but it is nonetheless an intellectually and morally superior form of government. The ratifiers of our Constitution (not only the Anti-Federalists but also the great majority of the Federalists and the many who occupied the political ground between the two contending groups) agreed emphatically, and so approved our federal system.

But the prolonged dispute over ratification of the Constitution made it clear to many that the document had many defects, or at least many debatable or dubious features. Many surmised that the central government to be established by the Constitution posed a serious potential threat to the self-government of the states, and that the central government could become a danger to justice and to Americans' freedom. These deep concerns produced hundreds of proposed amendments to the Constitution offered by the states' ratification conventions. Although the ratification struggle was over, Anti-Federalists still believed that their fears about the new governmental system were prophetic. Those who had taken neither side in the debates, but had been convinced that ratification of the Constitution was the best practical alternative, still wondered if the Anti-Federalists' predictions would prove right. Federalists who had convinced enough people (and pulled enough political shenanigans) to get the Constitution ratified wanted to allay public fears of the new governmental system. Consequently the members of the First Congress under the new Constitution distilled the hundreds of proposed amendments to the Constitution into a dozen proposed amendments, which they sent to the states to be considered for addition to the Constitution. The ensuing deliberations in the states' legislatures reduced that dozen proposed amendments to ten, our Bill of Rights.

Capping that Bill of Rights was a guarantee that the federalism of our Constitution would (or should) be preserved: our Tenth Amendment, which declares that the powers which the states have neither delegated to the central government in the Constitution, nor forbidden to themselves in the Constitution, are reserved to the respective state governments, or to the people of each respective state. That precious amendment does not guarantee that all legislation in every state will be morally as pure as the driven snow; nothing in this fallen world of civil governments of fallen men over fallen men can guarantee that. But the Tenth Amendment does guarantee that, insofar as it is obeyed, the foolish destructiveness of centralized injustice will be avoided, and the greater justice of laws based on knowledge of local conditions will be preserved, and local concerns will more likely be managed well and justly.

23

Freedom to Experiment

The results of experiments can be good or bad. Experiments can work to discover or produce desired—or desirable—results. Or (assuming, for the sake of argument, "good" intentions on the part of the experimenters) they can work to produce undesired, unexpected, and undesirable, even evil, results. This is as true in social, political, and economic sciences as it is in the physical sciences.

Whether peoples should engage in collective social, political, and economic "experiments"—and if so, the extent to which they should undertake such experiments, and the kinds of social, political, and economic "experiments" they should engage in—is problematic and involves serious ethical consideration, whether or not the would-be "experimenters" acknowledge the fact. Civil government is a ministry of God to people who are created in His image, and therefore civil governments are to be careful to obey God's standards of good and evil in order to serve and glorify Him, in order to protect and give praise to those who do good, and in order to punish, and thus restrain, those who do evil (Romans 13:1-7). Civil government is to obey God's law, for that is love, and love, obedience to God's holy law, works no ill or evil to one's neighbor (Romans 13:1-10). If social, political, or economic "experiments" work ill or evil to one's neighbors, they should not be conducted—particularly by civil governments, which have "the power of the sword."

On an individual level too we are to obey God's law, and thus to work no evil to our neighbors. Generally speaking, we cannot as individuals do as much evil to our neighbors as we could as a group. And as a group endowed with the authority to use the "sword," the means of legal force or coercion, we can potentially do much greater evil to our neighbors than an individual can, and even more than a group without the power of the sword can. On a social and governmental level we are to obey God's law. That prevents us from harming our neighbors by implementing ungodly laws, plans, and policies through our civil governments. It also prevents us from engaging in ungodly "experiments."

There are at least two kinds of social, economic, and political "experiments." (Since we are considering civil government, not voluntary social or economic experiments engaged in by people, whether they are social or economic experiments, both kinds of "experiments" are done by the coercive power of civil government and not by persuasion, so they must be termed *political*. Since social experiments affect economic life and economic experiments necessarily affect social life, social and economic "experiments" are linked.) One kind of social and economic "experiment" is simply trying another way to do something, another approach to solving a problem, alleviating an ill condition, or achieving a desired result. This is an approach which does not involve the intention to manipulate people or remake the social and economic, and perhaps religious and cultural fabric of society. This approach does not necessarily involve civil government in violating God's law.

The other kind of social and economic "experiment" does involve the intention to manipulate people and to remake the social and economic, and probably also the religious and cultural fabric of society. This is the kind of experiment we saw in the French Revolution, in the Russian Revolution, and in any other communist revolution spawned by the two. This kind of social and economic experiment is a result of rationalism, faith in man's unaided reason, the belief that man's unaided reason can apprehend universally valid concepts upon the basis of which society and its economic (and/or religious, cultural, and political) life can, should, or must be reordered. It is a result of the belief that society is a relatively simple thing which can be taken apart and put back together with wonderful results—via the coercive power of civil government ruled by the possessors of such knowledge. This kind of experiment may also be a result of scientism, the belief that man can solve the problems of society by applying science to society through the coercive power of civil government, which amounts to faith in science for the salvation of man. This kind of social and economic "experiment" reduces people, who are created in God's image, to the status of objects to be manipulated or discarded or destroyed as desired by the "experimenters" in possession of the civil government's power, and it involves using this power to take people's property, liberty, and even lives in order to implement the rulers' plans.

Although the "experiment" may be done in the name of a rough equivalent of "love" (waging war on some evil condition, perfecting man and society, etc.), the "experiment" violates the law of love by the means which it uses, by what it does in order, purportedly, to solve the "problem" which it claims to seek to cure, and by its violation of God's laws. Legalized theft is not love. Legalized diminution of liberty is not love. Legalized enslavement of free people is not love. Legalized murder is not love. This kind of "experimentation" violates God's law and thus violates His law of love, for it works ill/evil to the people whom civil government is supposed to protect.

Though the framers and ratifiers of our Constitution had not seen the horrors that would result from the political ideologies spawned by modern rationalism (French "Enlightenment" rationalism, utopian socialism, liberalism, democratic socialism), scientism (positivism, National Socialism, fascism, Marxism, communism, etc.), and irrationalism (National Socialism, Fascism, Marxism-Leninism/modern communism, 21st century "progressivism")they were well aware of the political theories of the ancient and modern advocates of absolutist governments and of the disasters promulgated by ancient, medieval, and modern regimes which lacked adequate constitutional and institutional protections of justice and liberty. They were well aware of the destructive consequences of rule by men of bad character—especially by able men of bad character. Consequently they gave us a limited, expressed-powers Constitution, with many stipulated denials of power to the central government and the states' governments and a once-celebrated, once-honored system of separation of powers with accompanying checks and balances between and among our central government's branches and institutions, to prevent abuses of power by civil government.

This careful design also worked to prevent such abuses of power as the sinful socio-economic dreams of later rationalists and "scientists" would mandate. Rationalists and "scientists" (or "social scientists") have had to devise many cunning fables, to engage in many carefully calculated deceits, to play masterfully (and with Machiavellian duplicity) on the ignorance, cupidity, and envy of the American public, to adopt a Fabian strategy of piecemeal subversion of the Constitution, and at times to use great audacity in order to advance their desires and implement their "experiments."

Federalism allows the states to be free to govern themselves apart from unconstitutional intrusions and dictation by the central government, and was intended, as Madison said in Federalist No. 51, to provide a double security to the rights and liberty of the people by giving the states' people and officials both the personal motives and the constitutional means to resist abuses, usurpations, or concentrations of power by the central government.

An important aspect of this freedom and self-government is the right and ability of each state to engage in the good kind of experimentation. By freeing the states from central government dictation and allowing each to govern itself, federalism allows states to try different approaches to vexing problems and permits them to learn what works, what works well, and what doesn't work. It frees us from the "one-size-fits-all" approach of centralized government and allows us to produce our own solutions to soluble problems and, likewise, by our own methods to mitigate the consequences of any insoluble problems.

Our Tenth Amendment's statement that each state government retains all powers which it has neither delegated to the central government nor denied to itself in the Constitution protects the right of each state to govern itself and the right to engage in the good kind of experimentation. But these rights cannot be exercised if the people of each state and their elected officials do not understand, value, and exert themselves to guard their state and their liberty against both the usurpation of their powers by our central government *and* the dreams and deceits of those who would turn our central government into an engine for conducting the wrong kind of "experiments" on American society.

24

Freedom from Experiments

The wise Massachusetts statesman "Agrippa," speaking of the importance of bills of rights reserved against civil governments by the authority of the people, said of American liberty, "The separate governments know their powers, their objects, and operations. We are therefore not perpetually tormented with new experiments."[1] Bills of rights let both the rulers and the ruled know what powers a given civil government has and may legitimately exercise and what powers civil government does not have and may not exercise, especially with reference to the individual citizen. Our Tenth Amendment is, of course, a key amendment in our Bill of Rights, making it clear that the central government may not legally or constitutionally exercise the rights or powers reserved to, and therefore exclusively belonging to, the state governments or to the people of each state from whom, humanly speaking, each state government gets its authority or powers.

The Tenth Amendment forbids our national or central government from experimenting on the people of the whole nation because it makes it clear that the central government has only those powers expressly delegated to it by the states in the Constitution. Since the powers reserved to the states respect the authority of each state to govern its own internal affairs, the central government is forbidden to attempt to govern the internal affairs—or even to think about governing the internal affairs—of the states. Theoretically our central government may "experiment" in regard to foreign affairs or interstate commerce (commerce between or among states), but it is forbidden by the Tenth Amendment (and the nature and wording of the rest of the Constitution) from "experimenting" on the people of the whole nation by any means which involves its intervention in the domestic affairs of any state.

---

1. Letter No. XVII (January 20, 1788), in Kenyon, 150-151.

Under the Constitution, a state may "experiment" within its borders—so long as its "experiment" does not involve establishing a non-republican form of civil government or violating its own constitution or bill of rights or declaration of rights.

Part of the beauty of federalism is that although each state is free to govern itself no state is required to adopt the laws of another state. So if a state "experiments" and the results are good, other states are free to choose whether or not to adopt that state's law or laws. If the results are bad, no other state is required to adopt the law(s). Also, if a state "experiments" and the results are bad, or if a state is run by people who insist on "experimenting," or if a state is run by people who insist on doing unjust things, then people living in that state can escape that state. If a centralized government does any of these things the people living under it can (if possible) only flee the whole country—an undertaking much more difficult than moving across state lines. The state in a federal system, then, if it persists in "experimenting" on people or doing unjust things will reap unpleasant consequences for its actions: people will move to other states, or move their businesses to other states; the state will experience "brain drain" and loss of manpower; the state will lose capital; the state and its people will earn a bad reputation in other states. In a centralized system the disaster of civil government "experiments" is spread to everyone. In a federal system the disaster is confined to the state whose laws are the source of the disaster and the state is given incentives to improve its legislative behavior.

Another facet of the beauty of federalism, and of our Tenth Amendment, is that, by protecting the reserved powers of the states, it enables the people of a state to avoid "being perpetually tormented with new experiments." In our time, under the perverse influence of liberalism, "progressivism," Marxism, democratic socialism, and kindred ideologies, not only many of our states but also our central government is dominated by ungodly people who want us to be perpetually tormented with their wicked, destructive, often manifestly crazy "experiments" which they cram down our throats. The subversion and denial of the constitutional authority of our Tenth Amendment has been a crucial part of the experimenters' strategy to usurp the authority to "experiment" on the American people.

A large part of the remedy for this potentially deadly disor-
der of our body politic is copious ingestion and application of the
Anti-Federalists' antidote to "experiments": the Tenth Amendment.
Whatever the precise nature of their ideological origins, all national
"experiments" require centralized planning and controls to *impose* the
experimental plan on every person in the nation. Federalism renders
such an "experiment" impossible because it denies centralization of
government in principle, defends the governmental authority of the
people of the various states in principle, and defends the rights and
liberty of the people of those states—and thus the rights and liberty of
all the people of the nation—in practice. Federalism gives us freedom
from "experiments"—but only if it is understood, practiced, defended,
and maintained.

25

The Tenth Amendment and Economic Freedom

Our Tenth Amendment works to preserve economic freedom by preventing the central government from imposing economic regulations and restrictions on intrastate commerce. The "Commerce Clause" of the Constitution (Article I, Section 8, Paragraph 3) states that Congress shall have power "To regulate Commerce with foreign Nations, and among the several States, and with the Indian Tribes..." That clause gives Congress the power or authority to regulate commerce from state to state or among the several states (**interstate** commerce). It emphatically does *not* give Congress power or authority to regulate commerce within a state, commerce which does not cross state lines (**intrastate** commerce). Intrastate and interstate commerce are logically and constitutionally different.

The Commerce Clause forbids Congress from enacting any law which interferes with intrastate (internal) commerce, making explicit the fact that Congress has state-delegated authority to regulate only commerce **between** the states, not commerce **within** the states. The fact that the U.S. Supreme Court has "reinterpreted" the Commerce Clause to mean that Congress can enact outrageously intrusive intrastate laws, like prohibiting a farmer from growing wheat for his own consumption on his own property, signifies the extent to which Supreme Court majorities have usurped power, perverted our Constitution, and robbed us of our freedom. And it signifies the extent to which presidents and Congresses have acquiesced to or become co-conspirators in such abominations. It obviously does not mean that the framers and ratifiers of our Constitution intended the Commerce Clause to mean such a thing. The Supreme Court has no constitutional authority to amend our Constitution. Supreme Court decisions which violate our Constitution are void of constitutional authority. Congress has no constitutional authority to tamper with intrastate commerce.

Our Tenth Amendment, rightly called the Liberty Amendment, protects each state's authority over its internal economic affairs as well as the reserved powers already discussed. Consistent with the Commerce Clause and underscoring the central principle of that clause, it prohibits the national/central government from intervening in any state's internal economic affairs—only commerce which originates in a state but is directed beyond the state is constitutionally subject to central government authority.

This protection helps shield the private property rights of the people, including an individual owner's rights to control the uses of his own property, especially productive property which is used only in intrastate commerce. This obstructs social and economic engineering projects, programs, and "experiments" imposed by the central government, protecting the citizens of the states against the injustices, economic inefficiencies, costs, and subversions to liberty inherent in such programs. It allows the societies of the respective states to make their own economic and social adjustments at their own paces, and to make such changes based on moral suasion, not central government coercion. It lessens the likelihood of central government politicians pandering to special interest groups, thus creating or exacerbating hostilities between those who are not members of the privileged group—but pay the tax-burden of its favors—and those who receive those undeserved favors. The Tenth Amendment thereby contributes to economic freedom and prosperity, which benefit everyone in the state's society. Since the people who live in the state are also potential economic actors (producers, consumers, entrepreneurs) in interstate and foreign commerce, using the wealth that they have produced via intrastate commerce, this indirectly benefits people in the rest of the nation and in foreign lands as well.

Protection of intrastate commerce leaves each state free to craft its own economic regulations for its own internal economic life. But this does not leave a state absolutely free to do whatever its government officials desire concerning the state's internal commerce. Article IV, Section 4 of the Constitution requires the national government to guarantee to every state in the Union a republican form of government. And Article I, Section 10 of the Constitution prohibits a state from coining money, emitting bills of credit, making anything but gold and silver legal tender in the payment of debts, passing a bill of attainder, ex post facto law, or law impairing the obligation of contracts, and granting any title of nobility. These wise restrictions on the authority of state governments have important consequences for economic life and for liberty.

The Constitution requires that each state be a *republic*, not a *democracy*, to protect the form of civil government which is most conducive to the existence and preservation of liberty, including economic liberty. *The Federalist*, the authoritative exposition of the framers' intentions for the Constitution, and especially its most important essay and the key to the design of our Constitution, Federalist No. 10, makes it unmistakably clear that the protection of the property of all men—rich, middling, and poor—against private and governmental theft is fundamental to, and inseparable from, the establishment of justice and the protection of liberty. The opening and closing numbers of *The Federalist*, Nos. 1 and 85, emphasize that the essence of the framers' philosophy is encompassed in republican government, property, and liberty. What the framers intended at the national level they also intended at the state level, though they thought the state governments threatened property and liberty because they were too democratic (republics may be designed in various ways, some more aristocratic, some more democratic). Hence while they guaranteed a republican form of government to the states they also prohibited the state governments from doing certain things which undermine or destroy property rights, economic freedom, and liberty as a whole.

The Constitution prohibits a state from coining money, emitting bills of credit, or making anything but gold and silver legal tender to prevent state governments from debasing the currency through inflation, a form of legalized theft. These were protections for all property, whether it would be used in intrastate or interstate commerce; they were protections for economic freedom and efficiency by protecting the stability, soundness, honesty, and predictability of the currency.

Prohibitions of bills of attainder (laws aimed at punishing a particular man or group) and *ex post facto* laws (laws enacted to punish something already done but not previously forbidden) were meant to protect men's lives, liberty, and property. Thus these prohibitions, too, were protections of economic freedom against legalized theft.

Constitutional stipulations against impairing contractual obligations were meant to protect property against legalized theft and to foster productivity, capital accumulation, and wealth by requiring men to live up to their word—to fulfill their legal obligations in commerce.

Prohibiting the grants of titles of nobility was intended to preserve the biblical principle of equality before the law, and to keep state governments from giving special legal and economic privileges or advantages to a certain class of people, another form of legalized theft. The prohibition, however, was not motivated by egalitarianism, for it left people free to ascend or descend the social and economic "ladder" of society in accordance with divine providence and their own character and efforts.

Positively, leaving each state free to govern its own internal affairs meant that each state and its local governments would be free to enact and enforce laws which uphold God's moral law and thereby tend to teach morality and to protect the morality of the people of that state. Since the states were all (to one degree or another) Christian states with Christian constitutions, declarations of rights or bills of rights,[1] and laws,[2] this meant that, other things being equal, the states would continue to honor biblical morality in their own diverse ways. As early American political thought and public political discourse acknowledged, this

---

1. Archie P. Jones, *Christianity and Our State Constitutions, Declarations, and Bills of Rights, Parts I and II* (Marlborough, New Hampshire: Plymouth Rock Foundation, 1993).

2. W. Keith Kavenagh, ed., *Foundations of Colonial America: A Documentary History*, 3 vols. (New York: Chelsea House, [1974] 1983; Perry Miller, *The Life of the Mind in America: from the Revolution to the Civil War* (New York: Harcourt, Brace & World, 1965), 99-268; Steven Alan Samson, "Crossed Swords: Church and State in American History," (Ph.D. dissertation, University of Oregon, 1984); B. F. Morris, *The Christian Life and Character of the Civil Institutions of the United States* (Powder Springs, Georgia: American Vision, [1864] 2007); David J. Brewer, *The United States: A Christian Nation* (Powder Springs, Georgia: American Vision, [1905] 1996); and Archie P. Jones, "Christianity in the Constitution: The Intended Meaning of the Religion Clauses of the First Amendment," (unpublished Ph.D. dissertation, University of Dallas, 1991), 145-230.

meant that each state, like the nation, would be free to acknowledge its covenantal relationship with God, free to teach that the temporal blessings—including economic blessings—which it experienced were God's blessings for faith in Him and obedience to His commandments, to teach also that the temporal hardships which it experienced were God's chastisements on its people for their departure from faith in God and their consequent disobedience of His commandments, and free to enact and enforce laws based on God's law (see Leviticus 26 and Deuteronomy 28), laws protecting morality, private property and economic freedom.

A guarantee of a republican form of civil government, of course, was not a guarantee that a republican government would govern biblically or well; the Framers and Ratifiers were well aware of that! The people in a particular state might choose representatives who would govern poorly or wickedly, who would use their authority over the state's internal affairs to enact and enforce laws which would undermine property rights, economic freedom, and liberty in general. If so, the Constitution's limitations on state government's authority and the constitutional principle of federalism would limit the damage that wicked or incompetent rulers could do in that state to that state. Disaffected citizens of that state could move to other, better-governed states, and the offending state would suffer the consequences of its misgovernment in lost population, lost intellectual and commercial capital, decreased productivity and wealth, and the loss of its good name.

The chief benefit of our Tenth Amendment for economic freedom, however, is its reaffirmation of each state's authority over its own internal economic affairs. This operates against central government usurpation of authority over intrastate commerce, and the central government's use of that usurped authority to attack noneconomic as well as economic aspects of liberty. That benefit, however, is premised on the action of the states to defend their liberty against an unwise, unjust, or utopian central government, which action our Tenth Amendment exists to enable, protect, and promote.

26

Against Those Who Stoop to Misconstruction

Writing against Anti-Federalist criticisms of the "General Welfare Clause" (Article I, Section 8 of the Constitution) and denying their argument that the clause's vague wording lent itself to misconstruction by power-hungry federal government legislators, James Madison said in Federalist No. 41:

> Some, who have not denied the necessity of the power of taxation, have grounded a very fierce attack against the Constitution, on the language in which it is defined. It has been urged and echoed, that the power "to lay and collect taxes, duties, imposts, and excises, to pay the debts and provide for the common defence and general welfare of the United States," amounts to an unlimited commission to exercise every power which may be alleged to be necessary for the common defence or general welfare. No stronger proof could be given of the distress under which these writers labor for objections, than **their stooping to such a misconstruction.**
>
> Had no other enumeration or definition of the powers of the Congress been found in the Constitution, than the general expressions just cited, the authors of the objection might have had some color for it; though it would have been difficult to find a reason for so awkward a form of describing an authority to legislate in all possible cases. A power to destroy the freedom of the press, the trial by jury, or even to regulate the course of descents, or the forms of conveyances, must be very singularly expressed by the terms "to raise money for the general welfare."

But what color can the objection have, when a
specification of the objects alluded to by these general
terms immediately follows, and is not even separated
by a longer pause than a semicolon? If the different
parts of the same instrument ought to be so expound-
ed, as to give meaning to every part which will bear it,
shall one part of the same sentence be excluded altogether from a share in the meaning; and shall the more
doubtful and indefinite terms be retained in their full
extent, and the clear and precise expressions be denied
any signification whatsoever? For what purpose could
the enumeration of particular powers be inserted, if
these and all others were meant to be included in the
preceding general power? Nothing is more natural nor
common than first to use a general phrase, and then to
explain and qualify it by a recital of the particulars. But
the idea of an enumeration of particulars which neither explain nor qualify the general meaning, and can
have no other effect than to confound and mislead, is
an absurdity, which, as we are reduced to the dilemma
of charging either on the authors of the objection or
on the authors of the Constitution, we must take the
liberty of supposing, had not its origin with the latter.
[Emphasis mine. Spelling in the original.]

Madison's argument that those who look to the General Welfare
Clause (and by implication like clauses in the Constitution: the Commerce Clause, the Necessary and Proper Clause, the Supremacy
Clause, etc.) as a constitutional basis for justifying the exercise of
powers which are not stated in the Constitution are committing not
only a grammatical but also a constitutional absurdity ought to be
instructive to us when we are trying to understand the meaning of our
Constitution, and when we are considering the unconstitutional things
that men have tried, and still try, to force the Constitution to justify.
Madison's implication that the Anti-Federalist critics of the Constitution were deliberately misconstruing the General Welfare Clause adds
emphasis to his contention that men who attempt to draw such mean-

ings out of such grammatical constructions are engaging in unethical attempts to deceive us.

Such unethical approaches to construction of our Constitution ought to be viewed in light of the Constitution's requirement that all federal and state officials swear an oath (or make an "affirmation") to support the Constitution. (See Chapter 20.) Those who engage in unethical attempts to deceive us about the nature of our Constitution are also violating the oath that they swore (or affirmation that they made) before God when they assumed governmental office under the Constitution. They are thus invoking God's inescapable judgment and our temporal judgment for their perfidy—both of which judgments must be acknowledged just.

But Madison's argument about the ethics of deliberate misinterpretation of our Constitution's provisions also misses the Anti-Federalists' point. For the Anti-Federalists were saying that the framers of our Constitution should have taken the political consequences of man's fallen nature more seriously; that unscrupulous men will slyly pervert the meanings of the Constitution's clauses and words; that the Framers should have exercised much more caution in their wording of the document; that the Framers should have provided checks against what sinful, calculating men will do with words in order to get, keep, and increase power, make the exercise of that power arbitrary and unlimited, and use that power to do whatever they will. They were saying that power-hungry men will will twist words to gull the many gullible, call evil good and good evil, violate the Constitution's limits on civil government's authority, and work mischief with our liberty. They were saying that it is a duty of wise statesmen to protect the people against these fundamental facts of human nature and of history.

The Anti-Federalists were right. Throughout our history, calculating men—including not only congressmen and senators, but also presidents, federal judges and U.S. Supreme Court "justices," and not a few professors of law, history, and government—have "stooped to misconstruction." They have misconstrued and misused the General Welfare Clause, the Necessary and Proper Clause, the Commerce Clause and other clauses to advance their own political status and promote their own interests—and, particularly in the twentieth and twenty-first centuries, to advance their leftist ideological agendas. Throughout our history calculating, unprincipled, or falsely-principled men have used high-sounding rhetoric to cover their deliberate misinterpretations of various clauses of the Constitution to assault other Americans' property, liberty, and lives. Or, worse yet, to "transform" our constitutional law and order without submitting to the Constitution's prescribed methods of amendment. In the hands of mere selfish politicians this has meant more or less thoughtlessly eroding the Constitution's principles in order to buy votes, be reelected, and perhaps become famous as a man "of the people." In the hands of big government enthusiasts such as socialists, collectivist "liberals," "progressives," Marxists, and kindred egalitarian statists this has meant carefully calculated strategies and campaigns to pervert the meanings of not only such vaguely worded clauses as the General Welfare Clause, the Necessary and Proper Clause, and the Commerce Clause, but also of the amendments which were added to the Constitution to protect our liberty against centralized, arbitrary government.

Today "liberals," "progressives," and Marxists have "advanced" far beyond "stooping to misconstruction" of the General Welfare Clause and other such clauses in the Constitution. They have "progressed" to inserting phrases into our Constitution such as "the separation of church and state," which are plainly *not* in our Constitution or its First Amendment, in order to advance their own opinions about the place of "religion" in American law and public life and the relationship of God to American government, which opinions are manifestly alien to the Constitution's intentions. They have "progressed" to construing "penumbras" (such as "the right to privacy") and "emanations from penumbras" (the "right to abortion"—based on "the right to privacy") of the Constitution—clauses and "rights" found nowhere in the Constitution but invented by the "creative" minds of "liberals" and their ilk.

Although the most egregious perversion of the Constitution by a "liberal" U.S. Supreme Court majority was the 1973 decision creating a "right" to abortion, "liberal'" perversion of the Commerce Clause—a clause which was clearly originally intended to give Congress authority over **interstate**, not **intrastate**, commerce—can serve to provide a few examples of the devious workings of leftist lawyers and judges' minds. Under "liberal" court majorities' decisions, a restaurant is engaged in interstate commerce because the nails used in constructing its building might have come via interstate commerce. A business that is engaged only in commerce within the state where it is located must yield to federal regulation because the elevator in its building came via interstate commerce. And wheat grown on your own property for your own use is involved in "interstate commerce" because it might affect interstate commerce. Americans need protection against such nonsense, deceit, usurpation, and injustice. Our written Constitution was meant to be part of that protection, for all who can read and reason can detect such misinterpretations. Our directly and indirectly elected national government officials' oaths of office were intended to be another part of that protection. The original modes of electing our senators and President, and federal judges were conceived to be a third. The Constitution's famous system of separation of powers and checks and balances was designed to tie the self-interest of our officials to the performance of their duty to uphold the Constitution against the assaults of cunning usurpers. The federalism of the Constitution was meant to provide a double security to Americans' rights and liberty—and a double security against those who stoop to misinterpret the Constitution which they have sworn falsely to uphold—by establishing a system of separation of powers and checks and balances between the state governments and the central government.

The Tenth Amendment was added to the Constitution to help prevent misconstruction of the Constitution. It informs one and all that each state is a self-governing entity except insofar as it has delegated certain specific powers to the national government and forbidden itself to exercise certain other specific powers. This puts the central government on notice that it is not to usurp any of the reserved powers of the states from the states, nor to intervene in the states' sphere of authority. It makes clear to the civil government officials of each state that their state has a sphere of authority which is fundamentally off-limits to the central government, within which they are free to govern their own state. It also makes clear to state government officials that they have a duty to the people of their state to jealously guard the reserved powers of their state against intervention and usurpation by the central government. By implication it informs each state's civil government officials that they have a self-interest in protecting their authority and reserved powers against federal government power-grabs and fulfills the framers' principle of tying the self-interest of the civil government officials to the constitutional rights of their places of authority in our governmental system. The Tenth Amendment works thereby to incline them to serve the public good and the people's liberty by striving to protect those rights. It gives each state's civil government officials both constitutional and personal motives to be ever-vigilant to detect, combat, and defeat all attempts to misconstrue the Constitution by power-hungry central government officials—and power-philosophy ideologues and propagandists.

Our Tenth Amendment also puts the *people* of each state on notice that our system is a federal, not a centralized one, and therefore each state was intended to be, and still remains, a self-governing entity for almost all practical purposes. The Tenth Amendment similarly notifies the people of each state that their state officials—as well as the officials they elect to represent them in the national government—have a constitutional duty, and a moral and political duty to the people of their state, to protect the authority of their state against central government intervention and usurpation.

But, fundamentally, our Tenth Amendment tells the people of each state that *they* are the ultimate guardians of the authority and reserved powers of their states, and, implicitly, of all other states. It tells them that they must take care that their representatives will work to protect their state's authority and preserve their liberty against central government intervention. It warns them that they must choose representatives who will guard against misconstruction of the Constitution. It admonishes them that they themselves bear the ultimate responsibility for guarding the people and civil government of their state, and of all states, against those who stoop to misconstruction to break down the Constitution's barriers against centralized government and its threats to liberty.

27

Against Judicial Tyranny Via the Fourteenth Amendment

The Fourteenth Amendment has been a favorite target for mis-construction by various advocates of Big Government who seek to circumvent the small government intentions of the framers and ratifiers of our Constitution and its amendments. It was passed by the Republican-controlled Congress on June 13, 1866, and proclaimed to be "ratified" on July 9, 1868. It was ratified in violation of our Constitution. What devious judges[1] have done to it and with it is even worse.

The Fourteenth Amendment was one of the post-"Civil War" amendments, the second of the three Reconstruction amendments. Like the Thirteenth and Fifteenth Amendments, it was "ratified" under the pressure of Radical Republican Congressional domination and stemmed from their desire to "reconstruct" the South—although our Constitution does not grant the central government the authority to "reconstruct" any section of the country or any state.[2] It was a direct

---

1. While the misdeeds of judicial malefactors is the central theme of this chapter because judges have led the assault on our Constitution, our Tenth Amendment and federalism, a full account would have to include (limiting it to our national government) presidential malefactors, congressional malefactors, and bureaucratic malefactors in unconstitutional bureaucracies created by congressional malefactors with the approval of presidential malefactors. As later paragraphs make clear, these malefactors have been aided by academic malefactors.

2. Historian Clarence B. Carson *The Sections and the Civil War 1826-1877: A Basic History of the United States, Volume 3* (Wadley, Alabama: American Textbook Committee, 1987), 192, notes that the "Civil War" itself was unconstitutional: "There simply is no provision in the Constitution for the United States government to use force, i.e., make war, upon states. There are no provisions for the treatment of people within states when war is undertaken against them. And certainly there were no provisions in the Constitution for

assault on the authority of the U.S. Supreme Court.[3] The Supreme Court did not fight back because the Federal courts were hesitant to accept cases involving "political" issues raised by Congress's repeated violations of the Constitution. Congress, of course, attacked President Andrew Johnson for repeatedly stating constitutional objections to Congress's actions. Acting on its Article III authority, Congress in 1866 passed a bill decreasing the size of the Supreme Court by two members so that the president could not appoint anyone to the Court unless there were three vacancies on it.[4] In the absence of effective opposition—the Southern states were out of the Union and had no representation in Congress, and there was no effective opposition from the Northern and border states' governments—the Radicals in Congress flouted the Constitution by proclaiming these three amendments added to our fundamental law.

The Radicals violated the Constitution by using—and coercing—Southern states which had seceded from the Union to help ratify the 13th, 14th, and 15th Amendments. President Lincoln had claimed, contrary to the evidence of the original states' ratifications of the Constitution,[5] that the Union could not be dissolved and therefore no state could leave the Union. The Radical Republicans, who in principle agreed with Lincoln's erroneous assessment, claimed, paradoxically,

---

reconstructing states."

3. The Court's decision, in *Ex parte Milligan*, December, 1866, that it is unconstitutional to try a civilian in a military tribunal unless the case was connected with military operations in a state, angered the Radicals. Rep. John Bingham said that Congress should remove all appellate jurisdiction from the Court (which Congress has authority to do under Article III of the Constitution.; whether it should have done so is another question). Having passed the Habeas Corpus Act in 1867, in 1868 Congress removed all Federal courts' jurisdiction from all cases arising under the Habeas Corpus Act. Carson, 193.

4. Ibid., 192-193.

5. As we have seen above, New York, Rhode Island, and Virginia ratified but with the proviso that they could take back the powers which they had delegated to the central government in the Constitution if they decided that the national government was working to the detriment of their liberty. The same understanding was implicit in the ratifications of all the other states, which had just fought to win their independence from the tyrannical central government of Great Britain.

that the Southern states were *out* of the Union and were "conquered territories" which could not become parts of the Union until they were "reconstructed" and ratified the 13th, 14th, and 15th Amendments. Of course, constitutionally (Article VI) there is no provision for ratification of proposed amendments by "conquered territories" or by states which are not already in the Union, so on this ground alone not one of these amendments was ratified constitutionally. There is also no provision in our Constitution for coercion to be used to get a state to ratify a proposed amendment, so on that ground too none of these amendments was ratified constitutionally. Whether or not we approve of the content of these amendments,[6] it doesn't change the fact that the Constitution has absolutely no provision for adding even the best amendments to the Constitution by blatantly—or even subtly—unconstitutional means!

The means used to adopt the 14th Amendment were the most objectionable[7] of the three. The first (1866) version of the amendment was rejected by 12 states (Kentucky, Delaware, and every former Confederate state but Tennessee) and thus was not ratified. In the First Reconstruction Act (1867), Congress stipulated that no state could be restored to the Union until it had ratified the 14th Amendment and that no state could be "restored" to the Union until the 14th Amendment had become a part of the Constitution: until the amendment had been ratified. The Southern states were occupied by Federal troops, were already being taxed by the central government though not represented in Congress, and had the nature of their state governments dictated to them by Congress (none of which is constitutional), so, under this duress, their "reconstructed" governments "ratified" the amendment. Meanwhile, Ohio and New Jersey, which had previously ratified the amendment (constitutionally!) rescinded their ratifications. On July 9, 1868 Secretary of State William Seward proclaimed that the

---

6. For example, the present writer is glad that slavery was ended in these United States because by biblical law, which he is convinced is the best standard of law, slavery as it was practiced in these United States was immoral and criminal on several counts. From that conviction, however, it does not follow that slavery here was ended by appropriate means, or by constitutional means, nor that it should have been ended by such unconstitutional means.

7. Carson, 195, calls them "the most controversial..."

amendment was ratified—*if* the ratifications of all the Southern states (including the ones about the legitimacy of whose governments he had doubts) were counted. Not liking the uncertain tone of Seward's proclamation, the Radical Republican Congress passed a resolution stating that three-fourths of the states of the Union had ratified the 14th Amendment and therefore the Secretary of State should proclaim the amendment ratified. There were 37 states (counting the Southern states) in the Union at that time, but Congress only listed 27 states as having ratified the amendment. Since 27 is *not* three-fourths of 37,[8] by Congress's own reckoning the 14th Amendment had not been ratified, for the Constitution requires ratification by three-fourths of the states. Overlooking the Constitution's requirement, Congress proclaimed the 14th Amendment to be "ratified."[9]

Although the manner in which the 14th Amendment was "adopted" was grossly unconstitutional, "Big Government" politicians and judges (the two are often indistinguishable), aided by left-wing constitutional scholars, have used the 14th Amendment for even more grossly un-constitutional—even anti-constitutional—purposes than the Radical Republicans did.

Before the onset of the "Roosevelt Revolution" in the early 1930s the scholarship on the 14th Amendment (and the Reconstruction Amendments in general) saw our Constitution, as M.E. Bradford put it, as "defined by procedures, by a way of conducting official business, as opposed to a high-minded set of purposes hidden away beneath the surface like a ticking bomb."[10] The older scholarship knew and

---

8. *Twenty-eight* is the smallest whole number that could constitute three-fourths or more of thirty-seven.

9. Carson, 195.

10. Bradford, *Original Intentions*, 104. Bradford's simile, of course, signi-fies that if the framers and ratifiers of our Constitution had intended some unstated "high-minded set of purposes" or principles to trump the carefully crafted provisions of our Constitution, then they would have created a situ-ation in which their carefully-crafted work to limit and restrict the powers of our central government could and would be effectively destroyed anytime a politician or politicians could generate enough enthusiasm for using the power of our national government to advance or achieve one or more of those "high-minded...purposes." Thus the status of Americans' liberty would always

honored the purposes of the framers and ratifiers of our Constitution
and its amendments. It knew that they clearly did not intend to give
us a Constitution whose meaning is to be continually redefined to
enable Americans to collectively achieve—through civil government
coercion—some abstract, undefined or loosely-defined principles like
"equality," or "social justice" which the Framers and Ratifiers (not to
mention the Americans they represented!) did not seek to achieve
and would have rejected. Post-1932 scholarship, however, has been
dominated by the view that the fundamental law of a constitution, and
of our Constitution, exists and should attempt to "reform and reconstitute the society which it serves"[11] based upon "certain normative
[i.e., *leftist*] assumptions about the nature and destiny of man."[12] Such a
view of law requires a rejection of limited, constitutional government
in order to enable the government to do whatever its rulers find necessary to reform and reconstitute society in order to achieve its rulers'
vision—rather than, as Bradford says, to do "no more than protect and
institutionalize a known if imperfect felicity."[13]

Our Constitution was based on the older, **biblical** concept of law:
that society, a complex network of institutions, encompasses civil
government and respects the person. That concept requires limited
constitutional government, the protection of society as it is, and the
freedom of the people of society to shape their own society through
their voluntary interactions. Post-1932 constitutional scholarship has
been based on the view that civil government encompasses all things
and must function to make society conform to a particular view of the
nature of man and society.[14] Pre-1932 constitutional scholarship by
and large taught that our Constitution rightly gave us limited consti-

---

be subject to limitation, redefinition, or destruction at the whim of those with
the power to redefine such purposes.

   11. Ibid., 106.

   12. Ibid., 104.

   13. Ibid., 106.

   14. Basically a left-wing secular humanist notion that man is a product of
his environment, and hence that man and society are perfectible via use of the
power of civil government—in the hands of "liberals," "progressives," Marxists, etc.—to "transform" society.

tutional government which left society free to shape itself. Post-1932 constitutional scholarship by and large taught that our Constitution serves and should serve certain abstract principles stated in the Declaration of Independence, or which can be redefined from certain words and phrases in the Declaration; it therefore taught that our Constitution should not limit the authority and power of civil government but empower our national government to achieve the social, economic, and political objectives required by these abstract principles. The older constitutional scholarship said that our Constitution should be changed by the document's own processes stated in Article V. The newer constitutional scholarship has sought to justify and legitimize judge-made law, or judicial amendment of our Constitution on the ground that such "amendments" have been done in the service of enabling, encouraging, and requiring our central government to reshape America's social, political, and economic life.[15]

Some Radical Republicans intended to use the 14th Amendment as a device by which the central government could usurp the powers of the states and transform American society, and they justified their actions with essentially the same arguments as have been advanced by most post-1932 constitutional scholars—saying that there are certain abstract principles to which our society must conform, whether or not the Constitution actually recognizes those principles.[16] However, these radical "Radicals" were not the majority in the Congress which produced the Fourteenth Amendment, and their views did not represent either the majority view or the purposes of the Fourteenth Amendment.

But before considering the Fourteenth Amendment it is important to consider who is right about the fundamental purpose of our Constitution. Are the minority of Radical Republicans and the majority of post-1932 constitutional scholars right, or are the majority of pre-1932 constitutional scholars right? Was our Constitution intended to enable or require our central government to reshape our society in terms of abstract principles like "equality" which are not stated in our Constitu-

---

15. Bradford, *Original Intentions*, 104-107. Since our focus here is on the mischief wrought by judges, the writer has omitted similar justifications of mischief wrought by presidents and lawmakers.

16 Ibid., 104, 106.

tion or its Bill of Rights? Or was our Constitution meant to restrain our central government, protect our states' self-government, and preserve liberty for future generations of Americans?

Does Our Constitution Require or Permit Our Central Government to Reshape Our Society in Terms of Abstract Principles Not Stated in Our Constitution?

Now, it is relatively easy to know what the Framers and Ratifiers of the Constitution intended, for we have plenty of primary sources on the subject. We have the written Constitution and Bill of Rights. We have the volumes of debates for the Philadelphia Convention which drafted our Constitution. We have more volumes of the debates in the state ratification conventions—in which Framers and advocates of ratification of the Constitution explained the Framers' intentions about the document as a whole, answered questions raised by men who had doubts about certain features of the document, or argued against Anti-Federalists' criticisms. We have the voluminous writings of the Federalists for the Constitution and volumes of the Anti-Federalists' writings against it. The burden of all of this testimony is that our Constitution was intended to give us—and to keep for our posterity—a distinctly limited civil government, the rule of law, federalism, and freedom. The same, to say the least, can be said of our Bill of Rights! There is no way to square any of this with Big Government of any sort—much less with a centralized governmental system in which the current officials are free to redefine the terms under which they hold their authority, the purposes of our system of civil government, the limits of their powers, and the nature and content of our liberty—all without bothering to go through the difficult amendment or constitutional convention process of Article V, and all by discovering unstated (and not even implied) purposes in the Constitution.

The Framers did say in the Preamble that "We the People of the United States" ordain and establish this Constitution to (among other things) "establish Justice" and to "secure the Blessings of Liberty to ourselves and our Posterity," and they did not define either "justice" or "liberty" in the Preamble. But then they immediately, beginning with

Article I, set forth the governmental structure, institutions, and processes by which our civil governments are to function under our Constitution. As Bradford, citing constitutional scholar Philip B. Kurland, notes, "the 'public policy expressed' in the Constitution 'is essentially procedural rather than substantive': that 'almost all of the Constitution is procedural and not substantive in nature.'"[17] Why did the Framers (and Ratifiers) not define such terms as "justice" and "liberty"?

Did they not define them because they believed, as 19th and 20th and 21st century positivists, evolutionists, historicists, pragmatists, irrationalists, and other assorted Machiavellian intellectual and moral relativists believe, that justice and liberty are essentially meaningless terms whose meanings can and should be redefined by man—or by man's rulers—to suit men's or rulers' present views and purposes? Read their writings! The evidence is overwhelmingly and resoundingly "NO!" The Framers, Ratifiers, and people of their states were none of these things. Though intellectual and moral relativism had been around since ancient times and Machiavellianism had been around for nearly three centuries, the nature of their predominant religious beliefs,[18] education,[19] law, legal thought, and legal education,[20] made them highly adverse to intellectual and moral relativism. The Declaration of Independence which our early states' representatives wrote,[21] and signed as representatives of their re-

---

17. Ibid., 105.

18. Jones, *Christianity in the Constitution*, 145-230.

19. Ibid., 79-144.

20. Ibid., 145-230.

21. Jefferson wrote only the first draft of the Declaration, not the whole, completed document. The five-man committee of which he was a part revised his first draft, and the Second Continental Congress revised that to produce the document's ultimate version. A perusal of previous and subsequent documents and actions by the Continental Congress and the colonies' governmental bodies, not to mention of early American political writings, sustains Jefferson's modest statement that he had only written "the plain common sense of the matter" in penning the first draft of the Great Declaration. The vast majority of Jefferson's fellow representatives in the Second Continental Congress were Christians; the few, like Jefferson and Franklin, who were not (who were what would later be called Unitarians) nevertheless shared their more orthodox fellows' belief in God and in the existence of intellectual and ethical universal laws and rights.

spective states, belies the notion that they were motivated and sustained by intellectual and moral relativism or a belief that the principles for which they fought were essentially meaningless terms, or terms which men—especially rulers!—can legitimately redefine as it suits their social, economic, and political purposes. A term which can be redefined or which has a changing content is obviously not a universally true thing.

The Declaration's grounding of men's God-given, inalienable rights in "the laws of nature and of nature's God" and in Americans' legal rights from their providentially-given legal heritage from Britain, and its appeal to nothing less than God's divine Providence for the rectitude of their intentions in the outcome of their struggle for liberty and independence, are manifestly inconsistent with intellectual and moral relativism. The Declaration is therefore inconsistent also with the views of those who would use it to justify a continual redefinition of our nation's social, economic, and political purposes to make our Constitution mean the opposite of what it meant to its Framers and Ratifiers—and, as a consequence, a continuing negation of the principles and purposes of the Declaration—by the current possessors of power in our national government. Clearly, it was not intellectual and moral relativism which led the Framers to leave "justice" and "liberty" undefined in our Constitution.

A study of our early states' constitutions, declarations of rights, and bills of rights certainly confirms this. These were Christian documents, not Deist or rationalist ones. They were based upon Christian ethics and an old, well-established heritage of Christian legal and political thought which is easily traceable back through the colonial period, the Counter-Reformation, the Protestant Reformation, and the medieval period (and, before that, to the Bible). These documents were not the legal and political fruits of man-centered thought and intellectual and moral relativism but of Christianity. Their legal and political burden was *the limitation of the authority of civil government*, not the creation of excuses for civil government's rulers to increase their powers and decrease the people's rights and liberty.[22] In this light, it is manifestly absurd to think that the representatives of the states intended to bequeath to their posterity a fundamental law which could

---

22. Jones, *Christianity in the Constitution*, 339-394.

or should be gutted and redefined by officials of the very central government *it had created* whenever its original interpretation impeded that central government from gaining forbidden authority or powers.

The authors of our Constitution, like the authors of our Declaration (some of whom were the same men), did not define such terms as justice and liberty because *they and their fellow Americans knew and agreed upon the meanings of these terms.* Contrary to what we have been taught by historical revisionists, the vast majority of the Framers and Ratifiers were orthodox Christians—not Deists, rationalists, or unbelievers.[23] They did not conceive the terms justice and liberty to be plastic, malleable, or pragmatically "made true" by man. They believed that Truth—with a capital "T"— exists, can be known by man, and was known by them: via the Bible, "natural law" (as opposed to abstract "reason") God-given, God-ordained (providential) experience, and their inherited, providentially-given and hard-earned legal rights. They did not define *justice* or *liberty* because they did not need to define these terms for Americans—and, it must be admitted, they did not foresee the upshot of modern man-centered thought and how these self-destructive presuppositions would eat away at future Americans' moral certitude.

They also did not define such terms as *justice* and *liberty* because our Constitution's carefully designed system of governmental institutions, allocations of power, governmental procedures, limitations on power, and separations of power with accompanying checks and balances specifies and clarifies what they meant by *justice* and *liberty*. Clearly, as Madison set it forth so lucidly in Federalist No. 10, the key to that great exposition of the Framers' intentions for the Constitution and its institutions and powers, and as "Publius's" explication of the intentions behind our Constitution throughout the rest of *The Federalist* makes so manifest, the design of our constitutional system was meant to protect both justice and liberty. The Framers and Ratifiers and the Americans they represented believed that justice and liberty are cor-

---

23.   See Bradford, *Religion and the Framers: The Biographical Evidence.*
The evidence drawn from the existing records of their lives indicates that at least 90%, and probably more than 95% of the Framers and of the leading men in the states' ratification conventions were orthodox Christians.

relatives. Civil government must be designed to control the effects of "faction"—a group (majority or minority) united and motivated by some interest which is opposed to others' rights and/or what we might call the common good.

The causes of faction which are "sewn into" the nature of man, are three. First, man's reason is fallible (so much for rationalism, and so much for rule by a "wise man" or an intellectual elite!). Second, man's reason is connected to his self-love, so his opinions are inseparably connected to his passions and his opinions and passions have reciprocal effects on each other. (So much, again, for rule by one man or by an intellectual elite!) Third, men are fundamentally unequal, for they have "diverse and unequal" faculties or mental capabilities (so much for untrammeled majority rule and egalitarianism!). Through these diverse and unequal mental capabilities men acquire different degrees and kinds of property. Property may be physical or non-physical (knowledge, ideas, opinions, etc., and especially religious knowledge, ideas, and opinions). Men form minority or majority factions upon the basis of the different kinds and amounts of property which they possess— and not only upon the basis of material things, nor only upon the basis of those who have many material things and those who have few material things (contra Marxism!). Men have a right to the property they acquire through the honest use of their faculties, and it is the duty of civil government to protect all kinds and degrees of legitimately acquired property against the effects of factions (So much for socialism and all forms of legalized theft!). Factions oppose others' rights to the property they possess. Since the causes of faction are sewn into man's nature, civil government cannot remove them. Moreover, if civil government were to attempt to remove these causes its supposed "cure" would be worse than the disease of faction since liberty would be destroyed in the process. To the extent that a minority or majority faction in control of civil government attacks others' property, justice and liberty are destroyed. To the extent that justice is destroyed liberty will be lost.

Factions, moreover, destroy popular governments, and with them justice and liberty. They do so, says Madison, by introducing "instability, injustice, and confusion into the public councils": giving us ever-changing laws, unjust laws, and contradictory laws. So the Framers and Ratifiers *opposed* ever-changing laws, unjust laws, and contradictory laws. They therefore opposed the very kinds of laws which are made when rulers of a civil government redefine justice and liberty at their whim, the kinds of laws which, historically, have resulted in the misery of countless multitudes. Hence they opposed the very kinds of laws "liberal," democratic socialist, "progressive," and Marxist intellectuals and politicians—the motivators and shapers of modern American factions—have given us. Hence they also opposed easy or deceptive means of changing our fundamental law, our Constitution.

Since the causes of faction cannot be removed, and since civil government should not try to remove these causes—for that would involve removing the limits on government's authority and the creation of what would later be called an "omnicompetent" or totalitarian state—the only "cure" for faction is to control the effects of faction. As Federalist No. 10 and all the others of those great essays make clear, the complex, careful design of our constitutional system of civil government was done to create the greatest probability, within the context of American culture and politics, that neither a minority nor a majority faction would be able to dominate our central government and destroy justice and liberty.

This brief account of the Framers' and Ratifiers' reasoning makes it quite clear that the authority of the civil government established by our Constitution is limited, and that its power in practice must be limited. What we read in the rest of *The Federalist*, the writings of proponents and opponents of ratification of our Constitution, the debates in the Constitutional Convention, and especially the debates in the states' ratification conventions certainly confirms this. And all of this massive evidence gives the lie to the lie that those who gave us our Declaration and our Constitution really meant for our central government officials to redefine the purposes of our Constitution—without, of course, going through the document's own amendment process—and consequently to redefine and remove at will the limits on **their powers** which the Framers designed into our system of government to protect us and the people of our states against the effects of minority and majority faction.

The fact that our first Congress produced a proposed Bill of Rights—including our Tenth Amendment—and that our early states ratified that

Bill of Rights makes obvious the absurdity of the notion that the purpose of our Constitution was to enable the present possessors of power in our central government to redefine the fundamental purposes of our Constitution. For to have done so would have been to remove the limits which the Framers and Ratifiers of our Constitution and its Bill of Rights so carefully placed on the mere men in power in our central government.

The nature of our Tenth Amendment makes this even clearer, for it reaffirms the fundamental design of our governmental system as one having a pervasive separation of powers. Our Tenth Amendment therefore forbids the rulers of our central government to use "redefinition" of any kind to usurp any powers from our states' governments, or to augment their own powers at the expense of the states' governments. The powers of the central government must stay exactly what they were upon ratification of our Constitution, unless the people of those states, using the Constitution's own amendment or constitutional convention process stated in Article V of our Constitution, delegate more powers to the national government.

Therefore, our Constitution does not contain, nor was it intended to contain, principles which require regularly renewed redefinition by the officials of our central government who then must increase or enlarge their own powers to fulfill the demands contained in those new meanings. This notion is—at best—nonsense. It is also, to say the least, a defective foundation upon which to base constitutional scholarship.

Scholars and Judges Even Worse Than Radical Republicans

Unhappily, that has not stopped "constitutional scholars" or U.S. Supreme Court and Federal Court judges from inventing such "principles," inserting them into various clauses of our Constitution and its amendments, and creating new pseudo-rights of Americans and pseudo-powers of the central government by which to achieve them. Radical Republicans sought to use all of the "Civil War Amendments" to enable themselves to do things that the Constitution, for better or worse, did not entitle Congress to do. But not all Republicans were Radical Republicans, not all Radical Republicans were equally radical, and the radicals could not amend the Constitution by themselves but needed the help of conservative Republicans as well as Democrats to propose amendments and gather enough states to ratify them. Consequently, the amendments meant what the consensus of the two-thirds congressional majorities meant by them, not what a few Radical Republicans meant by them.

The Thirteenth Amendment was intended to free the slaves. It was enacted by a combination of Radical Republicans, Democrats, and conservative Republicans. Radical Republicans, such as Senator Charles Sumner, tried to attach "expansive interpretive statements and language from the French Revolution"[24] to the amendment, making the freed slaves socially equal to the whites, but were defeated by Democrats and conservative Republicans—whose constituents in the North would not support such a measure. Sen. Morrill of Maine said that Sumner could not find any such meanings in the text of the amendment itself, and the majorities in the House and the Senate agreed with him.[25] Sen. Henderson, who presented the proposed amendment to the Senate from the Senate Judiciary Committee, said that the amendment was intended only to free the slaves, and to leave any further measures concerning the status of the freedmen to the states.[26] Clearly, the 13th Amendment was intended only to free the slaves, not to do anything more, and not to empower federal government officials to increase their powers in the name of achieving grand-sounding, or even actually good, objectives.

The Fourteenth Amendment was intended to guarantee the basic rights of citizens to the newly freed slaves. Its first section is the most important, and though it was not then the most debated of the sections, it has become the most debated since the 1930s. For those who have sought to use it to "swallow up the rest of the United States Constitution"[27] have sought to use its language to negate all of our Constitution's limits on the power of our central government in order to enable the possessors of that power to achieve social and economic objectives not stated in the Constitution, not necessarily approved by most Americans, and not achievable at that time by amending the Constitu-

---

24. Bradford, *Original Intentions*, 110.
25. Ibid., 111.
26. Ibid.
27. Ibid., 119.

tion. The first section was meant to protect the Civil Rights Act of 1866[28] by declaring that anyone born in the United States is a citizen of both the state in which he was born and the United States, forbidding any state to make or enforce any law abridging the privileges or immunities of United States citizens, to deprive anyone of life, liberty, or property without due process of law, or to deny the equal protection of the laws to any person in its jurisdiction. The purpose of the amendment, on the evidence of its framers and ratifiers, was to enforce the *legal*, but not the *social*, equality of blacks and whites, which the amendment left to the states to decide for themselves.[29]

We know this because the Fourteenth Amendment was part of a very political process, a sequence of post-"Civil War" civil rights laws and amendments, which were meant to aid the political objectives of the Republican Party in the post-"Civil War" era. As M.E. Bradford put it,

> ...it begins in a tendentious political act, not in Olympian disinterestedness and spiritual triumph over racial animosity. This amendment had as its primary purpose a plan to do something for the Republican Party by controlling the rebellious South, which meant that it did incidentally a few things for blacks, whose help would be needed if Republicans were to stay in power. But not too much. And certainly not at the level of personal relations.[30]

Whether we like it or not, only a small minority of Americans or of their representatives in Congress wanted the Reconstruction amendments and Congress's civil rights laws of 1866, 1870, 1871, and 1875 to uplift black Americans to social equality with whites. Democrats, who would have been the national majority party if Republican legislation had not excluded so many supporters of the Southern war effort, generally opposed such laws. Some Radical Republicans wanted such

---

28. Woods and Gutzman, 44-46. Bradford, *Original Intentions*, 119, notes that "The Framers of this amendment (such as Senator John Sherman) thought it was "only an embodiment of the Civil Rights Bill."

29. Woods and Gutzman, 46-47.

30. *Original Intentions*, 119-120.

social reforms because of their egalitarian principles, but many Radical Republicans and abolitionists wanted blacks to be free but not equal. Some Northern judges and legal scholars wanted the social conditions of blacks improved—**if** the means by which that was achieved did not damage the Constitution's principle of federalism: each state's control over its own internal affairs. Other Republicans wanted these civil rights laws to win them blacks' votes—but not to cost them the votes of Northern whites. The majority of whites in most Northern states— Illinois, Indiana, Michigan, Ohio, Pennsylvania, New York, New Jersey, etc.—would accept such laws as punishments for Southern states and Southerners, but not if said laws would alter either the Constitution or Northern states' laws and blacks' living conditions in Northern states. During this time it was common for Northern states to exclude blacks from voting. The majority of whites in most Northern states approved of "reconstructing" the states of the South, but not their own states.[31] Moreover, after 1866, the Republicans in general and Radical Republicans in particular began to lose political support both to Democrats and to Republicans who were more interested in political power for its own sake (and the wealth that they could get from it) than they were in abolitionism or egalitarianism.[32]

Section I forbids any state to "deprive any person of life, liberty, or property, without due process of law [the Due Process Clause]; nor [to] deny to any person within its jurisdiction the equal protection of the laws [the Equal Protection Clause]." This wording was taken from Lord Edward Coke's great and influential commentaries on the Magna Charta (1215) and two fourteenth century English cases. This language had to do with things related to trial procedures—procedural, not "substantive" due process of law. It was meant as a negative, not a positive thing: not a license to judges to destroy our Constitution's limita-

---

31. Ibid., 108–109, 114–115. Bradford, 115, notes the political outworking of this: "In Kansas, Minnesota, New Jersey, and Ohio proposals for extension of the suffrage to blacks failed. Later they failed again in Michigan and Pennsylvania. Colorado and Nebraska applied to be admitted to the Union without giving a franchise to blacks." Historical reality does not match contemporaneous and subsequent partisan rhetoric. Neither Republicans nor Northern voters were as pure in motive as we are customarily told they were.

32. Ibid., 114–115.

tions on the power of our national government by "creative" judicial interpretation or the claim that the section embodies certain "general principles" not stated in its text. Instead it was meant to guarantee only equality regarding certain specific—specified—rights to residents of a state.[33]

We can understand the intended meaning of the Fourteenth Amendment—particularly of its first section—by studying the records of the debates in Congress (recorded in the *Congressional Globe* and *Congressional Record*) using the ordinary methods of analyzing literature, rhetoric, and historical events. We can study what Republican congressmen and senators, including, of course, Radical Republicans, said about their intentions for the Fourteenth Amendment. We can study then-contemporary newspaper accounts. We can study the papers of important participants in the process.[34] When we do this—when we study the actual historical record—we see that the amendment was not meant to affect social or political rights. Even the most consistent of the Radical Republican abolitionists, Thaddeus Stevens, agreed with this. Senator Charles Sumner of Massachusetts, a truly radical abolitionist, gave very little support to the amendment since he could not find the revolutionary revision of the Constitution that he wanted to find in the amendment's language. And Wendell Phillips and other radical abolitionists opposed the Fourteenth Amendment because its language did not go so far as they wanted it to go in enabling the central government to intervene in the sphere of the states' authority.[35]

But those who want to "transform" our system of civil government without having to resort to the amendment or constitutional convention processes of Article V—the advocates of centralized, unlimited power to be used in the "transformation" of American political, economic, and social life—have not sought to deal honestly with the historical record and the intentions it reveals for the Fourteenth Amendment. Instead they have deliberately distorted the meaning of the Fourteenth Amendment.[36] Consequently, as Bradford noted,

33. Ibid., 120.
34. Ibid., 123.
35. Ibid.
36. A summary of the divergent scholarly approaches to the meaning of

Our understanding of the Fourteenth Amendment, and especially of its first section, is beclouded by the greatest variety and volume of interpretive distortion attached to any component of the United States Constitution. What I refer to is a paragraph [the first section of the amendment] smothered over the generations by the concoctions of those advanced spirits always more interested in speaking of what it should have meant, or might become, or of the "general principles" concealed beneath it than they are in what the law, interpreted through what the Republican majority in the Congress in April, May, and June 1866 might have been politically free to undertake, means on its face.[37]

Those who want the 14th Amendment to be "broadly construed" have attempted to achieve this obfuscation by focusing on the speeches of unrepresentative Republican politicians such as Rep. John Bingham of Ohio and Sen. Jacob Howard of Michigan.[38] Another method of deception is to use the Democrats' exaggerated objections to the first section of the amendment—"objections that attribute to it a centralizing power which few Republicans wished it to include"[39]—without informing their readers that Republicans denied that the language of the first section was intended to give the central government such power, and without telling their readers that the Republicans ultimately defended their intentions for the meaning of the first section of the amendment by going directly to the explicit, restrictive language of the 1866 Civil Rights Act. Since this language defeats their purpose, they tell us that we should interpret the Fourteenth Amendment in terms of

---

the Fourteenth Amendment and the issue of its "incorporation" of the Bill of Rights and requirement that federal courts apply it to the states in order to produce one kind or another of "equality" is contained in Richard B. Bernstein with Jerome Agel, *Amending America: If We Love the Constitution So Much, Why Do We Keep Trying to Change It?* (New York: Times Books, 1993), 337n.

37. Bradford, *Original Intentions*, 123.

38. Ibid., 124.

39. Ibid.

the supposed "principles" which underlie the Constitution[40] but which, of course, are not stated in our Constitution. Another approach is to argue that the intent of the amendment's framers cannot be known, so today's judges should not be bound by it.[41] A related approach is to argue that the debates in the 39th Congress which produced the Fourteenth Amendment contained "vague, open-ended, and sometimes clashing principles" which make the job of the federal courts to "reconcile its ambiguities and its conflicting meanings."[42] Their usual tactic is to tell us that the framers of the Fourteenth Amendment put "language that is capable of growth" into it because they meant the meanings of their words to "evolve" or "expand" with changes in time and circumstances.[43]

What such "interpretations" of the supposed intentions behind the Fourteenth Amendment do, of course is: (1) evade (or attempt to evade) the evidence of the political realities within which the debates on the amendment took place, (2) obfuscate the evidence of the winning side's intentions for the meaning of the amendment, (3) free federal courts (and legislators and presidents)[44] from the constraints of the evidence, and therefore (4) free federal judges (legislators, and presidents) to do whatever they can deceive the public and its diverse representatives into accepting, though grudgingly. The consequence of this, of course, is that federal judges and other federal officials are free to do whatever they will to invade the sphere of the states' authority in order to mandate ever-new concepts of "equality," "rights," and the like. This despite the fact that the evidence is clear and overwhelming that the framers of the amendment intended to protect only a limited category of rights, did not dare to claim that the amendment's purpose

40. Ibid.

41. Alexander M. Bickel, "The Original Understanding of the Segregation Decisions," *Harvard Law Review* 69 (1955), 1-65.

42. William E. Nelson, *The Fourteenth Amendment: From Political Principle to Judicial Doctrine* (Cambridge, Massachusetts: Harvard University Press, 1988), 62-63, quoted in Bernstein with Agel, *Amending America*, 105.

43. Bradford, *Original Intentions*, 125.

44. Our focus is on the courts because the courts have been the chief vehicle for amending our Constitution without using its own amending process.

was to promote political or social equality, and certainly did not mean
to have the central government invade the states' sphere of authority
other than in the very limited way specified in the amendment.

Again, the issue is not what the framers of the Fourteenth Amendment **should have done** but **what they actually did**. By falsely and
deceitfully claiming that the framers of the Fourteenth Amendment
intended to do what a later generation of Americans or their representatives **thinks they should have done**, federal judges (and others) have
falsified the historical record and used that falsified record to usurp
power from the states, violate the Tenth Amendment, and make war
on Americans' liberty. The ultimate consequences of such usurpations
are nothing less than judges making the Fourteenth Amendment the
effective destroyer of the Tenth Amendment, and so of federalism.
This means that the Fourteenth Amendment has been made a vehicle
for the creation of the very kind of centralized government and tyranny against which the Anti-Federalists warned—an engine for the
destruction of every American's liberty.

The notion that the framers and ratifiers of the Fourteenth
Amendment intended it to "evolve" or be "reinterpreted" by later
government officials is absurd, of course. For not even the Radical
Republicans intended such a thing: they wanted their words to mean
what they meant by them, not what others could or would twist them
to mean. Moreover, the whole idea of carefully writing a constitution,
or an amendment to a constitution, and then permitting later officials
of the civil government established by and under that constitution to
give new meanings to the carefully, laboriously chosen words of that
constitution or amendment is self-contradictory. Why go through the
elaborate process of debating the meanings of words if the underlying
"principles" of a constitution or amendment necessitate or permit later
occupants of governmental office to change the meanings of those
words? Worse yet, why go through the difficult process of carefully
selecting the words of a constitution or amendment if subsequent
officials of its civil government can destroy the meanings of those
words—and thus the intentions behind those words—by simply redefining those words? Why not simply state that the equivalent of a
"royal prerogative" is henceforth given to future government officials

and they are free to do whatever they want to do? As indicated (re-peatedly!) above, the notion that civil government officials can change the meanings of the words of the constitution under which they are to govern is profoundly anti-constitutional. It is fundamentally hostile to the consent of the governed and to constitutional government, and favorable to arbitrary, anti-constitutional, absolutist government. It is hostile to justice and to liberty, and it is certainly hostile to the philosophy upon which our Constitution was based and which our Constitution and its Bill of Rights embody.

Had the Fourteenth Amendment been understood to have contained such a constitution-destroying "principle" as allowing subsequent central government legislators or judges to redefine that amendment's words, that amendment would never have made it out of Congress, much less survived the ratification process. For such an amendment would have destroyed both federalism and our Constitution itself. Not even the most radical Radical Republicans in Congress wanted that, and no states would have ratified such an amendment.

Judicial Tyranny via the Fourteenth Amendment

What such "broad" interpretations—self-conscious, deceitful distortions—of the Fourteenth Amendment do, of course, is to make the Fourteenth Amendment a vehicle for destroying constitutional government, our Tenth Amendment, and our Constitution. For if the Fourteenth Amendment meant that the constitutional duty of our national government is to use its power to pursue and implement "principles" which are not stated in our Constitution, and which in fact are manifestly opposed to the design and historically identifiable purposes of our Constitution, then the Fourteenth Amendment would destroy our Constitution's carefully crafted system of separation of powers and checks and balances, and destroy the document's explicit and implicit limitations on the powers of our central government. With that destruction the Fourteenth Amendment would also destroy our Tenth Amendment, and with it that amendment's protections of federalism, federalism's system of separation of powers and checks and balances between the central government and our states, and the liberty and justice which our Tenth Amendment was created to protect and preserve.

The Radical Republicans and those who collaborated with them in the "adoption" of the Fourteenth Amendment set a terrible precedent by adding amendments to our Constitution by unconstitutional means. In doing so, they broke their oaths of office by violating our Constitution. Yet their purposes (the purposes of the majority, not the purposes of the really radical Radical Republican minority) in creating and adopting the Fourteenth Amendment were limited and represented only very limited intrusions into the states' sphere of authority.

What the left-wing "scholars," lawyers, and judges have done with the Fourteenth Amendment is much more sinister and much more dangerous. Even if we grant the purity of their motives, their actions to achieve their goals have been filthy and destructive. They have followed in the Radical Republicans' footsteps in amending our Constitution by unconstitutional means, but have gone farther in that they do not even pretend to use our Constitution's own amendment process. They have amended our Constitution by means of judicial legislation—an obvious perversion of the function of judges in our constitutional system—and by means of judicial legislation masquerading as judicial decisions. In the process, of course, the judicial "legislators" (and those in Congress and the White House who have supported them) have violated their oaths of office—their affirmations to God and to the American people. Worst of all, they have perverted the manifest meaning of the Fourteenth Amendment (the meaning its framers and ratifiers intended it to have) to create pseudo-constitutional goals which give unlimited authority to our central government, and particularly to federal judges, to remake American social, economic, and political life; to violate the legislative, executive, and judicial rights of our states to govern themselves; and, in principle, and often in practice, to destroy justice and liberty for people of all races in our country.[45]

But despite the deceitful obfuscations of leftist legal scholars, historians, "political scientists," judges, presidents, and legislators, the

---

45. Woods and Gutzman, 41–70. This passage summarizes the Supreme Court's and federal courts' twisted logic, perverted constitutional reasoning, violations of states' authority over their internal affairs, and practical injustices to blacks and whites in regard to racial discrimination, school busing, and the like.

overwhelming historical evidence indicates that the intentions behind the Fourteenth Amendment were not to destroy, but only to adjust constitutional government, our Constitution, federalism, and our Tenth Amendment. The Tenth Amendment remains a vital part of our Constitution. And thus it remains a vital means of defending ourselves and our neighbors against the perverted dreams, deceitful arguments, and the "legal" machinations of the anti-constitutional, anti-liberty forces of our day: in our courts, our civil governments, and in our society.

We have the evidence to refute their arguments. We still have our states' governments through which we can revivify federalism, defend what remains of our liberty, and restore the rest. Do we have the will to resist judicial tyranny and restore our lost freedom?

28

Interposition and Constitutional Interpretation

A n understanding of the intentions behind our Tenth Amendment and of the biblical doctrine of interposition helps us to discern true and false theories of constitutional interpretation.

The Tenth Amendment was added to our Constitution to protect the non-delegated powers—the reserved powers—of the state governments, or of the people of each state; to protect the liberty of the people of each state and therefore of all Americans; and to protect justice and liberty against the ill effects of central government usurpation of power from the states.

The doctrine of interposition is based squarely on the Bible's teaching about the nature and duties of God's ministry of civil government and the duties of His ministers, civil government officials. It requires civil government officials to use their authority and power to protect the people under their authority against ungodly laws, policies, and actions, including usurpation of power and the abuses of power which result from such usurpation.

Our whole constitutional system of separation of powers with accompanying, carefully designed checks and balances, is a system of interposition, or at least of limited interposition, or, at worst, if our elected representatives are not doing their jobs, of potential interposition. Federalism was intended to be "a double security to the rights of the people," as Madison said in Federalist No. 51. Our constitutional system is designed to have the officials of our various institutions (House vs. Senate), branches of civil government (legislative vs. executive vs. judicial), and civil governments (national vs. state) oppose usurpations, abuses of power, and the exercise of unconstitutional power by other institutions, branches of government, or civil governments. It also is designed (how well-designed is

175

debatable, but the intention is indisputable) to use the self-interest of civil government officials to oppose unconstitutional, and/or unjust actions by other officials in our governmental system. Our constitutional system, based on an awareness of the sinful nature of man, is designed to enable and incline all officials of civil government—in our national government and in our state governments—to interpose their authority in order (1) to protect their own, or their own institution's, authority against usurpation of power, and (2) to protect justice, liberty, and the rights of the people against usurpation of power, unjust laws, and tyranny.

Inasmuch as our Constitution requires all officials of our civil governments to swear an oath (or make an affirmation) to support the Constitution, our system requires all of our civil government officials to interpose their authority and power against usurpations and injustices by other officials, institutions, branches of government, or governments in our governmental system.

Although our Constitution requires all officials of our civil governments to swear an oath (or make an affirmation) to support the Constitution, the Constitution does not state clearly that any one person or institution is the final authority on the meaning of the Constitution or of any disputed part of the document.

This has given rise to different theories of who, or what institution, has ultimate authority to interpret or declare the meaning of the Constitution or of any disputed portion of it. Advocates of some theories have claimed that it is absurd that there should be no ultimate authority to declare the meaning of a constitution, and that therefore the national/central government, and/or some institution in it, must be the ultimate authority in interpreting the Constitution. Although it has been fashionable for many decades now to treat the U.S. Supreme Court as the final authority on the meaning of the Constitution, Robert Yates, the framer of the Constitution whose brilliant "Letters of Brutus" opposed the Constitution and presciently warned against the Supreme Court's future distortions of the Constitution and usurpation of powers, saw Congress, as it is directly accountable to the people, as being the final authority for interpreting the Constitution.[1]

---

1. Kenyon, 323.

But the idea that there should be no ultimate authority in determining the meaning of the Constitution is not absurd if one realizes, as did its Framers and Ratifiers, the sinful nature of man, the biblical duties of civil government, and the rightness and constitutionality of the doctrine of interposition.

For the fact that all men are sinful means that they naturally want to be as God, determining the definitions of good and evil for themselves—and not obeying God's definitions of good and evil written on man's heart and revealed most clearly and fully in the Scriptures. Applied to civil government, this means that the power of all men must be limited and checked. It also means that the craftiness of man in inventing pseudo-justifications for his usurpation and abuse of power must be taken into account in the framing of constitutions as well as in the functioning of civil government. And it means that the biblical duties of civil government require carefully conceived checks against civil government's officials' usurpations and abuses of power. As James Madison said so memorably in Federalist No. 51,

> ...the great security against a gradual concentration of the several powers in the same department, consists in giving to those who administer each department the necessary constitutional means and personal motives to resist encroachments of the others... Ambition must be made to counteract ambition. The interest of the man must be connected with the constitutional rights of the place. It may be a reflection on human nature, that such devices should be necessary to control the abuses of government. But what is government itself, but the greatest of all reflections on human nature? If men were angels, no government would be necessary. If angels were to govern men, neither external nor internal controls on government would be necessary. In framing a government which is to be administered by men over men, the great difficulty lies in this: you must first enable the government to control the governed; and in the next place you must oblige it to control itself.

The doctrine of interposition is both solidly based on the Bible and an integral part of our Constitution's system of civil government. The doctrine of interposition makes it the duty of all officials of civil government to protect those under their authority against injustice and tyranny, to protect them against laws, policies, and actions which protect and/or praise the evildoers and/or restrain and punish those who do that which is good. Our system of separation of powers and checks and balances requires officials of the various institutions, branches, and governments (federal and state) to protect the liberty of those under their authority against usurpation of power, unconstitutional actions, and tyranny. Federalism gives us a dual system of separation of powers and checks and balances to protect the liberty of the states to govern their own internal affairs and the liberty of the people of the several states against usurpation, injustice, and tyranny by the central government and its institutions.

Our Constitution does not designate any institution of the central government, nor even the state governments, as the final or highest authority on the meaning of the Constitution because all of these institutions are supposed to be obliged to prevent the others from usurping power, abusing power, and threatening justice and liberty. If any one institution had been designated as the highest authority on interpreting the meaning of the Constitution, then that institution, administered by mere sinful men, would be in a position to twist the interpretation of the Constitution to augment its own power at the expense of the other institutions, to sooner or later rule over them, and thus threaten or destroy Americans' rights and liberty.

The Anti-Federalists warned against the danger of Congress, the Presidency, the federal judiciary and the Supreme Court, and the central government in general taking advantage of the powers given to central government and its institutions, and of vaguely worded clauses in the Constitution to threaten justice, the authority of the state governments, and the rights and liberty of the people. Though the Federalist advocates of the Constitution's ratification denied the validity of these criticisms, many Americans doubted the Federalists' arguments and feared that the Anti-Federalists' were right. Consequently, the Bill of Rights was drafted to protect our rights and liberty against the national government, including the Tenth Amendment as an unmistakable statement of the right of each state to retain all powers which it had neither delegated to the central government nor forbidden to itself in the Constitution.

The Tenth Amendment also made it clear, by implication, that the people of each state, or their state's government's officials, have a right to interpret the Constitution in order to protect their rights and liberty against misinterpretations and deliberate misconstructions of the Constitution by the central government or its officials or institutions. Thus, by protecting federalism, the Tenth Amendment provides a double security to the rights of the people by protecting the Constitution's complex system of interposition through protecting the authority of the state governments to interpose themselves between the central government and the people of their respective states.

The result does not provide an easy, efficient way to resolve differing interpretations of particular clauses of the Constitution, as do theories which place such supposed authority in the central government or (despite overwhelming evidence to the contrary) the Supreme Court. The Constitution implicitly gives "we the people of the United States" the authority and duty to interpret the Constitution's meaning—for it is we who directly or indirectly elect the representatives who administer all our civil government institutions. Through the congressional districts in our states we directly elect our representatives in the House of Representatives. Originally indirectly through our state's legislature, now (since the Seventeenth Amendment) we directly elect our state's two U.S. senators. Indirectly, through the Electoral College, we elect the President. Through the President and the Senate we elect (by two degrees of separation) the Federal court and U.S. Supreme Court judges. Having the power to elect the people who run our government, we can remove them from office and replace them with men who have a sound understanding of the Constitution and the will to preserve the Constitution: *if* we have the knowledge, the courage, and the perseverance to do so.

And as the Federalists, who had to defend the Constitution against Anti-Federalists' charges that the opening words of the Constitution's Preamble implied a governmental system based on national majority rule, repeatedly said, "We the people of the United States..." meant "We the people of the several states of the Union," not "We the majority of the people in the Union." "We the people of the United States..." were intended by the Constitution's Framers and Ratifiers to work to preserve our liberty primarily and ultimately through our own states.

The Constitution provides the amendment or constitutional convention process as the way to resolve different interpretations of the Constitution. It is a complex, difficult process that is designed to require the agreement of unusual majorities of our representatives in Congress (two-thirds of both houses)—and in our states' legislatures (three-fourths of them)—to any proposed change or clarification of the Constitution's meaning. This process requires the consent of an unusual majority of the states to any change in the Constitution. This ensures, by original intention, that it is difficult and often time-consuming to amend the Constitution. The process has been criticized of being inefficient. But it was not designed for efficiency or speed, but to preserve liberty for American citizens and their posterity. Further, it *was* designed to be efficient in preventing ill-considered changes and craftily-calculated usurpations of power.

Without the Tenth Amendment's guarantee of federalism we would have perhaps less than half the means of checking usurpations of power by the central government or its institutions because those institutions would find it easier to circumvent and circumscribe the powers of the states. The Tenth Amendment's emphasis on the importance of the reserved powers of the states, or of the people of each state, reinforces the importance of the states in the amendment process, and makes the states more conscious of their duty to defend the liberty of their people. It should also make us more conscious of our duty to know the Constitution, and to insist that our representatives in state and national governments interpret it aright, and do their constitutional duty.

29

The Tenth Amendment and Changing The Constitution

We have long been told that our Constitution must be a "living" document, with its meaning changing as dictated by time and circumstances, or men's responses to those changed circumstances. This is, in practice, our civil government officials' responses to changed circumstances based on these men's political philosophies and political self-interest. Such a standard of constitutional interpretation removes the restraints of law upon the desires of the men who have been chosen to serve in our central government. Such a standard is a pseudo-standard of constitutional interpretation, for it destroys the purpose for which our Constitution was so carefully framed and ratified, replacing the rule of law with the rule of men.

Our Constitution was intended—as rightly it should have been—to give us the rule of law, not the rule of men. The rule of law is the rule of fixed, known principles of law. The rule of men is of ever-changing rules being continually, arbitrarily reinterpreted by civil government rulers or officials. The rule of law requires that rulers obey the fundamental rules or law-principles of their political order. The rule of men frees rulers from the restraints of the fundamental laws of their political order, thus freeing rulers to decrease or extinguish the freedom of the people over whom they rule. The rule of law—depending on the content of the law, of course—prevents rulers from decreasing or abolishing the freedom of the people over whom they rule, thus preserving and protecting liberty (if the content of the fundamental law in question is compatible with liberty). The rule of men is opposed to liberty and attacks liberty. It is totally contrary to the rule of law when civil government officials arbitrarily change the meaning of the fundamental laws of their political order, or redefine their own authority, power, and duties: this is the rule of men, and not of law.

The rule of law is violated, not upheld, when a judge or Supreme Court majority attempts to characterize its unconstitutional decision as "constitutional."

Biblically and constitutionally, the rule of law is primarily and fundamentally **a content, not a process**. God did not command His people to go through a given process of making and enforcing laws: he commanded them to obey **His laws**. And He attached concrete, tangible historical sanctions to national obedience or disobedience to His laws. Clearly, the framers and ratifiers of our Constitution were concerned with the process by which our national laws are to be made under our Constitution. But the framers and ratifiers were particularly concerned with the **content** of the process: amendment or constitutional convention, not congressional legislation, presidential executive orders, or judicial fiat. And their concern with the content of the process of changing our Constitution was manifestly focused on protecting the **content** of our constitutional law and the **content** or meaning of the justice and liberty which they meant themselves and their posterity to have via our Constitution and our Bill of Rights.

"Liberals" and their ilk want to change the **content** of our Constitution by effecting a new **process** for changing our Constitution—and to deceive us about what they are doing.

"Liberals" and their co-conspirators often deceive conservatives into supporting "liberal" judicial amendments of our Constitution by appealing to the English Common Law and American legal principle of *stare decisis*, "let the decision stand." This principle requires that in deciding a particular case judges must let a previous decision on a similar case, a legal precedent, stand, making their ruling conform to the rule laid down by a previous court. For a court to overturn such a decision is "judicial activism" and a violation of legal precedent. "Liberal" courts' decisions which overturn legal precedents that are based on our Constitution are instances of judicial activism as well as violations of the principle of *stare decisis*. But having thus overturned legal precedents based on our Constitution (and violated their oaths of office to support our Constitution), "liberal" courts then establish new precedents—which "liberals" and their kindred ideologues then want to be honored and obeyed by subsequent courts. Then they complain

against conservatives or constitutionalists who want to overturn the
"liberals'" unconstitutional precedents: accusing those who want to
return to constitutional principles of "judicial activism" and violation
of *stare decisis.*

But overturning an unconstitutional legal precedent by replacing
it with a decision actually based on our Constitution is **constitutionalism**, not judicial activism. No legal precedent which is against the
principles of our Constitution should be permitted to stand. It does
not matter, in principle, that the overturned decision has the seeming
sanction of time or of numbers (exempting, of course, the numbers
which our Constitution requires to amend it): lies and deceit are lies
and deceit no matter how many judges and civil government officials support them. All such violations of our Constitution should be
overturned. The rule of law in our constitutional system is not a mere
loosely-defined process.

The rule of law in our political order is compatible with changing
the Constitution only by the Constitution's own processes for changing it: amendment or constitutional convention. The rule of law is **not**
compatible with changing the Constitution by "evolution" or the self-
servingly convenient "interpretation" of those in possession of temporary political power—as legislators, as the chief executive, or as judges.

Since they are but men who are put (or put themselves!) in a position of changing our Constitution by "interpreting," not amending
it, James Jackson Kilpatrick's argument is very much to the point:
the men who framed and ratified our Constitution and Bill of Rights
were great men, well-educated men, thoughtful men, men learned
in the experience of the ages, so "We ought to honor them. By what
presumption—by what giddy conceit—do today's political scientists,
uneducated editors, witless politicians, and other ignorami assert a superior wisdom?"[1] American education today may be superior to early
American education in the "hard" sciences, but it is greatly inferior
in virtually everything else, particularly religion, ethics, history, gov-

---

1. "The Case for 'States' Rights,'" in Robert A. Goldwin, ed., *A Nation of
States; Essays on the American Federal System* (Chicago: Rand McNally & Co.,
[1961] 1969), p. 90.

ernment, and economics[2]—not only in the secular humanist, leftist-dominated "public schools," but also in our colleges and universities.[3] *The Federalist Papers*, the classic essays by Hamilton, Madison, and Jay explaining the Constitution, advocating its ratification, and answering its critics, were primarily written for upstate New York farmers. Today college students have great difficulty understanding them (in the rare courses in which any of them are taught!), and they are seldom read (much less studied) by graduate students in Political Science or History. [4] Very few of our political "leaders" write their own newspaper columns or speeches—and not just because they are busy not reading the bills on which they are to pass judgment. Given the left-wing ideological composition of the faculties in most colleges, universities, and law schools, our politicians' (and journalists', "social scientists'", educators', etc.) "education" has been more like an indoctrination in the logically contradictory notions of intellectual and moral relativism and the pseudo-imperatives of leftism's social, economic, and political agenda

---

2.   Yes, economic thought and textbooks are much more developed than they were when our Constitution was framed, but economic thinking and instruction then were much less perverted by socialistic notions.

3.   David L. Goetsch and Archie P. Jones, *Liberal Tyranny in Higher Education; How You Can Fight Back* (Powder Springs, Georgia: The American Vision, Inc., 2009).

4.   When the present writer taught an introductory course in American National Government at a large state university in the middle and late 1970s, he assigned his students some 40–45 of the 85 essays of *The Federalist*. He was virtually the only one in the Political Science department who required (or tried to require) students to read any of that great work. Graduate students taking a graduate course in American Government were required to read Federalist No. 10, the most important of *The Federalist Papers*, but the professor who taught that course misread or plainly misinterpreted Federalist No. 10, making it out to have an essentially economic determinist or pre-Marx Marxist view of politics. Graduate students studying American government and the Constitution thus read only one of the 85 essays in *The Federalist*—and absolutely nothing from the debates in the Constitutional Convention, not to mention the debates in the state ratification conventions in which advocates of ratification had to explain every item in the Constitution questioned by anyone and answer all criticisms by articulate, learned Anti-Federalists.

and its periodic crusades.[5] Such pseudo-education, devoid of truth and wisdom, ignorant of and hostile to the Bible, the experience of the ages, and the principles of our governmental and legal heritage, has ill-equipped our current political, educational, and journalistic leaders to criticize, much less improve upon, our Constitution.

Those who call for us to make our Constitution a "living Constitution" do so because they consider it too difficult to change the Constitution via the document's own process for changing itself. They want to make the Constitution much easier to change—and much easier for **them** to change. They know that they cannot persuade enough Americans, or enough Americans in enough states, to make the changes that the advocates of the notion of a "living Constitution" want to make, so they adopt the deceitful strategy of telling us that we must make our charter of liberty a "living" document by permitting those in power to change its meaning at will.

A key reason that they have been unable to persuade enough Americans in enough states to adopt the changes that the "living Constitution" spokesmen want to make is that those changes are inimical to the original intentions of the Framers and Ratifiers of our Constitution and most Americans, despite being miseducated and propagandized for decades, do not want to embrace such radical changes. So "living Constitution" propagandists have adopted an "end-run" strategy of persuading Americans to let them change the Constitution by redefining its meaning (or some carefully selected provisions' meaning). But their method masks their true intention, which is to change the Constitution radically. **Their method of making our Constitution a "living Constitution" kills the Constitution** by discarding the carefully crafted meanings agreed upon by our Constitution's Framers and Ratifiers and removing the restraints which they intended to place on our presidents, legislators, and judges.

---

5. If "everything is relative," and there is no such thing as Truth, then there can be no moral imperatives upon which to base any social, economic, or political crusade. If there is no Truth, then there cannot be any objective reason why anyone should be morally concerned about anything, much less concerned enough to participate in a crusade.

Note that such "interpretation" of our Constitution is to be done by those who are currently in possession of the authority of offices in our central government (unless, of course, they disagree with the "living Constitution" advocates' social, economic, and political philosophy and agenda). Obviously, such men stand to gain power (at least power, but probably wealth also) by usurping the power to amend the Constitution from the institutions which the document itself authorized—and alone authorized—to change the Constitution. Ultimately this is usurpation of the authority of the people whose representatives framed our Constitution. What Raoul Berger said of the U.S. Supreme Court's attacks on federalism is true of all changes in our Constitution made by unconstitutional means: the facts show that "in revising the Founders' design for federalism, the Supreme Court has usurped power the people reserved to themselves."[6] Now, what sort of changes in the Constitution do you think the current possessors of power in our central government will want to make? It would be astounding if they did not want to make changes which would increase their own power. Such changes, however, would jeopardize justice and liberty in America, and the greater the changes, in all likelihood, the greater the threat to justice and liberty.

The Framers and Ratifiers of our Constitution gave us a far better means of changing our Constitution than "interpretation" by current, self-interested holders of federal government office. They spelled out the means of changing our Constitution in Article V of the Constitution:

> The Congress, whenever two thirds of both Houses
> shall deem it necessary, shall propose Amendments
> to this Constitution, or, on the Application of the Leg-
> islatures of two thirds of the several States, shall call
> a Convention for proposing Amendments, which, in
> either Case, shall be valid to all Intents and Purposes,
> as Part of this Constitution, when ratified by the Leg-
> islatures of three fourths of the several States, or by
> Conventions in three fourths thereof, as the one or the
> other Mode of Ratification may be proposed by the

---

6. Berger, 7.

Congress; Provided that no Amendment which may be
made prior to the Year One thousand eight hundred
and eight shall in any manner affect the first and fourth
Clauses in the Ninth Section of the First Article [The
Ninth Section states certain specific limits or prohibitions on the authority, powers, and acts of Congress;
its first clause concerns the importation of slaves.]; and
that no State, without its Consent, shall be deprived of
its equal Suffrage in the Senate.

Our Constitution's means of changing our fundamental law is the
amendment or constitutional convention process. The amendment or
constitutional convention process is carefully designed to admit only
thoughtfully considered changes to our fundamental law. This was
done with wise purposes in mind: to create the greatest probability of
making sure that changes to our Constitution are products of "the deliberate sense" of the people of our nation and of our states in order to
defend that justice and liberty for which the Constitution was framed
and ratified.

As Article V makes quite evident, "the deliberate sense" of the
people of America includes—and is inseparable from—the deliberate
sense of the peoples of the several states, and thus from the system
of separation of powers and checks and balances between the central
government and the states which is federalism. For **federalism is inseparable from the Constitution's methods of changing the Constitution**. Amendments may be proposed by two-thirds of both houses
of Congress, each of which is filled with elected representatives of
each state. And it is not a mere majority of those representatives in the
more democratic House of Representatives and in the more aristocratic Senate who must agree to a proposed amendment; instead it is an
unusually large majority of each house which must agree to a proposed
amendment: a majority larger than the "super majority" of sixty of the
one hundred senators which our U.S. Senate requires today for certain
legislative purposes. In the constitutional convention process, amendments may be proposed by "the application of the legislatures of two-
thirds of the several states," followed by a constitutional convention for
proposing amendments. Here again an unusually large majority of the

legislatures of the states is required to even submit a proposed amendment. In either case, ratification of proposed amendments must be "by the legislatures of three fourths of the several states" or by conventions in three quarters of the states (depending on the mode of ratification chosen by Congress). Our Constitution requires an even larger majority of the states' legislatures or conventions (three-fourths) to ratify a proposed amendment than to propose an amendment (two-thirds).

These majorities are not popular majorities, nor are they popular "super majorities." They are not based on votes of the people of the nation as a whole, nor even on the direct votes of the people of each state. They are unusually large majorities of the elected representatives of the people of each state—in Congress and in each state's legislature or ratification convention. These majorities are steps away from the majority-rule democracy which leftists love to praise in the abstract and thwart when the majority cannot be duped into supporting their aims. They are different in at least six ways.

First, these majorities are not based on the will of the national majority of voters. Second, they are not composed of popular votes but of majorities of representatives who, having been chosen by the people of their respective states, meet, deliberate, and then vote whether to ratify a proposed amendment. Third, they are composed of representatives chosen by the people of each state who in turn decide whether to approve a proposed change in our Constitution. Fourth, they are not simple majorities but unusually large majorities: majorities unusually difficult to achieve. Fifth, two different majorities, of different, hard-to-achieve sizes—one to propose amendments and one to ratify them—are required in order for a proposed amendment to be ratified. And sixth, the majority required to propose an amendment (two-thirds of both houses of Congress or of the states' legislatures), while difficult to achieve, is neither so large nor so difficult to achieve as the majority required to ratify a proposed amendment (three-fourths of the states' legislatures or of their ratification conventions).

Since even all the people of the largest or most populous state are a minority of the people of the Union, each of these steps away from majority-rule democracy is a step in defense of federalism and a protection of justice, liberty, and the self-government of the minorities who are the people of the respective states.

Article V's amendment or constitutional convention (which should be called a "constitutional amendment-proposing convention") process was designed to include the sense of the people of each state—with the approval of at least of the representatives of three-quarters of the states—in order to protect, preserve, and defend the liberty, justice, and local self-government for which the Constitution was framed and ratified. In this way, too, federalism provides a double security to the rights of the people. And in this way, too, our Tenth Amendment powerfully buttresses our Constitution's protections of federalism.

The framers of our Constitution certainly knew that the flow of history would produce changed circumstances in these United States, and that those changed circumstances would necessitate changes in our Constitution. They also knew full well that they had neither produced a perfect document nor given us a fundamental law which would never require changes to meet unforeseen future conditions facing the Republic. But they did not include in our Constitution any provision for changing the meaning of our fundamental law by "evolution" or anything of the kind. They did not do so because they knew that changing the meaning of a document by "evolution"[7] is changing it by interpretation, and "interpretation" can be, and often is, done deceitfully, unwisely, and/or unjustly.

The argument that the Constitution must be changed by the actions of our current officeholders without resorting to Article V of the Constitution because of "necessity" is debatable. First, whether anything is necessary is debatable, and people's conclusions about whether something is necessary depend on their premises as much as or more than on the information available to them. The argument from "necessity" is also deceitful, for it begs the question—assuming that a given thing is really necessary—and it deliberately obscures the

---

7. Yes, the pseudo-scientific notion of evolutionism got a huge boost from the publication of Charles Darwin's *Origin of Species* in 1859, but the concept had been present in European thought for a couple of centuries by then. Early Americans and their elected representatives were, as their religious views and public documents make clear, creationists, not evolutionists—a fact which has profound ethical, political, and legal implications.

issue of whether proclaimed necessity (or, for that matter, real necessity) does or should trump the Constitution. The Constitution has a mechanism for enabling necessity to trump the Constitution: change the Constitution! But that change is supposed to occur by means of the Constitution's own amendment or constitutional convention process, not by allowing civil government officials to "redefine" the document's meaning and, in the process, their own powers' limits, Americans' liberty, and the effective structure of our governmental system.

Men do not always agree on what changes are required by changed circumstances, so it is not wise to permit changes in fundamental law to be made quickly or easily. Interpretation of what is "required" by changed circumstances may be done by one man in a position of governmental power, a minority of men in possession of such power, or a majority. It may be done to increase the power of the individual or group in power. It may be done deceitfully or upon the basis of naked temporary power. It may be done by calculation, incrementally, and more or less slowly, to increase the power, or establish absolute, tyrannical power in the hands of the possessor(s) of one office or institution, or of the governmental apparatus as a whole. Or it may be done precipitously, in a real or manufactured crisis or series of crises (by one man or a few men), with or without the intention of augmenting the power of an institution or office, but with an unwise or dangerous result or set of results for the governmental system—and for justice and liberty. It may be done by manipulating public opinion. And it had been done so many times in ancient, medieval, and modern history, as our well-educated Framers and Ratifiers well knew.

That is why the framers of our Constitution designed the amendment or constitutional convention process into the Constitution (Article V). That process was designed to take a longer time than ordinary legislation. It was designed to require unusual majorities of more than one institution—two-thirds of both houses of Congress or of the states' legislatures, three-quarters of the states' legislatures or ratification conventions—to produce the change involved. It was designed to increase the probability that the deliberate sense of the American community or nation, reflected in and mandated by those required unusual majorities, would be the basis of the change. Serious public debate and deliberation, not popular passion, manipulated precipitous action, or factional animosity, was what they wanted the change to be based on. Agreement by a "super-majority" of three-quarters of the states was an essential—and inseparable—part of their definition of such serious public debate.

The statesmen who ratified our Constitution would never have accepted the notion that the officials of our national government should be granted permission to amend the Constitution by interpretation or "evolution." As a group, they were far more diverse than the framers of the Constitution and contained far greater percentages of serious opponents of the Constitution, and far more men in the middle, men who had some doubts about various provisions of the Constitution and about the document as a whole, men who needed to be persuaded In order to support ratification of the Constitution.[8] The Anti-Federalist opponents of ratification of the Constitution included many thoughtful, learned, highly articulate men, like George Mason and the great Patrick Henry of Virginia, who had weighed the Constitution as a whole and its various provisions, had found them wanting, and had voiced insightful criticisms of the defective provisions as well as of the document as a whole. They were even more distrustful of the nature of man, and particularly of men in possession of the authority of civil government power, than were the Federalist supporters of ratification of the Constitution. The burden of their criticisms was that the Constitution was too poorly designed, too loosely worded, and too trustful of the nature of man to be accounted useful for the protection of Americans' liberty and the states' authority against tyranny. They

---

8. On the struggle over ratification of our Constitution, see Jeffrey St. John, *A Child of Fortune: A Correspondent's Report on the Ratification of the U.S. Constitution and Battle for a Bill of Rights* (Ottawa, Illinois: Jameson Books, Inc., 1990) and M.E. Bradford, *Original Intentions: On the Making and Ratification of the United States Constitution* (Athens and London: The University of Georgia Press, 1993). On the ratification of the Bill of Rights, see Robert Allen Rutland, *The Birth of the Bill of Rights, 1776-1791* (New York: Collier Books, 1962). In order to understand the intentions behind the Constitution and the Bill of Rights it is essential to read what is known as *Elliot's Debates,* the classic compilation of the debates in the states' ratification conventions: Jonathan Elliot, ed., *The Debates in the Several State Conventions on the Adoption of the Federal Constitution,* 5 vols., (published in various editions).

wanted more protections of liberty and against tyranny, more detailed, explicit restraints on governmental power and the power of the central government's institutions, than the Constitution contained.[9] Changing our Constitution by "interpretation" was exactly what they had in mind in opposing ratification of the Constitution. They would never have approved a provision allowing the possessors of civil government power to claim "interpretation" in order to define an "evolution" of the meaning of the document meant precisely to restrain that power.

The notion of an "evolving" constitution is, of course, either a delusion or a deceit. An "evolving" constitution is one with no inherent meaning, no fixed principles, and consequently no means of protecting or promoting justice, liberty, or traditional or legally-denominated divisions of authority and power. An "evolving" constitution is a meaningless document: it is no true constitution, for its meaning cannot be determined from its text, but originates in the current desires of those in possession of civil government power. Those who believe that the possessors of civil government power should be permitted to continually redefine their authority and powers are deluded about the nature of man and the allure of governmental power to fallen man. They are also profoundly ignorant of history. At least some of them are profoundly deceitful. Those who seek unlimited, arbitrary power over others champion such notions to deceive any who might stand in their way.

From the fact that our system of civil government has "evolved" in the unmistakable direction of greater and greater centralization of power and increased arbitrariness in the exercise of such power it does not follow that such an "evolution" is or has been either necessary or desirable.

---

9. On the Anti-Federalists' arguments, see Herbert J. Storing, ed. *The Complete Antifederalist*, 7 vols. (Chicago: University of Chicago Press, 1981), Cecelia M. Kenyon, ed., *The Antifederalists* (Indianapolis: The Bobbs-Merrill Co., 1966), Joseph Michael Bordelon, "Antifederalists and the Agrarian Republic: Securing the Blessings of Liberty through a Less Perfect Union." unpublished Ph D. dissertation, University of Dallas, 1975), and Jackson Turner Main, *The Anti-Federalists: Critics of the Constitution—1781–1788* (Chapel Hill: University of North Carolina Press, 1961). The late M.E. Bradford did insightful biographical sketches, published in various venues, which contain pointed distillations of many of the leading Antifederalists' political thought and views about the Constitution and Federalism.

And in passing let us note that the use of the term "evolution" or "evolving" to describe such centralization involves deceptive rhetoric. For the term "evolution" carries with it the meaning and the connotation of progress "onward and upward," so to speak.[10] But since the issue, or at least a fundamental issue, in dispute is whether the centralization of power in the history of our governmental system is good or not, the use of the term "evolution" to describe this series of developments is begging the question, prejudicing the debate over the issue.

And similarly disapproving things can be said about the increasingly arbitrary nature of the augmented power in our central government. Certainly if freedom is the criterion (or a criterion) by which we should measure the effects of arbitrariness of power, then arbitrariness has been bad, for it has clearly decreased individual freedom (and, along with it, the freedom of institutions such as the family, the church, and voluntary associations) as well as federalism's principle that freedom includes the freedom of the people of each state to govern their own internal affairs.

The intrusion of the central government into the affairs of the states is massively real, but it is not justified by its own existence. For the original intention of the Constitution's Framers and Ratifiers was plainly **to prevent the central government from making such intrusions**. Or, if any such intrusion were made, to first require it to be justified by an explicit change in the Constitution made via the amendment or constitutional convention process. Precisely what is at issue is the rightness of such interventions, and the official standard by which we Americans are to evaluate the rightness of any and all such interventions is our fundamental law, the Constitution. By the Constitution's own standard, central government interventions which transgress the Constitution's boundaries are wrong, not right, for they are unconstitutional.

---

10. In this the term "evolution" benefits from the survival of older, largely Christianity-influenced views of the world, life, and history being inherently meaningful and containing knowable ethical standards. The inherently irrational, and increasingly militant atheistic nature of evolutionist thought, of course, renders the world, life, and history meaningless, without objective ethical standards, and hence logically destroys the idea that "evolution" does or can contain any ethical improvement, no matter what results "evolution" produces.

Just because the American people have, in general, approved the expansion of the central government by voting to accept the money and "services" provided by the central government, it does not follow that the expansion of central government is, or has been, good—or constitutional. Nor does such a conclusion follow from the fact that states' governments have all too often sought or accepted centralization in order to get "federal" money (that is, money taken from the citizens of other states). Neither the Framers nor the Ratifiers of our Constitution, nor the people of their respective states, believed that the majority is always right, or that the *majority will* is always good, wise, just, or necessarily consistent with liberty. The Constitution was not based on the premise that the majority is sinless, nor that the majority should rule unchecked, but rather that the national majority must never be permitted to control all areas of life. And on that premise, the several states are to govern themselves within the boundaries of their respective states without coercion from the national majority will. As the Tenth Commandment's prohibition of covetousness reminds us, just because people want something, it doesn't follow that they are entitled to it.

The principle of the Tenth Commandment cannot be circumvented by the fact that most, if not all, of the things that the majority of Americans have approved from the hands of the central government over the decades have been preceded by educators' arts of preparation, politicians' arts of persuasion, and lawyers' and judges' arts of deception. Our Constitution was also based on the premise that a minority will—including that of judges—must never be permitted to control all areas of American life. Immoral rhetoric plus central government usurpation of the states' powers—no matter how, or under what guises it is accomplished—does not, and cannot equal constitutional government or policy.

Our Tenth Amendment was intended to buttress both federalism and the Constitution's own, deliberately complicated, state-oriented process of changing our fundamental law against both majorities and minorities who would subvert federalism and our Constitution. It is a reminder to the people of each state, as well as to the people of the Union formed by those states, that each state is a self-governing entity with authority over almost everything that occurs within its borders, and that the central government has very little authority over what occurs within the borders of any state. In reminding the people of each state of the breadth of that state's authority over its own internal affairs and the narrowness of the national government's authority over what occurs in a state, the Tenth Amendment reminds the people of the goodness and importance of federalism, and of federalism's importance to justice and liberty in the American system of civil government.

Whenever we are considering proposed changes to our Constitution we must therefore also consider the importance of federalism to justice and our liberty. The federal features of our amendment process were meant to enable the states to effect desirable changes in our fundamental law, but also to prevent undesirable changes—whether those changes are achieved via constitutional or unconstitutional means.

30

Arguments Against The Tenth Amendment Answered

1. The Tenth Amendment and federalism are outmoded today.

We have long been told that our Tenth Amendment is outmoded today because it is a relic of the past. America, we are told, is radically different today than it was when the Tenth Amendment was framed and ratified: It is much more populous, industrialized (or post-industrialized), ethnically and religiously diverse, etc., etc. Therefore the Tenth Amendment is unnecessary today. A variation of this argument is that ours is an age of globalism, while the Tenth Amendment would turn us back to localism.

Though America may be radically different, in some ways, today than it was when our Constitution, Bill of Rights, and Tenth Amendment were framed and ratified, it does not of necessity follow that we should not have the Tenth Amendment. Nor that the principles of the Tenth Amendment, or of federalism, are inappropriate for the governance of our nation of states today.

There is nothing in principle new under the sun, as Ecclesiastes reminds us. The nature of man has not changed, nor has the word and law of God which applies authoritatively to all aspects of the governance of man. Man is still fallen in sin, and the effects of God's imputation of Adam's sin to all of us are at least as evident as they ever were. Man still loves power and lusts after power, wanting to lord it over others. Man still wants the kingdoms of this world and all that is available through them, yielding more or less eagerly to the temptation which Christ resisted and rejected. There are still advantages of local government to justice and liberty, and still disadvantages of centralized government to the same. Hence it is still true, as the great Christian historian and political thinker Lord Acton said, that power tends to corrupt man, and absolute power corrupts him absolutely. It is still essential to do what is necessary to protect those who are ruled by civil government from evil done by the officials of civil government.

The limitations which God's word and law require on the scope and functioning of civil government are still the same today as they were when the Lord inspired the writers of the Bible. For God, who does not change, remains the same; and His word remains the same; and His law remains both the same and binding on all men, including the rulers of civil government. Civil government remains God's ministry. He remains in authority over it. Its rulers, therefore, remain required to function in terms of His standards of good and evil. As Romans 13:1-10 makes clear, they are required by God to protect and praise those who do what is good and to restrain, by punishing, those who do evil. Since it is God, and no mere man, ruler of civil government or not, who is sovereign, it is God's word and law, not man's, which defines good and evil. So it remains the duty of rulers to refrain from substituting their own definitions of good and evil for God's, to make their every action conform to God's moral definitions, and to protect those who do what God's law defines as good, and to punish those who do what God's law defines as evil. Thus it remains their duty to keep the authority and power of civil government, and the legislative, executive, and judicial actions which are done upon the basis of that authority, *limited*.

So from the fact that these United States of America have changed it does not follow that the basic moral and legal standards which we should follow have changed. It does not matter that our population is many times (about 100) that of the United States when the Constitution was framed, nor that we Americans are much more ethnically diverse than the generation which gave us our Constitution. The moral content of law is neither affected nor determined by the size, ethnicity, or diversity of population. Our population is still composed of human beings—and gives no sign of being composed of anything else. And national origin and ethnicity do not nullify God's word and law—and do not nullify our Constitution unless the American people decide to change our Constitution according to its own processes. It does not matter that we *were* an agricultural society and are now an industrial, or "post-industrial," society. The moral content of law is not a product of the economic structure or makeup of society (sorry, Marxists!); it is independent of such things because its origin is in the only place whence objective morality can have its origin—in God and His word and law.

Now, the notion that the Tenth Amendment should be abandoned (by "interpretation" or otherwise) because America has changed and the change has made federalism outmoded, is based on the notion that there are no knowable, universal ethical laws upon which laws should be based. It presupposes things that the Framers and Ratifiers of our Constitution and Bill of Rights rejected: that God has not communicated any universal ethical laws to man, that God's law is not the measure of ethics or law, that autonomous man's word is the standard of law. It presupposes that man has no universally true standards of law, or, as per historicism, that "truth" is an ever-changing thing. Or that, as per pragmatism, "truth" is a man-made thing.

Of course, if these things were so, then we would face insoluble problems trying to determine what our fundamental law should be. For if there are no universal truths or standards of ethics and law, then there can be no way to objectively tell what the law should be at any given time. If there are no universal truths, then there can be no objective way to tell what today's, or any other time's, "truth" is because there would be no universal standard by which to distinguish between truth and falsehood. So if there are no universal truths there can be no universal ethical truths, and thus there can be no objective way to tell what is "outmoded" and what is not. What is "outmoded" for one man is not outmoded for another. And if "truth" is man-made, then man can make what was once the "mode" for man the "mode" again (although such is certainly not the intent of advocates of an "evolving" Constitution).

And what are we doing when we place "modes" above our Constitution—or any constitution? We are abandoning critical thinking and discernment. We are refusing to ponder the principles of our Constitution and fundamental law. On a deeper level, we are abandoning the revealed word and law of God in favor of the word of sinful, finite men. We are setting the ever-changing opinions of men, intellectual and cultural fashions and fads, above our country's fundamental law and all God-given laws or principles of law. Yes, God-given laws or principles of law are more fundamental, and more authoritative, than our country's fundamental law, but our country's fundamental law, our Constitution, (though it certainly was neither divinely inspired nor perfect!) is founded on the fundamentals of God's law. When we place "modes" above our Constitution we are abandoning constitutional government for unquestioning faith in the word of one or more intellectuals, propagandists, and/or rulers of civil government who claim authority to dictate to the rest of us. That is surely the way to become serfs and slaves to civil government.

The principles of our Constitution—the original intentions of its Framers and Ratifiers—remain knowable, remain the same, and remain true. They have not been invalidated by time or the changes which time has wrought. By definition they also remain applicable to civil government.

And our Constitution is and was obviously intended to be **a written constitution**. Our Constitution's Framers and Ratifiers intended the Constitution to be the guide to our civil government and a statement of the limits on its authority and powers. What use (other than as a deceitful façade) is a written constitution if its words can continually be redefined? No good use. If its words can continually be redefined, then it has no inherent meaning. If it has no inherent meaning, then it is useless as a guide to government and worse than useless as a statement of the limits on government's authority and powers. If it has no inherent meaning, then the civil government it describes has no inherent limits on its authority and powers. Such a "constitution" cannot serve to form a more perfect Union, establish justice, ensure domestic tranquility, provide for the common defense, promote the general welfare, or secure the blessings of liberty to the present generation or to that generation's posterity. Such a "constitution" is not worth the paper it is written on, for it might as well have nothing written on it if the words written on it are meaningless.

Our Constitution was not intended to be a meaningless document. It was not designed so carefully on the premise that there is no ultimate meaning, that there are no fixed truths or moral laws, or that justice and freedom are achieved by removing all limits on the power of those who are in positions of governmental authority.

Freedom is still a crucial ethical principle to be achieved through our Constitution. It does not become "outmoded," nor do its blessings cease to be blessings because we have more people or because they are from different countries than were the Americans who gave us our Constitution and Bill of Rights. Freedom does not become less important because the peoples of the world are "closer" together now than they used to be when they had much less technology and much less convenient means of travel and communication. Freedom is as important now as it ever was. And with the theoretical foundation of modern totalitarianism having been established in nineteenth century thought (though it can easily be traced back to previous centuries' man-centered thought), and totalitarianism's horrific practice having come to fruition in the twentieth and twenty-first centuries, freedom is more important now than it ever has been.

And the means of protecting and preserving freedom remain at least as important as they ever were. Our Constitution and its Bill of Rights are the tangible means of preserving Americans' freedom designed by our early statesmen. Constitutional government, a written constitution, a carefully designed system and set of institutions of civil government, separation of powers, checks and balances, a bill of rights, and federalism: these were the governmental features designed by those statesmen and approved by other statesmen from their respective states to create the greatest probability of establishing justice and securing Americans' rights and liberty.[1] Americans' faith in God ("religion") and consequent obedience to His commandments (moral

---

1. The Framers knew quite well that they could not create a perfect governmental means of establishing justice and securing present and future Americans' rights and liberty. They knew that they were fallen, imperfect, human beings framing a constitution for fallen, imperfect human beings. They knew that the Constitution which they had laboriously produced was imperfect but was the best that Americans and their states would accept. Contrary to the analysis of some commentators on their intentions, they knew that the governmental system alone was insufficient. They knew that the religion and morality of Americans was fundamental and essential to the preservation of justice and liberty for present and future generations of Americans.

virtue) were the intangible means of protecting and preserving our liberty and that of future generations of Americans—as virtually all early American statesmen of our "founding era" believed and George Washington noted in his now long-neglected "Farewell Address."

Our Tenth Amendment was created to provide a double security to the rights of the American people, and, in the process, establishes justice by protecting federalism, the people's rights in each state to govern themselves through their representative state governments which have the constitutional right to govern affairs within their boundaries on the basis of their own superior knowledge of local conditions and their own political tradition. Liberty and justice are no less essential today than they were when the Tenth Amendment was framed and ratified. In fact, with the growth of theories and the practice of unlimited government, centralized government, social and economic salvation by systematic government intervention, and even totalitarianism, the need for federalism to preserve freedom is far greater than it was 220 years ago when the Tenth Amendment was framed.

From the fact that worldwide communication and transportation are far easier today than they ever have been it does not follow that localism is no longer good and useful. Goods and services are still produced locally though they can be marketed internationally and globally. Localism—and, in the United States, federalism—enable the people of a local town, city, or county, and on a larger scale, a state to enjoy the greater freedom, job-creation, productivity, capital accumulation, and wealth which are the results of local and state governments' imposing fewer regulations and taxes on the people of a particular locality or state. Localism and federalism also allow people to flee high-regulation, high-tax localities and states and move where they are free (or freer) to fulfill at least the economic part of their God-given duty to have dominion over the earth and its creatures.

And what is true of economics under localism and federalism is also true of non-economic facets of life: religious freedom, culture, the arts, education, invention, and many other things.

"Globalism" moves to subordinate the "sovereignty" of the United States to an international or one-world governing authority only make the problems of justice and liberty worse—and the need for honoring

the Tenth Amendment more intense. The religions and cultures of the
many peoples of the world are fundamentally different, not similar,
and most of the world's people worship false gods (including man).
The most common political result of these false religions and their
false ethical systems—in the West as well as elsewhere, throughout
history—is tyranny, not liberty. To subordinate our civil government
to an international or one-world government is to discard federalism's
partial sovereignty of our states over themselves along with our nation's sovereignty over itself. To subordinate our nation's civil government to an international or one-world government is also to exchange
our liberty for tyranny.

Consequently, the need for obedience to the Tenth Amendment is doubly important. It is needed to protect liberty and justice
against abuses of power by our own central government, and it is
needed to protect against our own central government yielding its
sovereignty—and our liberty—to a larger central government entity,
international or worldwide.

The Constitution—its original wording—remains the same as it
was in 1791: the Tenth Amendment has not been amended away. It is
still there in the Constitution; still comprehensible; still authoritative
today. The fact that our legislators, presidents, judges, and bureaucrats
do not obey the Tenth Amendment does not mean that it is no longer
binding on them. It only means that they lack the knowledge—or integrity—to obey their oaths of office. Or that they hold to an ideology
which claims that it is legitimate for them to deceive those who elect
them in order to acquire and retain the political power necessary to
use civil government's "power of the sword" to accomplish whatever
their ideology requires. It means that we the people who directly or
indirectly elect or appoint them lack the knowledge, character, and
commitment to liberty and justice to make them obey their oaths to
support the Constitution.

The fact that federal judges have interpreted the amendment's authority away does not mean that their interpretations are true or authoritative.
A federal court or Supreme Court proclamation that something is constitutional or unconstitutional does not make it so. The federal courts at all
levels, like presidents and federal legislators, are bound by their oaths to

support the Constitution—not to subvert it. The fact that they do subvert it in the name of interpreting it does not exactly strengthen their case. Moreover, mindless "conservative" judicial theorists to the contrary not withstanding, subsequent courts' obedience to earlier courts' unconstitutional decisions is not the rule of law but the continuation of the rule of men, violation of the judges' oath to support the Constitution, complicity in judicial usurpation, judicial deceit, and collaboration in a conspiracy to commit evil. There is no constitutional reason why our current president, congressmen, senators, or any other civil government officials should honor or obey unconstitutional Supreme Court or federal court decisions. The Constitution does not obligate anyone to obey unconstitutional laws, orders, or decisions. It does obligate all our officials to obey the Constitution's fundamental principle of federalism.

The Tenth Amendment exists to help them—and us—remember our duty, and to help us retain the means to oppose those who would, through ignorance or malevolence, destroy federalism and thus our liberty.

2. Interpreting the Tenth Amendment as the Framers and Ratifiers intended is incompatible with the evolution of federalism.

How many times have we been told that we should abandon federalism because our governmental system has "evolved" away from the framers' intent? The argument usually goes something like this: Due to the intellectual, cultural, historical, economic, and political forces in our political history, the meaning of "federalism" has evolved. This has affected the functioning of our governmental system as, over the decades, the central government has found it necessary to extend its power, laws, and programs into the internal affairs of the states. This process, though often accompanied by political and legal battles, has been sanctioned by widespread public approval of the growth of the central government as the public has repeatedly voted to accept, or demand, the services provided by the central government. Therefore the Tenth Amendment, or at least the original meaning of it, should be abandoned.

We should answer that this is but a variation of the argument that our Constitution must be a "living" document, with its meaning dictated by changing times and evolving circumstances; the upshot of this, remember, is that the Constitution's meaning is dictated by our civil government officials' responses to changed circumstances based on their political philosophy and political self-interest.

The "living Constitution" argument is really, at bottom, a rejection of constitutionalism. For it replaces a constitution, in this case our Constitution, with the judgments of civil government officials: legislators, presidents, judges. In so doing it replaces the well-considered judgments of the great statesmen who framed and ratified the original Constitution and Bill of Rights (and subsequent amendments) with the judgments of current government officials—who stand to profit, at least in terms of power, from the change(s) which they seek to make in the Constitution.

The "evolution of federalism" suffers from the same intellectual, moral, and political malady as its philosophical cousins, for the established fact that federalism has "evolved" far from the Framers' and Ratifiers' intentions about the function and importance of the state governments does not necessitate that this development has been an "evolution" of progress rather than a *devolution*. The "evolution of federalism" has been accomplished by usurpation of authority and power from the state governments, not via constitutional means (excepting the Seventeenth Amendment, which took election of each state's U.S. senators out of the hands of the state's legislature). Under the influence of central government socialistic legislation, it has also been accomplished by appeals to greed, envy, and legalized theft and, in the hands of the Federal courts, by manifest dishonesty in interpreting our Constitution. The means have not been admirable.

Moreover, the results of "evolution" by usurpation have been the growth of civil government power, the concentration of power in the central government, the diminution of the states' governments, the diminution of justice, and the decline of liberty. The ends, therefore, have not been admirable either. The rejection of constitutionalism and the abandonment of the well-considered decisions of our Constitution's Framers and Ratifiers is intellectually, morally, and practically repulsive. Here, as in so many other areas, what has been proclaimed as "progressive" "evolution" has, in reality, been regressive devolution.

By discarding the well-considered judgments of the statesmen who framed and ratified our Constitution, the "living Constitution" philosophy necessarily also disregards the well-considered judgments of the people of the states—whose elected representatives framed and ratified the Constitution and its amendments. It thus replaces a prolonged, very high-level process of *public* deliberation by public officials and the people whom they represented with a comparatively *private* process of deliberation by public officials: congressmen, senators, presidents, judges (and their advisors). It cuts out the public debate and deliberation of the Congress's proposal of amendments, of the legislatures of two thirds of the states calling for a convention to propose amendments to the Constitution, of the publicly-elected representatives of those conventions, and concludes by cutting out the public deliberations of the states' legislatures, or of three-fourths of them, which are necessary under our Constitution to ratify amendments.

By cutting out all these kinds of public debate and deliberation, the "living Constitution" philosophy does more than violate the Constitution. It radically simplifies the process by which our Constitution is changed, and in the process it excludes voices, viewpoints, and arguments which the Framers and Ratifiers intended to include. It replaces the Constitution's super-majorities of each house of Congress and of the states' legislatures or ratification conventions with the opinion of a federal judge or panel of federal judges, or the opinion of a majority of the U.S. Supreme Court, or the President, or simple majorities of both houses of Congress (agreeing, tacitly, to enact an unconstitutional law). The deliberations of a federal judge or panel of judges, or of a U.S. Supreme Court majority, or of a President composing an executive order, or of the leaders of the majority in Congress are much inferior to those of two-thirds of each house of Congress plus those of three-quarters of the states' legislatures or ratification conventions. By such exclusions of the people's elected representatives (regardless of the actual outcomes of this conveniently simplified process), it undermines the liberty of the people of the several states and thereby also the liberty of the people of the nation by stealing from them the ability to contribute to these momentous constitutional decisions.

A similar argument "justifies" such patently unconstitutional abominations as Reconstruction or "Black Reconstruction," etc. as procedures which should have been carried out because they "fixed" a great problem or set of problems.[2] Whatever we think of Reconstruction or "Black Reconstruction," and whatever good things they accomplished (let it be noted that they also accomplished a lot of bad things), they were certainly gross violations of the Constitution. The argument that such things should be considered constitutional because they were intended to do good things or in fact did good things is simply another instance of the argument that the end justifies the means. Good intentions do not justify evil actions. As the saying goes, the road to Hell is paved with good intentions.

Certainly the gross violations of the Constitution by Lincoln and then the Radical Republicans paved the way to the destruction in principle and near-destruction in practice of federalism, resulting in the centralization of power in our national government, presidential dictatorship, congressional tyranny, the abandonment of the Constitution's restrictions on central government power, and the rhetorical justification of further violations of the Constitution in the name of high-sounding purposes. By such an argument virtually any action by our central government—no matter how much it violates the Constitution, what it does to justice, or what it does to liberty—can be "justified" or made "constitutional" because of the alleged high purpose (or even a genuinely high purpose) for which it is said to be undertaken or was actually undertaken. Such an argument in effect junks the Constitution and constitutional government in favor of coercive action to achieve any high-sounding purpose claimed by those in possession of power in the national government. The argument that "the end justifies the means" is a notion which spells the end of constitutional government and the rule of law, and ushers in the arbitrary rule of men and thus tyranny.

Our Constitution was intended—and should have been intended— to give us the rule of law, not the arbitrary, changeable rule of men. The rule of law is the rule of fixed, known principles of law, not of ever-changing rules being continually reinterpreted or redefined by civil

---

2. See Page Smith, *Trial by Fire: A People's History of the Civil War and Reconstruction*, vol. 5 (New York: McGraw-Hill Book Co., 1982), 990.

government officials. The rule of law is not merely a process. The rule of law is a process with content. It is a process by which the officials of civil government function under the authority of the fundamental law and within the limits of the content of that law. The rule of law is not the unlimited, arbitrary rule of the officials of civil government with those officials being free to do whatever they think is best. The rule of law is compatible with changing the Constitution by the Constitution's own processes for changing it: amendment or constitutional convention. The rule of law is **not** compatible with changing the Constitution by "evolution" or the self-servingly convenient "interpretation" of those in possession of temporary political power.

Those who want to justify changing the Constitution by "interpretation" want to junk the Constitution's process of amendment and replace that process with an act (or at most "process") of "interpretation." They want to replace the document's own somewhat complex, difficult process with a simple, easy process which will make it easy to gut the content of our Constitution and replace it with alien ideas. They want to replace our Constitution's honest process with a dishonest process. Moreover, they want to clothe their pseudo-process with the authority of constitutionality, to cloak low illegitimacy with high legitimacy, to hide their assault on our Constitution behind a veneer of legal respectability.

Our Constitution's amendment or constitutional convention process was wisely designed to admit only carefully considered changes to our fundamental law. It was designed to require the consent of unusually large majorities to fundamental changes, but it was concerned with more than mere numbers. It was concerned with requiring more time to make momentous decisions, but it was concerned with more than time. It was crafted to require unusually large numbers and greater amounts of time in order to achieve a greater quality of deliberation to arrive at wiser, more just decisions. It was crafted by the framers to prevent hastily-considered, ill-conceived changes to our Constitution; to involve multiple key institutions in the consideration of proposed fundamental changes; to create the greatest probability of making sure that changes to our Constitution are products of "the deliberate sense" of the people of our nation of states in order to defend justice and liberty.

As Article V makes evident, "the deliberate sense" of the people of America is inseparable from the deliberate sense of the peoples of the several states, and thus from federalism, for federalism is inseparable from the Constitution's methods of changing the Constitution. Amendments may be proposed by two-thirds of both houses of Congress, each of which is filled with elected representatives of each state (they may serve in our national Congress, yet they are not elected by the vote of the national majority, but of the voters or legislators of their own states), or, in the constitutional convention process, by "the application of the legislatures of two-thirds of the several states," followed by a constitutional convention for proposing amendments. In either case, ratification of proposed amendments must be "by the legislatures of three-fourths of the several states" or by conventions in three quarters of the states (depending on the mode of ratification proposed by Congress).

Article V's amendment process was designed to include the sense of the people of each state (or at least of three-quarters of the states). This was not so demanding a process as that of the Articles of Confederation, which required the unanimous consent of the states in order to amend the Articles. Yet Article V's process was clearly meant to utilize the federal principle to protect, preserve, and defend the liberty and justice for which the Constitution was designed, framed and ratified, which included liberty and justice for the people of each state. In fact, in this way, too, federalism, as Madison, "the Father of the Constitution," proclaimed in Federalist No. 51, provides a double security to the rights of the people.

The framers of our Constitution certainly did not expect all, or anywhere near all, of the conditions in the world or in these United States to remain forever the same. They were well aware that history would produce changed circumstances, and that some of those changed circumstances would necessitate changes in our Constitution. Indeed, they had not tried to produce the perfect constitution but only the best constitution that the people would accept. Still, they did not include in our Constitution any provision for changing the meaning of our fundamental law by "evolution" or anything of the kind. It was not only because they did not believe in evolutionism that they did not do so. They did not do so because they knew that changing the meaning of a document by "evolution" is changing it by interpretation, and "interpretation" can be done deceitfully, unwisely, and/or unjustly—and is usually done with disastrous consequences to justice and liberty.

The argument from "necessity" is debatable and deceitful, as has already been discussed. Our Constitution has no provision or implication permitting "necessity" to trump the Constitution. It says nothing to justify suspending the Constitution in an "emergency" situation. It does not create any special office (such as temporary dictator) or institution to rule in unforeseen or "emergency" circumstances. It simply provides means for changing the Constitution. But that change is supposed to occur constitutionally, by means of the Constitution's own prescribed process, not by allowing civil government officials to "redefine" the document's meaning and, in the process, their own powers' limits. Those who want to have such an office or institution to cope with unforeseen circumstances and "emergencies" should create one; define its functions, powers, and limits carefully; define "emergency" or the special circumstances in which such an office or institution temporarily replaces the Constitution, and submit the proposal to the Article V process.

But "living Constitution" advocates do not want to create such an official office or subject such a proposal to the criticisms of others in the Article V process. They want to permit—or urge—our elected officials to in effect discard Article V, in order to make up the rules as they go along. They do not want proposed changes to be submitted to formal, clearly-defined convocations of the people's elected representatives for debate, consideration, and decision. They particularly do not want such changes to be submitted to the representatives of the people of the states for debate, consideration, and decision. They also want to justify past usurpations of power and violations of our Constitution after the fact—and to praise their heroes who have committed such acts—thereby paving the way for future usurpations and violations.

That is why the Framers designed the amendment or constitutional convention process in the Constitution (Article V) to require both an unusually large amount of time and unusually large majorities of opinion at both the national and state levels of government.

This design increased the probability that the deliberate sense of the American community or nation—including the deliberate sense of the people of the states which compose the nation—reflected in those un-usual majorities, would be the basis of any change. The changes would require serious public debate and deliberation, not popular passion, "crisis"-inspired action, or factional animosity—and emphatically not the will of those in power in the central government. Agreement by a "super-majority" of three quarters of the states was an essential part of their definition of such serious public debate—and it should be of ours.

The Ratifiers of our Constitution would have rightly said that the notion of an "evolving" constitution is a delusion or, more likely, a deceit. As has been said, those who believe that the possessors of civil government power should be permitted to continually redefine their authority and powers are deluded about the nature of man and the al-lure of governmental power to fallen man. Those who seek power over others deceive men with their notions of "living" constitutions so they can, at best, acquire the power to launch some legislative plan which is forbidden by the Constitution, or, at worst so they can acquire unlim-ited, arbitrary power in order to do evil things with it.

3. The Tenth Amendment would prevent the national government from establishing justice throughout the nation and make it impossible for its programs to be effective.

Although "to establish justice," as stated in our Constitution's Pre-amble, is one of the most fundamental principles of our constitutional system of civil government, the concept of justice in our Constitution is more complex than is implied by the belief that federalism impedes the national government's establishment of justice. The argument presumes that the national or central government is the only vehicle in our governmental system for establishing justice. It presupposes that the states' governments are inherently defective in, or even opposed to the establishment of justice. While it is true that the majority of our Constitution's framers thought that their carefully designed central government would be more likely to promote justice than the state governments, it is also true that the framers knew that the central government would not be an infallible fount of justice, that the state governments were essential to justice, and that the state governments and federalism would give us a double protection of both the rights of the people and justice. Moreover, it is certainly true that the majority of the Framers—not to mention the Ratifiers!—of our Constitution considered that the self-government of the states (free from all but stated, limited central government authority) was *essential* to justice. The notion that federalism is inherently inimical to justice is refuted by the fact that the Framers and Ratifiers of our Constitution deliberately gave us a federal form of civil government.

The Tenth Amendment, of course, protects federalism, one of the most fundamental principles of our Constitution, and one without which our Constitution would never have been ratified. The Framers and Ratifiers of our Constitution certainly intended to preserve federalism. This was partly of necessity, for the states would never have approved a constitution which abolished the state governments and gave us a centralized government. But it was also largely for the sake of principle, for the Framers and Ratifiers saw federalism as a positive good. The existence of our Tenth Amendment proves that the Framers and Ratifiers valued federalism as beneficial to the establishment of justice.

Federalism was meant to leave the states in control (with exceptions stated in the Constitution and other exceptions stated by the states in their particular bills or declarations of rights) of their own internal affairs. Now, it is certainly true that a state government can enact and enforce unjust laws within its borders. We have plenty of examples of that from our history. We have plenty of examples of that today with federalism seriously weakened by many decades of central government usurpation and widespread public "education" about the Constitution through an educational system dominated by secular humanism, intellectual and moral relativism, and socialism. Within the legitimate bounds of its constitutional authority, the central government in our federal system can and should check against unjust, unconstitutional state laws.

But the legitimate bounds of the central government's authority are, and were intended to be, limited. The central government may not constitutionally intervene in a state's internal affairs in any area over which the Constitution does not give it authority. Each state government retains authority over all areas of life within its borders over which it has not delegated authority to the central government in the Constitution, forbidden to itself in the Constitution, or forbidden to itself (or which the people of the state have not forbidden to their state's civil government) in its state constitution or bill of rights. Now, it is more than possible that the officials of a state's government may enact and enforce one or more unjust laws. But an unjust law is not necessarily an unconstitutional law, and our Constitution does not authorize the central government to intervene in a state government's reserved area of authority (reserved powers) to right every wrong which a state may commit. The Constitution does not authorize such intervention because the Framers, Ratifiers, and people did not want a centralized system of government, but instead wanted each state to be free to govern itself, within limits. Such a system, as has been noted above, enhances justice by permitting state and local governments, whose officials know state and local circumstances far better than central government officials can or do, to deal with their state's own internal issues.

We should not want unjust laws in our states either, so our federal system is designed to create negative consequences for state governments which produce and enforce unjust laws. Unjust laws create hostile reactions from those who suffer under them, and from those who love justice and hate injustice. Among other possibilities, people flee from states which have unjust laws, and would-be immigrants are encouraged to settle elsewhere. Those states then lose population, and with population intellectual and moral capital, labor, and economic capital. Those states will then lose present productivity, wealth, capital accumulation, future increased productivity, and future increased wealth. They will also lose their good names, which Scripture tells us are more valuable than economic wealth. And, of course, the states to which the oppressed flee and immigrants flock will, by their more just laws, reap the blessings of their justice. Unjust laws in a federal system have adverse consequences for the people of the states which produce them, but at least these laws are kept within the boundaries of the state *by federalism*.

Moreover, from the fact that a state government may enact and enforce unjust laws it does not follow that a central or national government, even **our** national government, will never enact and enforce unjust laws. Nor does it follow that our central government will be more likely even to enact and enforce *a greater percentage* of just laws than will the states' governments. It does not even follow, in fact, that our central government will become anything other than a mighty engine of unjust laws, effectively imposing injustice unilaterally on all the states. A key reason why we have federalism, the Constitution's long-neglected second system of separation of powers and checks and balances, is so that state governments can check central government usurpation of power, centrally-imposed injustice, and central-government-imposed confusion.

Neither the Framers nor the Ratifiers of our Constitution supposed that the officials of our central government would be exempt from human nature, that is, from the sinful nature of man. Nor were they foolish enough to suppose that even their carefully designed central government would attract to federal government office, or get in national office, men exempt from original sin. Yes, they designed our national government to create a greater probability that its offices would attract, and tend to get, more intellectually and morally excellent men than did the states' governments. And they meant this to produce wiser, more stable, more farsighted, more just, laws. But they knew and said that this was but a greater probability, not a certainty.[3] They knew and said that the design of our governmental system was not enough in itself. They knew and said, on good biblical grounds, that the preservation of liberty depends also on "religion" (Christianity) and morality: that a people must remain morally virtuous if it is to remain free.[4]

---

3 See Paul Eidelberg, *The Philosophy of the American Constitution: A Reinterpretation of the Intentions of the Founding Fathers* (New York: The Free Press, 1968), and Paul Eidelberg, *A Discourse on Statesmanship.*

4 See, for example, Leviticus 26; Deuteronomy 28; and Judges. On the relationship between "religion" (Christianity), moral virtue, and liberty in early American political thought, see Ellis Sandoz, *A Government of Laws: Political Theory, Religion, and the American Founding* (Baton Rouge and London: Louisiana State University Press, 1989) and John Eidsmoe, *Christianity and the Constitution: The Faith of Our Founding Fathers* (Grand Rapids: Mott Media, 1987). Wilmoore Kendall and George Carey, *Basic Symbols of the American Political Tradition* (Baton Rouge: Louisiana State University Press,

The Tenth Amendment was rightly understood by its Framers and Ratifiers to assist in establishing justice precisely by protecting federalism, for federalism gives the people of each state the possibility of protecting themselves against unconstitutional and unjust laws, programs, and the like coming down on the people of the states from the central or national government.

Concerning efficiency and effectiveness, the intention of the Framers and Ratifiers of our Constitution was *not* to make the new central government effective in everything its officials might take it into their heads to do. They did not intend the central government to be effective in enacting and enforcing unwise, unjust, liberty-threatening, unconstitutional laws, plans, or programs—nor should they have been!

Efficiency was not the primary objective of the Framers and Ratifiers. Far from it! They did not want to create an effective mechanism for tyrants, nor one that could be converted into an efficient engine (or any kind of engine!) of tyranny—of one man, of a minority, or of the majority. The Framers and Ratifiers intended only to make the central government efficient in doing what it is constitutionally authorized to do—and even then they deliberately compromised its efficiency (as, for example, in legislation) by including protections for the authority of the states over their own internal affairs. They designed the Constitution's famous system of separation of powers with accompanying checks and balances into the structure of our central government, and carefully designed the various legislative, executive, and judicial institutions of our central government, precisely to produce the greatest probability that our central government would not be efficient in enacting unwise, unjust, or unconstitutional laws. They deliberately created the Constitution's complex governmental system to diminish the efficiency of any central government that was trying to produce or enforce laws tending to instability, injustice, or confusion. **Justice and liberty, not justice and efficiency, were their ruling purposes**. Liberty was far more important to them than efficiency—especially the oppressive efficiency imagined by utopian theorists and desired by calculating tyrants.

1970) found the theme of a virtuous people to be the central symbol of the American political tradition.

And as Federalist No. 10, the key to understanding the framers' purposes in designing the Constitution's governmental system, makes clear, justice and liberty were inseparable correlatives for the Framers and they wrote this correlation into the Constitution. They gave us a written constitution, very carefully designed, with a mixed form of government—a partly democratic, partly-aristocratic bicameral legislature, aristocratic federal courts, and a partly monarchial, partly-aristocratic, partly-democratic president[5]—as its central government precisely to increase the probability that our central government would **not** be efficient in producing unjust, liberty-destroying laws. They gave us what the people of the several states and their state governments demanded, a federal system, to double the security of the people's rights, to provide a double security to liberty.

Then, under the pressure of the states' legislatures and/or specially elected ratification conventions (which is to say, of the people of their states), our early statesmen in the central government and the states gave us a Bill of Rights emphatically to ensure that the central government would not be efficient in producing unjust, liberty-destroying, rights-violating laws. So concerned were they to protect justice, liberty, and the blessings thereof for present and future generations of Americans that they made sure that the ninth of these amendments was a blanket-statement protecting all the rights of Americans which had not been stated in the preceding amendments. And they were also decidedly concerned with protecting the principles of liberty and justice as they had understood them, e.g., that liberty includes the freedom of each state to govern itself, that justice includes laws enacted and enforced by those who are familiar with local conditions, and that the protection of liberty and justice requires a systemic horizontal and vertical separation of powers with checks and balances. Thus, they gave us the Tenth Amendment to embody these principles and provide

---

5. The best works on the design of our system of civil government, though they are weak on federalism, are Paul Eidelberg, *The Philosophy of the American Constitution* and *A Discourse on Statesmanship: The Design and Transformation of the American Polity*. On federalism, see Raoul Berger, *Federalism: The Founders' Design* and Felix Morley, *Freedom and Federalism* ([1959] 1981).

further constitutional protection of federalism and the reserved powers of the states.

The Framers and Ratifiers of our Constitution and our Bill of Rights rightly avoided giving us a centralized governmental system, a system with an excessively-powerful central government, or a system which would tend to permit designing politicians to concentrate power in the central government. They—and the states and people they represented—did not want us to have a government that would be efficient in imposing its will on every area of Americans' lives, so they limited the authority and powers of our central government and created a federal system in which the states would be able to resist unconstitutional, unwise, and/or unjust laws which our central government might seek to impose on the people of the states. They did not want us to have a central government that would be able or permitted to impose one-size-fits-all legislation on the diverse peoples, governmental traditions, and conditions of the states which compose these United States. They wisely gave us a federal governmental system to be efficient in protecting the right of each state to govern itself, for they were convinced that that right is essential to the protection of individual liberty as well as of justice.

4. The interpretation of the Tenth Amendment you are espousing would reverse the last 50-75 years of Federal jurisprudence.

Is truth determined by the date on which its words were uttered or published? Does the fact that something is old make it true, or more likely to be true than something new? There were a lot of false words spoken and written in ancient times. Does the fact that something is new make it true? Or make it more likely to be true than something old? There is and has been a lot of nonsense spoken and written in modern times, and since we of the modern era have vastly more means of publication, it is a safe bet that we have a vastly greater amount of published nonsense, and probably a vastly greater percentage of it, than can be counted against the ancients. Truth is not determined by when something was said or published. It is determined by its content, which is to say, by its correspondence to reality.

The federal jurisprudence of the past 50-75 years is not, and should not be, the standard by which we determine what is constitutional and what is not. That is, not if we are following the words of our Constitution. Nowhere does our Constitution say that federal judges or court decisions are the final standard for interpreting the Constitution or any of its amendments.[6] So whether the federal jurisprudence of the last 50 years, or any other span of time, is right or wrong is beside the point. Since federal jurisprudence is not the standard by which constitutionality should be determined, it does not matter, constitutionally, whether the concept of the Tenth Amendment set forth in these pages agrees with federal jurisprudence—from the last 50–75 years or from any other span of time since the Constitution was framed and ratified. Rather, *the Constitution* is the standard by which federal jurisprudence, from any span of time, should be measured.

Nor does the fact that Constitutional Law is and has long been taught via the "case law" method, and not by a study of the original intentions behind the document as a whole and its clauses, phrases, and words, justify the notion that recent judicial decisions should trump the intentions of the men who gave us our Constitution and its various amendments. The "case law" method was introduced in the 1870s by Christopher Langdell, dean of the Harvard Law School, as the means of shifting the philosophy of law from one based on the view that the ethical principles of law are unchanging to one based on the Darwinian evolutionist view that the principles of law are products of an evolutionary process.[7] The "case law" method was designed to shift both

---

6. This is self-evident from merely reading the Constitution attentively. However, since much "scholarship" of the past century has been devoted to making the U.S. Supreme Court the final arbiter of the meaning of the Constitution, it is worth reading works on this issue which are based on the Constitution and the manifest intentions of our early statesmen. See Edward S. Corwin, *Court Over Constitution* (New York: Smith, 1950), Hon. Robert K. Dornan, M.C. and Csaba Vedlik, Jr., *Judicial Supremacy: The Supreme Court on Trial* (Plymouth, Massachusetts: Plymouth Rock Foundation, [1980] 1986), and Thomas J. Higgins, S.J., *Judicial Review Unmasked* (West Hanover, Massachusetts: The Christopher Publishing House, 1981).

7. John W. Whitehead, *The Second American Revolution* (Elgin, Illinois:

the philosophy of law and the philosophy of American constitutional law away from the philosophy of law which had traditionally been taught to Americans and away from the Constitution's philosophy of government and law. It was meant to free judges and other civil government officials to recast themselves into perpetual constitutional conventions by removing them from under the law or Constitution and placing them over the law—setting them up as continual revisers of the law and the Constitution. The "case law" method subtly and deceptively teaches a philosophy of law which holds that there are no universal intellectual and moral laws or principles of law—without necessarily explicitly analyzing that philosophy and its logical and practical consequences.

The fact that a judge—even a federal judge or a U.S. Supreme Court "justice"—says that something is so does not make it so, even if he or she says it from the bench! When judges (or "justices") decide constitutional issues on the basis of a judicial philosophy which is opposed to submission to our Constitution and the intentions of those who framed and ratified it, they are violating their oaths of office and attempting to deceive the people whom they represent. When they make decisions on this basis their decisions are neither explications of the meaning of our Constitution in particular instances nor constitutional in any sense. Rather, they are violations of our Constitution. The "case law" method is thus a chronicle of the deliberately deceitful decisions of the majority of the denizens of our U.S. Supreme Court. It is a record of judicial perfidy and violations of the judges' oaths of office—whether they are creating "emanations" from "penumbras" of the Constitution or lesser perversions of our fundamental law. On a deeper level, it is a guilt-soaked record of the judges' that the God, whom our Constitution does acknowledge to be over our nation and its civil governments in Article VII, will judge: a record of their bearing false witness against their neighbors, the American people, by lying to them about their fundamental law; of their making themselves accessories before the fact to "legalized" theft; and in the case of such pro-abortion decisions as the abominable Roe v. Wade case, accessories before the

David C. Cook Publishing Co., 1982), pages 46-47.

fact to "legalized" murder. (Legislators' and presidents' acquiescence or submission to such decisions does not make such violations of our Constitution legitimate; rather, it makes legislators and presidents accessories after the fact to the Court's violations of their oaths of office and our Constitution.)

In the context of our Constitution, the method justifies—even urges—judges and other civil government officials to violate their oaths to uphold our Constitution by changing the meaning and intentions of our Constitution, and so redefining and increasing their own office's powers, without submitting to the Constitution's own amendment process. And the method craftily seduces students of our laws to accept the ultimate authority and legitimacy of these judges and other civil government officials, these self-proclaimed constitutional-conventions-of-one, who are both violating their oaths of office and disregarding the original intentions of the Constitution and its amendments by amending the meaning of the Constitution without bothering to change its content through the Constitutionally prescribed, and alone legitimate, amendment process found in Article V.

The Constitution does not explicitly place ultimate authority for determining its meaning in any institution or official created or recognized by the Constitution. It neither stipulates nor implies that governmental or popular acceptance of unconstitutional usage constitutes the equivalent of constitutional amendment. Every representative and official in the United States government—including the President, congressmen, senators, and all federal judges—and **every** official in the state and local governments—must swear an oath (or make an affirmation) to support the Constitution. **Each of them**, having sworn to support the Constitution, is responsible to interpret the Constitution's meaning in order to discern between constitutional and unconstitutional ideas, laws, and practices. If every official were not required to interpret the meaning of the Constitution, our system of separation of powers and checks and balances would make no sense, for it would then become precisely what James Madison inveighed against in Federalist No. 51: a mere *paper barrier* against the gradual concentration of powers in any one branch of the government.

The Tenth Amendment, of course, emphatically concerns the Constitution's somewhat complex system of division of powers, with its accompanying checks and balances between and among the institutions of the central government and the central government and the states' governments. That amendment reminds us of and protects federalism. It is a reminder to every American official—in the central government no less than in the state governments—of the centrality of federalism to our system of civil government, a reminder of the intentions of the Constitution's framers and ratifiers. It is thus a reminder that our Constitution is a system of limited, divided, powers with means for the possessors of those powers to defend their powers against usurpation by other institutions in our central government and by that central government itself. It is therefore also a reminder to all of their duty to honor our Constitution's federal system of civil government. In being so it provides protection for our once-cherished federalism and the justice and freedom it was meant to protect.

As a matter of fact, the mainstream of federal jurisprudence of the last 50-75 years or so, going back to the Roosevelt Administration, is quite contrary to the manifest intentions of the Framers and Ratifiers of our Constitution, and our Bill of Rights including the Tenth Amendment. For although F.D.R.'s infamous Court-Packing Scheme of 1936 failed, beginning with the Roosevelt Administration it has been the goal and practice of "liberals" to appoint to the Federal Courts and especially to the U.S. Supreme Court judges who will labor to amend the Constitution by interpretation, following a strategy of gradualism to mask their intentions. Liberal Democrats have, of course, excelled at this, but "Me Too" Republicans have helped the process, as have thoughtless Republicans who either want to be "bipartisan" or give a Democrat president whatever appointees he wants in the vain hope that Republicans will receive the same treatment when they hold the White House. All these have shamelessly violated their oaths to support the Constitution, or, in the case of the President, to "preserve, protect, and defend the Constitution of the United States" (Article II, Section 1, Paragraph 8).

In the service of such desires, "liberals" of both major parties and "liberals" on the bench have violated or subverted virtually every principle intended by the Framers and Ratifiers of the Constitution and the Bill of Rights. Among those principles—and certainly not the least among them—is the absolutely fundamental principle of federalism, which inseparably includes the right of each state to govern its own internal affairs and the corresponding duty of the central government to avoid intervening in those internal affairs where the Constitution does not give it a clear right or duty to intervene. As noted in a previous chapter, they have perverted the Interstate Commerce Clause (Article I, Section 8, Paragraph 3) to allow the central government to regulate all commerce within a state. They have twisted the General Welfare Clause (Article I, Section 8, Paragraph 1), and the Necessary and Proper Clause (Article I, Section 8, Paragraph 19) to justify central government programs which usurp the states' internal authority. They have violated the state governments' authority in a myriad of ways, approving "federal" agencies or bureaucracies, programs, and laws which plainly go against the Framers' and Ratifiers' intention to preserve federalism by permitting or requiring federal government intrusion into the states' sphere of authority. In so doing they go against the mainstream of previous federal jurisprudence, which had protected federalism[8] over the course of our legal history.

So the fact that our reading of the Tenth Amendment goes against the jurisprudence of the last 50-75 years is insufficient reason to abandon the truth. The truth is that the federal judiciary's jurisprudence of the last 50-75 years goes against both the intentions of the statesmen who gave us our Constitution and the mainstream of previous American federal jurisprudence.[9] The truth is that, wherever there may be

---

8. In order to simplify the legal history here and to keep our focus on the federal courts, particularly the U.S. Supreme Court, and federal jurisprudence, we will omit the roles of Congress and the President in centralizing power in Washington, D.C., and will therefore not go back to the Missouri Compromise (1820) or the tragic years of the War Between the States and Reconstruction. Until well into the twentieth century the federal courts protected federalism, the right of each state to govern its own internal affairs.

9. Two good old works which present an accurate picture of the main thrust of federal jurisprudence of the last fifty to seventy-five years are Rosalie M. Gordon, *Nine Men Against America: The Supreme Court and Its Attack on American Liberties* (New York: Devin-Adair, 1958), and L. Brent Bozell, *The Warren Revolution: Reflections on the Consensus Society* (New Rochelle, New

disagreement, the Constitution trumps, and must trump, federal juris-prudence from the last 50-75 years as well as from all of our previous legal history. The result of our federal courts' and U.S. Supreme Court's abandonment of the Constitution has been judicial tyranny.[10] The plain truth is that the federal courts, including the U.S. Supreme Court, have no authority to "interpret" our Tenth Amendment and federalism out of existence, and their efforts to do so have been disasters for justice and liberty as well as for personal and judicial integrity.

York: Arlington House, 1966).

10. The consequences of the federal judiciary's and U.S. Supreme Court's deliberate, dishonest perversion of our Constitution have been well-sum-marized in Carrol D. Kilgore, *Judicial Tyranny: An Inquiry into the Integrity of the Federal Judiciary published at the beginning of the Third Century of American Independence* (Nashville and New York: Thomas Nelson Inc., 1977). When we speak of the federal judiciary and the U.S. Supreme Court, we do not, of course, mean all federal judges or all Supreme Court justices, but rather those who have self-consciously substituted their intentions for the intentions of the men who gave us our Constitution and its amendments. Though Kilgore's book is more than thirty years old, his description is apt— and all too frighteningly apparent in our day.

31

Virtue, Liberty, and The Tenth Amendment

arly American political thought was overwhelmingly Christian. This point can be established easily if one is willing to search the primary source documents: early American political writings, including the thousands of public political sermons preached in The Middle States and the South as well as in New England.[1] Early American thought was not rationalistic,[2] nor

---

1. The best scholarly work on this is Sandoz, *A Government of Laws*, especially pages 83-217, which provides a fine description of the relationship of Christianity to early American political thought. Donald S. Lutz and Charles S. Hyneman, "The Relative Influence of European Political Writers on Late Eighteenth-Century American Political Thought," *American Political Science Review* 189 (1984), 189-197, established this by an analysis of the sources cited as authoritative by early American political writers. John Eidsmoe, *Christianity and the Constitution: The Faith of Our Founding Fathers* (Grand Rapids: Baker Book House, 1987), especially pages 51-53, shows the connection of this to our Constitution. A great old work, B. F. Morris, *The Christian Life and Character of the Civil Institutions of the United States* (Powder Springs, Georgia: The American Vision, 2007), proves beyond any doubt that Christianity was the fundamental and dominant influence on our government in and under our Constitution. Early American law, legal thought, and legal education also affirmed the dominant Christianity of the American people, the American states, and the American nation; early American laws were fundamentally Christian and based on Christian ethics and our Christian heritage of the Common Law of England, modified by our American circumstances. On Christianity and early American law and legal thought, see Perry Miller, *The Life of the Mind in America: from the Revolution to the Civil War* (New York: Harcourt, Brace & World, 1965), 99-268, Archie P. Jones, "Christianity in the Constitution," 145-230, and Steven Alan Samson, "Crossed Swords: Church and State in American History" (Ph.D. dissertation, University of Oregon, 1984).

2. Rationalism is faith in the autonomy, or self-sufficiency of man's unaided reason (unaided by God's redemptive grace or His revelation of His word and moral will in Holy Scripture). It is based on a denial that man's reason has been adversely affected by Original Sin. Rationalism holds that somehow there are universal intellectual and moral principles which are designed into, or present in the

225

religiously "neutral."[3] It was also, like English political thought at the time, solidly republican. Because of our English political roots as well as our saturation with Biblical teaching, early American political thinkers held it to be absolutely fundamental that the people of a republic could preserve their freedom only by preserving their virtue—and that the bedrock of moral virtue was "religion." In other words, for the people living under a republican government to remain free they must remain virtuous, and for them to remain virtuous they must remain "religious." As George Washington declared in his Farewell Address (1796):

> Of all the dispositions and habits which lead to political prosperity, religion and morality are indispensable supports. In vain would that man claim the tribute of patriotism who should labor to subvert these great pillars of human happiness, these firmest props of the duties of men and citizens. The mere politician, equally with the pious man, ought to respect and cherish them. A volume could not trace all their connections with private and public felicity.

When early Americans used the word "religious" or "religion," they did not mean any and every religion: they did not believe that all religions are even remotely equal, equally true, or equally good in their doctrines or their moral and practical effects. The great majority of them, after all, had read their Bibles and therefore knew that men have conceived many false religions in rebellion against God and His law;

---

constitution of being or the nature of things; that these universally valid principles are knowable by man's unaided reason; that man can both know these principles and live by them, individually and collectively; and that man should do so.

3. In the broadest sense, every view of the world and life, of God, men, and things, is religious; for man is finite, not infinite, so he must think about the world and life upon the basis of unproven, presupposed ideas about the fundamental nature of reality, about God, men, and things. These world-views are logically incompatible. Hence it is logically impossible to be neutral among them: the affirmation of one denies the truth of the rest. Even in the more common, restricted sense of "religion," "religious" views certainly hold to diverse propositions about God, men, ethics, and things. Hence even "religious" systems of thought are logically and philosophically incompatible. Thus neutrality among them, while it may sound nice or high-minded, is a logical and practical impossibility.

that these false religions involve many unethical or immoral practices; and that such practices, in a God-ruled world, have, to say the least, destructive social, economic, and political consequences. When early Americans (or the great majority of them) said that someone should "get religion," they did not mean that he should latch onto just any religion, old or new; they meant that he should believe Christianity ("that old time religion"). When the great majority of early Americans said that "religion" is necessary for a people to be moral and that morality is essential to the preservation of liberty, they did not mean that just any old or new religion would serve the purpose. They meant that Christianity (or, at the most, a religion with the same moral imperatives as Christianity) is necessary for a people to be moral, and is thus necessary to the preservation of a people's liberty.

Willmoore Kendall and George Carey's *Basic Symbols of the American Political Tradition* maintains that the central symbol of the American political tradition is *a virtuous people*. Unlike many modern intellectuals and their followers in our populace, early American statesmen and the people who elected them did not divorce morality from civil government, law, or their concept of liberty.

Constitutional Thought

Our Constitution's system of civil government was and is republican. Ours is a republic of republics: an "extended republic," our national government, sharing civil governmental authority and power with the "small republics" which are the several states—with the states having the lion's share of governmental authority over the lives of the people who are within their respective boundaries.

The governmental institutions of our national "extended republic" are republican, not democratic (except in the sense of "democracy" meaning all forms of popular government including republics). The Framers and Ratifiers intended to give us, and gave us, a republic, not a democracy (a civil government ruled directly by the majority). *The Federalist*, the finest primary source explanation and defense of our Constitution, makes it clear in its introductory and concluding essays (Numbers 1 and 85) that the Constitution protects republican government, property, and liberty. The Framers and Ratifiers of our

Constitution put a great deal of mental effort into designing for the people of these United States the best form of republican government which those people would accept. That republic was a mixed form of government, what Aristotle called a "polity," which he considered the best form of government in practice. That republican government combined "democratic" features (as in the House of Representatives), aristocratic features (as in the Senate, the Federal courts, and the U.S. Supreme Court), and monarchial features (in the Presidency) in order to create the greatest probability (not, the Framers knew, a certainty!) of both emphasizing the advantages and attenuating the disadvantages of each of these forms of civil government.[4] Our central government's republic also was designed to have a well-working system of separation of powers with accompanying checks and balances between and among the three departments of government—legislative, executive, and judicial—in order to create the greatest probability of maximizing justice and preserving liberty. It was a federal republic, or as "Publius" (the pen name of Hamilton, Madison, and Jay, the authors of *The Federalist Papers*) often put it, using a phrase which emphasizes the federalism of our governmental system, a "con*federate* republic." That confederate republic was intended to provide a double security to the rights and liberty of the people by constituting a second system of separation of powers and checks and balances between the national government and the state governments. It was also intended to secure to the state governments their authority and right to rule their own internal affairs—and to provide them with the means to protect their authority over their own internal affairs.

The "small republics," our states, were more democratic (more based on majority rule) than our national government but were democratic **republics**, not majority-rule democracies. These republics, too, had mixed forms of government: typically a more democratic lower house of the state legislature, a more aristocratic upper house of the state legislature, an aristocratic council of revision to advise the governor about laws, and a somewhat monarchial unitary chief executive, the governor. These state governments, too, had their own systems of separation of powers

4. See Eidelberg, *A Discourse on Statesmanship*.

with accompanying checks and balances; and these were designed into their respective state constitutions for the same basic reasons which led the Framers to construct our central government's more famous system of separation of powers and checks and balances.

Knowing this before they framed our Constitution, the Framers gave us a national republic composed of the representatives of republics (the states) with a system of separation of powers within that national republic. Joined to that they gave us a system of internally self-governing republics, each of which had its own system of separation of powers with checks and balances. And the "confederate republican" or federal system by which the state republics and the national republic were joined contained its own system of separation of powers and checks and balances between the central government and the state governments.

So much has been made of the brilliance of the Framers' and Ratifiers' design of our system of government that many have lost sight of the "other half" of the Framers' and Ratifiers' intentions for our governmental system. That commonly neglected "other half" is the importance of the people being virtuous. In subtle ways, *The Federalist* presupposes that its authors are addressing a virtuous people. The authors' approach is frank and straightforward. They do not flatter "the people"—or the aristocratic minority, or anyone else.[5] They speak openly of the shortcomings, fallen nature, and moral and political sins of the majority in general and in the histories of particular peoples.

---

5. Various potent quotations could be compiled from *The Federalist*, also known as *The Federalist Papers*, but perhaps the best and most widely read example is Christian statesman James Madison's analysis of the causes of the problem of "faction"—the effects of which destroy popular governments, justice, and liberty—in Federalist No. 10. These causes are the fallibility of man's reason, the connection between man's reason and his self-love, and the diversity and inequality of the "faculties," or mental capabilities, of men. This analysis is consistent with biblical teaching about man's nature in his fallen estate. Madison makes it clear that these causes cannot be removed (nor should civil government try to remove them!): for they are "sewn into" human nature. This unflattering analysis crushes at once arguments for rule by one man, by an elite of men, or by a majority of men. It also repudiates notions of the perfectibility of man by man—by civil government. And it lays the foundation for the limited, constitutional government and liberty which the Framers and Ratifiers intended to give us.

They tell the people that they—"the people"—are not exempt from the characteristics and sins of majorities throughout history. They emphasize the inherent inferiority, characteristic weaknesses, and historic failures of democracy—the form of civil government based on direct majority rule. They tell the people (all the readers of such Constitution-defending-and-explicating works as *The Federalist Papers*) that they have given us a republic, not a democracy, and why they have done so. They set forth rational arguments based on evidence for their readers to consider. They engage the Anti-Federalists' arguments against the Constitution and its features, replying with logic, analysis, and evidence. They defend the Constitution's mixed form of government which had (and has) some positively non-democratic features which were intended to give the American Republic some beneficial characteristics which democracies (majority-rule governments) do not inherently possess—and thus to create a greater probability of avoiding the defects of democracies.

Advocates of ratification of our Constitution could make such arguments because they knew they were addressing a Christian, moral, and well-educated people. *The Federalist Papers* and other efforts to explicate the Constitution were efforts to help the people of the states which were considering whether to ratify the Constitution understand the principles and purposes of the document so that they could (if enough states ratified it) act to defend it and its principles against attack, subversion, decline, and perversion. Throughout *The Federalist* its Christian authors[6] imply and occasionally state explicitly (as has been noted previously) that the people of the nation—and of the states—have a duty to defend their Constitution against usurpation of power and its ultimate result—tyranny.

The people's duty to "keep" the Republic and our liberty, as Benjamin Franklin famously put it, was based "half" on the complex system of civil government which the Framers and Ratifiers gave us—with its system designed to incline civil officials to serve the public good out of

6. Like 90–95+ percent of the Framers and Ratifiers of our Constitution, Alexander Hamilton, James Madison, and John Jay, were Christians—not rationalists (as some have claimed). They were not sinlessly perfect (especially Hamilton), but the evidence of their beliefs indicates that they had firmly Christian minds.

self-interest if they lack higher motivation, but was also based "half" on the virtue—and thus on the religion and morality—of the people of the nation and the people of the several states.

Those states were in fact, and were intended to be, far more than half of our system of civil government so far as civil government was meant to affect the lives of Americans. In terms of our federal system, the states were also intended to be the other "half" of the Constitution's system of separation of powers and checks and balances: providing a double security to the rights and liberty of the people by using their representatives in the national government and their reserved powers to check central government usurpation and tyranny. In order to do so, however, the people and their elected representatives in their states' governments would have to be virtuous as well as knowledgeable about the principles, purposes, and functioning of our federal system of government.

Our early American States' Christian constitutions, with their declarations of rights or bills of rights, implicitly and explicitly taught that "religion," Christianity, is basic to virtue, and that virtue is necessary to liberty.[7] These constitutions, declarations of rights, and bills of rights honored God, explicitly recognizing His existence, importance, and attributes. Various ones recognized God as good, Almighty, as one God, as Creator, as Governor of the Universe, as Divine Providence, as the Great Legislator of the Universe, as Inspirer of the Scriptures of the Old and New Testaments, and as Savior and Lord, and therefore as the One whom men have a duty to worship. Many of them implied that the people of a given state are in a covenantal relationship with God: God rules history; God has a relationship with the people of a given state; man and civil government are under His authority and the authority of His standards of law and justice; and God

---

7. For a slightly fuller treatment of the relationship of Christianity and our early states' constitutions, declarations of rights or bills of rights, see B. F. Morris, *The Christian Life and Character of the Civil Institutions of the United States* (Powder Springs, Georgia: The American Vision, [1864] 2007), 267-292; Paul Eidelberg, *The Philosophy of the American Constitution*; and Archie P. Jones, *Christianity and Our State Constitutions, Declarations, and Bills of Rights, Parts I and II* (Marlborough, New Hampshire: Plymouth Rock Foundation, 1993).

will enforce His covenant, punishing them for their sins and rewarding them for their faithful obedience via His providential rule of history.[8]

This covenantal view of the relationship of the people of a given state with God is particularly clear in light of numerous statements concerning the relationship between religion, virtue, and liberty. The Pennsylvania Declaration of Rights (1776), for example, declared:

> XIV. That a frequent recurrence to fundamental prin-
> ciples and a firm adherence to justice, moderation,
> temperance, industry, and frugality are absolutely
> necessary to preserve the blessings of liberty, and
> keep a government free: The people ought there-
> fore to pay particular attention to these points in
> the choice of officers and representatives, and have
> a right to exact a due and constant regard to them ,
> from their legislators and magistrates, in the mak-
> ing and executing such laws as are necessary for the
> good government of the state.

Section 45 of the Pennsylvania Form of Government (1776) stated that:

> Laws for the encouragement of virtue, and prevention
> of vice and immorality, shall be made and constantly
> kept in force, and provision shall be made for their due
> execution: And all religious societies or bodies of men
> heretofore united or incorporated for the advancement
> of religion or learning, or for other pious and charitable
> purposes, shall be encouraged and protected in the en-
> joyment of the privileges, immunities and estates which
> they were accustomed to enjoy, or could have enjoyed,
> under the laws and former constitution of this state.

These instruments spoke of "rights," "natural rights," and "the law of nature," but the context of these statements made it clear that these rights, and this moral law, are from God—not, contrary to early

---

8. Deuteronomy 8 and 28, and Leviticus 26 are the classic passages—among many—conveying this teaching.

modern political philosophers, from man's mere desires. They spoke of rights, but they also spoke of duties and of virtue. They proclaimed the importance of "religion"—in their context, Christianity—to the maintenance of virtue, and thus of the importance of Christianity and Christian morality to the preservation of liberty. For example, the Massachusetts Declaration of Rights (1780) declared:

> III. As the happiness of a people, and the good order and preservation of civil government, essentially depend on piety, religion and morality; and as these cannot be generally diffused throughout a community, but by the institution of the public worship of God, and of public instructions in piety, religion and morality: Therefore, to promote their happiness and to secure the good order and preservation of their government, the people of this Commonwealth have a right to invest their legislature with power to authorize and require, and the legislature shall, from time to time, authorize and require, the several towns, parishes, precincts, and other bodies-politic, or religious societies, to make suitable provision, at their own expense, for the institution of the public worship of God, and for the support and maintenance of public protestant teachers of piety, religion and morality, in all cases where such provision shall not be made voluntarily....

Article X of this Declaration made it explicit that individuals' rights entail serious duties:

> Each individual of the society has a right to be protected by it in the enjoyment of his life, liberty, and property, according to standing laws. He is obliged, consequently, to contribute his share to the expense of this protection; to give his personal service, or an equivalent, when necessary....

And Article XVIII, in words which we should heed today, reiter-

ated and reemphasized the crucial importance of "religion" and virtue
to the preservation of liberty:

> A frequent recurrence to the fundamental principles
> of the constitution, and a constant adherence to those
> of piety, justice, moderation, temperance, industry, and
> frugality, are absolutely necessary to preserve the ad-
> vantages of liberty, and to maintain a free government:
> The people ought, consequently, to have a particular
> attention to all those principles, in the choice of their
> officers and representatives: And they have a right to
> require of their lawgivers and magistrates, an exact and
> constant observance of them, in the formation and ex-
> ecution of the laws necessary for the good administra-
> tion of the Commonwealth.

Some state constitutions sought to buttress the connection between "religion," virtue, and liberty by means of manifest connections
between Christianity and civil government. Some required Christian
oaths or affirmations of public officials. These oaths of office required
affirmation of belief in Christianity, Trinitarian Christianity, or Protestant Christianity. Most—ten of the original thirteen states—had
pluralistic establishments of Christianity, or of Protestant Christianity,
as the religion of the state. Seven had established churches, or laws
which were close to constituting an established church. Three other
states had definitely Christian provisions and requirements for public
office, though they had no established or quasi-established church. The
remaining three states were closer to having "full religious freedom,"
but none really separated Christianity from civil government or law.
Virginia's Declaration of Rights spoke of men's duty to practice "Christian forbearance, tolerance, and charity" toward others. Rhode Island's
Charter, which it used as its constitution until 1842, was a Christian
document. And New York's constitution, authored by John Jay, the first
Chief Justice of our U.S. Supreme Court, had a Protestant provision
requiring naturalized citizens to renounce allegiance and subjection
to all foreign ecclesiastical and civil princes and potentates, and had a
Protestant test oath for public office until 1806.

These states' fundamental laws were concerned with liberty and sought to maintain their citizens' traditional, hard-earned rights. They were limited-government documents. Though they were concerned with the virtue of the people, they sought to promote it, not to coerce it: they were not "statecraft as soulcraft" documents.

These limited-government Christian documents presupposed parental authority over the education of their children and so did not attempt to permit the state government to usurp that authority. These fundamental laws also presupposed the kind of education extant among early Americans of all colonies and states, in the settled areas and on the expanding frontier. That education, though mixed with the study of classical writers, was distinctly and overwhelmingly Christian in every kind of school, at every level, and everywhere. The classical component of that education combined history and politics with ethics. That education was closely connected with ethics, even, perhaps especially, at the college and post-graduate level. Its political teaching was Christian, republican and strongly ethical. Education was supplemented by many public political sermons, preached by the most outstanding local ministers, given in every colony and state, before various kinds of audiences on diverse occasions, and often published. This education, and these sermons, conveyed the traditional republican teaching that a people must be virtuous if they are to retain their liberty. Early Americans' education both produced and reinforced the teaching of their states' constitutions, declarations of rights, and bills of rights.

These states' constitutions, declarations, and bills of rights all plainly implied the view that it is the right and duty of a virtuous people to resist injustice and tyranny, even to the point of taking up arms to throw off tyranny—an old and distinguished Christian legal and political doctrine[9]—for they were made in the process of the colonies' struggle for independence from British tyranny. The Maryland Declaration of Rights (1776) stated it most boldly:

---

9. The Christian legal and political doctrine of the right and duty of resistance is easy to trace back from the teachings of American colonial pastors and political thinkers through seventeenth-century British political thought, the Roman Catholic Counter-Reformation, the Protestant Reformation to medieval legal and political thought, and back through that to the Bible.

IV. That all persons invested with legislative or executive powers of government are the trustees of the
public, and, as such, accountable for their conduct;
wherefore, whenever the ends of government are
perverted and public liberty manifestly endangered,
and all other means of redress are ineffectual, the
people may, and of right ought, to reform the old or
establish a new government. The doctrine of non-
resistance, against arbitrary power and oppression, is
absurd, slavish, and destructive of the good and happiness of mankind.

What these state documents affirmed, their representatives did
not deny when they framed or ratified our Constitution. In fact, they
formed a system of civil government through the Constitution which
was designed to enable the American people and their states to resist
injustice and tyranny emanating from our central government. In fact,
as has also been seen above, the authors of *The Federalist* and other
advocates of ratification of our Constitution endorsed the Constitution's system of civil government as the best means of protecting the
semi-autonomy of the states as well as the rights and liberty of their
people against injustice, arbitrary power and oppression coming from
our central government.

Federalism, Virtue, and Liberty

Thus the theory and practice of American federalism and Americans' liberty was inseparable from the presupposition that ethics is basic
to politics.[10] Our American predecessors knew that the mere processes
of popular government are not enough; that although republican government is the best form of civil government, republics decline and fall
when their people turn from virtue to vice; and that in order to keep

---

10. In this it is unlike the teachings of so-called "Political Science," which
positivistically claims that we cannot have objective knowledge of "values" or
ethical laws or principles and implicitly denigrates ethics—even though most
"political scientists" are "liberals" or leftists who push left-wing agendas and
crusades.

their liberty the people must remain virtuous. They knew that while the form of civil government is important, the virtue of the people is ultimately at least as important. They read it in their Bibles, in classical history, in Montesquieu, and in virtually all of their favorite political thinkers. They knew that federalism was fundamental to their liberty in the American system of government, but they knew that the virtue of the people is essential to preserve federalism and liberty.

What was true when our Constitution, our Bill of Rights, and our Tenth Amendment were framed and ratified is still true today, for the character of God, the nature of man, and the nature of things has not changed. Virtue is still necessary for the preservation of liberty. A vicious society is concerned mainly with the gratification of its desires. The individuals who compose it are concerned with doing whatever they will, and with the means to enable them to do whatever they will, regardless of whether the means to do so is supplied at the expense of others. A virtuous society is concerned with doing right, and being free to do right. The individuals who compose it do not want their civil government to do wrong and call it right, to steal from some in order to give to others, or to violate people's freedom in order to subsidize false charity. A vicious people want the rule of men and largesse from the government. A virtuous people want the rule of law and liberty. So a vicious people will have their short-run largesse provided by civil government, at the expense of others—and will in the long-run have neither material well-being nor liberty. A virtuous people will act to defend its liberty and, if it can do so successfully, in the long-run will have both liberty and prosperity.

Do we have enough virtuous people today to defend federalism, our states' rights to rule their own internal affairs, and Americans' liberty?

32

Let's Put The Tenth Amendment To Work Today!

Though the Tenth Amendment is old, its principles are perennial, for they are drawn from the permanent things. The principles of the Tenth Amendment are ours: they are the warp and woof of our governmental system. But the Tenth Amendment is not merely a matter of history; it is of vital importance today, for liberty is of vital importance today and always, and our American liberty has long been under attack and is now under assault as never before. Those of us who understand and love the Tenth Amendment must act to defend it, and to put it into practice for the good of all Americans, and for the good of all throughout the world who still look to America as a beacon of liberty.

What Individuals Can Do

Humanly speaking, all social and political action begins with individual action, with individuals' choices to believe, think, and act in a certain way or set of ways. Yes, you are only one person, yet one person can do a great deal if he or she resolves to.

1. Begin With Study.

Inform yourself first, then inform others. Study the Bible and learn what it says on civil government, law, and public life. It does speak to these things, and is philosophically the most authoritative source of standards for civil government, law, and public life. The Bible was the foundation of American liberty. It was the foundation of the overwhelmingly dominant religion of early Americans, the Framers and Ratifiers of our Constitution, and the statesmen who gave us the Bill of Rights and the Tenth Amendment. It was the foundation of early American political and legal thought, and of our law. It was far and

239

away the most authoritative source cited by early American political writers, and was basic to the thought of the great majority of political and legal writers cited by early American political writers. To understand what the Bible has to say about ethics in general and legal and political ethics in particular is to understand the thinking which undergirded our Constitution. If you don't want to study the Bible to see what it says about these things, then you should begin at the second step: study our Constitution.

2. Study our Constitution, our Bill of Rights and our Tenth Amendment.

First study the Constitution itself, as it was before the first ten amendments, the Bill of Rights, were added to the Constitution. Know the provisions of each article of our Constitution. What does the Preamble say are the purposes for which our Constitution was framed? What does each of these purposes mean? How is each to defined and put into practice by the Constitution?

What does Article I deal with? Why was the legislature put first, before the executive and judicial departments? Why is Congress's function more important than the President's law-enforcing function and the federal courts' law-adjudicating function in our governmental system? What lawmaking authority does Congress have (Article I, Section 8)? What lawmaking authority does Congress **not** have? (What powers are not stated in Article I, Section 8? What does Article I, Section 9 forbid Congress to do by law?) And what are the states/state governments forbidden to do (Article I, Section 10)? What authority does Article I give Congress to intervene in or regulate the internal affairs of a state?

What does Article II deal with? (Section 1) What does the President do in our governmental system? Why was the Executive Branch the second branch of the central government dealt with by the Constitution and not the first? Why is the President's function less important than Congress's function in our governmental system? How is the President elected? Is his election purely democratic? Is it based on the will of the majority of the American voters? What part do the states have in the "Electoral College" (the system or institution by which the President is elected)? What part did the individual state legislatures originally have in the election of our President? Was this method "democratic"? Was it based on the direct will of the majority of American voters? How did this method of election enable the states to check against abuses of power by our central/national government, and against usurpations of power from the states by our central/national government? How did the Seventeenth Amendment affect this?

What does Article III deal with? Why was the Judicial Branch of our central government the third branch of our national government dealt with by our Constitution—and not the first or second? Why is the federal courts' (and U.S. Supreme Court's) law-adjudicating function less important than Congress's lawmaking function and the President's law enforcement function in our governmental system? In which section of Article III is the U.S. Supreme Court (or any federal court) given the authority to amend our Constitution? Is the Supreme Court (or any federal court) given the authority to amend our Constitution anywhere in our Constitution? (Look ahead at Article V. Is the Supreme Court (or any federal court) given such authority in Article V?)

What does Article IV deal with? How is what it says about the authority and powers of the state governments relevant to our Tenth Amendment?

What does Article V deal with? Exactly how is our Constitution to be changed? How, according to Article V, do "interpretation," "evolution," "reinterpretation," and like terms figure in Article V's explanation of how our Constitution is to be changed? How about such things as "majority will" or "the will of the people"? What about things such as "the opinions or views of the intellectuals" or "political scientists," or "legal scholars," or "Federal judges," or "the U. S. Supreme Court"? Is the U.S. Supreme Court (or any federal court) authorized by Article V to amend our Constitution? What about "the will of Congress"? Does Article V authorize Congress to amend our Constitution? Does Article V give Congress only a part in amending our Constitution, or the ruling influence in amending our Constitution? What about "the will of the President"? What about "presidential executive orders"? Does Article V authorize the President to amend our Constitution? And what about agencies or bureaucracies created by the federal government? Are they authorized to amend our Constitution?

How do the states fit into our Constitution's system of changing our Constitution? How does the states' part in our system of changing our Constitution enable the states to protect themselves and their people against abuses of power or usurpation of power by the central/national government?

What about Article VI? The second and third paragraphs are particularly pertinent. The second paragraph contains what is known as "the Supremacy Clause": "This Constitution, and the Laws of the United States which shall be made in Pursuance thereof; and all Treaties made, or which shall be made, under the Authority of the United States, shall be the supreme Law of the Land..." Does this mean that the laws of the United States (the national government) which are **not** made in pursuance of our Constitution "shall be the supreme law of the land"? Are the states bound by this clause to obey laws **not** made in pursuance of our Constitution? What are the states obligated by this clause to do about laws that violate our Constitution? How are the states to tell the difference between laws made in pursuance of our Constitution and laws not made in pursuance of our Constitution? Are they to go by what Congress tells them? By what the President tells them? By what a Federal judge tells them? By what the U.S. Supreme Court tells them? By what federal bureaucrats tell them? Or are they to study the Constitution for themselves and base their determination on that?

Consider the third paragraph. Its first clause requires all legislative, executive, and judicial officers of the nation (the United States) and the states to be bound by oath or affirmation "to support this Constitution..." Does "support" mean "to change the meaning of" (or any similar idea) without amending the Constitution? What does this clause require those national and state government officials to do in regard to matters of civil government which violate the Constitution? Does this clause require all national and state government officials to support everything that is done **in the name of the Constitution** regardless of whether it is consistent with the Constitution or not? And which official or institution of our governmental system does this clause—or any other clause in our Constitution—make the final and highest authority on the meaning of our Constitution? Does this clause require any state or national government official to yield to any other state or national government official in disputes about what is constitutional and what is not constitutional? Does this clause imply that state government officials are constitutionally or morally justified in resisting national government officials who are doing things which violate the Constitution?

What about Article VII? Is it basically unimportant? What is important about its first paragraph? What is significant about the fact that our Constitution had to be ratified by the conventions of at least nine states in order for the Constitution to be established?

Now consider its second paragraph. What does it imply about Jesus Christ when it says that the Constitution was "Done at Philadelphia, in the year of our Lord one thousand seven hundred and eighty-seven, and of the independence of the United States the twelfth"? Is there a reference to God in our Constitution after all (despite what we've been told about it for so long)? And to whom does "our Lord" refer? What are the implications of this statement for history? What are its implications for our civil governments?

Now consider the signatures of the states' delegates to our Constitutional Convention who signed our Constitution. (Not all reprints of our Constitution include these signatures. All should.) These delegates signed in groups, according to the states that they represented. What is the significance of this? What does this imply about the origin of our Constitution? What does it imply about the importance of the states in our constitutional system of government?

In summary, consider the "big picture" of our Constitution. What place did the states or state governments have in the constitutional governmental system? Consider: representatives and representation in the House of Representatives; how congressmen are elected; representation of states by U.S. Senators in the Senate; how U.S. senators were originally intended to be elected; the scope of state government powers under our Constitution; the scope of central/national government powers under our Constitution.

On our Constitution the best primary source is Alexander Hamilton, James Madison, and John Jay, *The Federalist*, or *The Federalist Papers*. The best edition is the Liberty Fund, Inc. paperback (2001) edited by George Carey and James McClellan. If you cannot get this one, get an unabridged edition containing all of the 85 essays. Also get an edition edited by someone who is not seeking to denigrate the authors or the original intentions of our Constitution. Some editions also have selected writings of Anti-Federalist critics of the Constitution; these are worthy of thoughtful reading. So are larger collections of the writings of the Anti-Federalists. As indicated in some previous chapters, the Anti-Federalists' criticisms of the Constitution are well worth pondering—partly for their own worth; partly for what they indicate about early Americans' political thought; partly because supporters of ratification of our Constitution had to and did respond to them; and partly because time has taught us of their insight, foresight, and wisdom. And there is no better source than *Elliot's Debates*, the notes on the debates in the Constitutional Convention and the state ratification conventions—for in these debates the framers and advocates of ratification of our Constitution had to justify the document as a whole and each of its provisions in the face of Anti-Federalist criticisms and other concerns.

Then study our Bill of Rights: What did each amendment say? What did each one protect? Against whom or what did each of these amendments protect? What did the Ninth Amendment protect, and against whom or what? Why did they add this amendment to the Constitution? What does the sum and substance of these amendments indicate about Americans' intentions for our Constitution? What do these amendments indicate about what Americans who gave us our Constitution and Bill of Rights feared our central/national government would do if the Constitution were not amended? What do they indicate about how early Americans wanted our national government's legislators, presidents, and judges to carry out their constitutional functions? Do these amendments indicate that early Americans did not mind if their national government officials "reinterpreted" or played "fast and loose" with our Constitution and its offices? If they indicate something else, what do they indicate? And were early Americans' views on these things wise or unwise?

Now consider our Tenth Amendment: What does it say? What does it protect? Against what, or whom, does the Tenth Amendment protect the states? Consider how these ten amendments changed the original Constitution. Did they change it? How did they change the

Constitution? Why is the Tenth Amendment included in the Bill of Rights if our Constitution already contains the principle of federalism?

3. **Study early American political and legal thought—the background of the Constitution, the Bill of Rights, and the Tenth Amendment.**

This is helpful, but not mandatory for an understanding and a defense of our Tenth Amendment. In your study, consider whether early American political and legal thought generally advocates or opposes: big government; arbitrary government; the right of the officials or institutions of civil government to redefine their own authority and powers, removing limits on their authority as they see fit; unlimited government; law based on the will of the rulers; centralization of authority and power; federalism; the authority of the states to govern themselves; the use of civil government to solve the "problems" of man and society; individual liberty.

4. **Consider the impact of the adoption of the Seventeenth Amendment in 1913.**

What impact did this have on federalism? What did selection of a state's U.S. senators by the state's legislature enable the state to do in regard to the central government? What did the Seventeenth Amendment's replacement of the state legislature with the vote of the majority of the state's voters do to the ability of the state governments to check and balance the central/national government?

5. **Study the arguments for and against taking the Tenth Amendment seriously.**

Know what the enemies of the Tenth Amendment, constitutionalism, and our Constitution have argued and are saying today. Ponder their arguments and the evidence they adduce to support their arguments. What do their various arguments presuppose? What premises do they state openly? Ponder the counter-arguments made by advocates of states' rights and federalism. What do they presuppose? What premises do they state openly? What arguments for or against federalism are popular today? Which arguments are better? Why?

6. Pray without ceasing.

The Bible makes it clear that God rules history and all things by His divine providence, sustaining and directing all things by the word of His power. Scripture makes it manifest that God hears and answers prayer. It also makes it clear that civil government is a ministry of God, and that His ministry of civil government should function in terms of God's law, His infallible, revealed standards of ethics and law. If you believe these things, you should pray for our people, for those in positions of authority in the various civil governments of our land, and pray against those who are motivated by evil designs or are deluded by false arguments.

The statesmen and people who gave us our independence, Articles of Confederation, Constitution, Bill of Rights, and Tenth Amendment certainly believed in the necessity and efficacy of prayer. They were, overwhelmingly, Christians, not rationalists or Deists. Overwhelmingly, whether they were Christians or not, they believed that God rules history by His divine providence. Even non-Christian statesmen like Franklin and Jefferson believed that God is over our communities, states, and nation, ruling our history by His divine providence. So they believed that He is accessible to us by prayer, and that we can and should pray for His guidance, protection, and blessings on our local communities, states, and nation—and on the officials of their civil governments. The officials of our early American local and state governments, before and after the adoption of our Constitution and Bill of Rights, including the First Amendment, did not separate "religion" (in practice, Christianity) or God from civil government, law, or public life. Nor does the First Amendment—that is, the intentions of the framers and ratifiers of both our Constitution and what became our First Amendment—require this. And this was true of the conduct of our national government under the Constitution and the Bill of Rights. Hence they provided for chaplains for each house of Congress, prayer in each house of Congress, chaplains for our military units, and public worship in the halls of Congress. So there is good precedent for prayer for, as well as by, our civil governments and their officials.

Still, if you do not believe in prayer but do believe in federalism, freedom, constitutional government, and honesty in the conduct of civil government, you should work to protect and use the Tenth Amendment.

7. Teach others.

Talk, converse, argue, speak, debate, write; produce audios, videos, and art on the Tenth Amendment and related issues. Make sure they are accurate, truthful, and understandable by the audience to which they are directed.

8. Join with others to gain and promote an understanding of our Constitution and our Tenth Amendment.

Meet, organize, plan strategy, tactics, and projects; carry out those projects. Or join existing organizations and work in and through them.

9. Use the Internet.

Research, write, learn from others, communicate, network, organize, work with people elsewhere who are knowledgeable about federalism, our system of federalism, and the threats against federalism—and active in defense of federalism and the use of its principles to affect our governments' policies.

10. Act politically. Educate and influence the public in your state and in other states. Public knowledge and opinion is the foundation of the election and support of local, state, and national officials who will honor and obey our Constitution and our Tenth Amendment.

Elect civil government officials at all levels who know the importance of our Tenth Amendment and are willing to act in obedience to the Tenth Amendment.

Every civil government—at every level—is a ministry of God. It is a means of serving and glorifying Him, of protecting those who do that which is good and of restraining those who do that which is evil, of working no evil to our neighbor and of making sure that no evil is done to him (Romans 13:1-10). Every civil government, at every level, is under God's authority and so is obligated to act in terms of God's definitions of good and evil. Every civil government is important.

Act at the local level: Local government, a part of state government (created by the state government), is protected by the Tenth Amendment—and harmed by central government intrusions when and where the Tenth Amendment is neglected or abandoned. Local government officials can influence local people, people in their own state, and state and national government officials from their state. Local government office is both a "pulpit" and a stepping stone to state and national government office. Do all you can to make sure your local government officials understand, value, and support our Tenth Amendment. Do all you can to inform or oppose those who do not.

Act at the state level: State governments are protected by our Tenth Amendment—and harmed by central government neglect or violation of the Tenth Amendment. State government office is "a bully pulpit" (not so big a pulpit as the Presidency, but bigger than local government office). State government officials can influence, educate, and motivate the public—in your state and in other states. State government officials (and the laws, resolutions, and policies they produce, the lawsuits they launch against central government abuses of power, and the constitutional amendments they propose and support) can influence local, state, and national government officials. State governments can work directly to influence and oppose national government laws, judicial decrees, and policies. They can also work with other states' governments to oppose unconstitutional national government laws, plans, programs, judicial decrees, and the like. State government office is a stepping stone to more powerful state government offices and to national government office. Do all that you can do to make sure that your state government officials understand, value, and support our Tenth Amendment—and will use it to do what our Constitution requires. Inform or oppose state government officials who do not, or will not, meet these requirements.

Act at the national level: Establish contacts and working relationships with like-minded people and national government officials in your state and in other states, or join and get active in organizations which maintain such contacts and working relationships. Find out where your local congressman and your state's senators stand on federalism and our Tenth Amendment. Do the same with your state's other congressmen. Work to support those who are squared away on these principles; work to educate or oppose those who aren't. Work with or support any and all local and state government officials who are trying to get your state's (and/or other states') congressmen and senators to support our Tenth Amendment. Work with and support those who are trying to work with other states' officials to protect states' authority against unconstitutional federal government plans, programs, decrees, and the like.

Establish contacts with like-minded individuals and civil government officials in other countries and/or join organizations which have such contacts. Get and share information, ideas, data on the consequences of laws and policies, pertinent literature, and the like. Let their knowledge, experience, and intelligence supplement and reinforce yours, and yours theirs.

Question civil government officials at all levels about the Constitution, the Tenth Amendment, and pertinent issues.

Communicate with your elected representatives: via telephone, e-mails, letters, personal visits, open letters, signs, and other means.

Attend and participate in your representatives' functions and events.

What Pastors and Churches Can Do

1. **Study the Bible on civil government, law, and public life.**

It speaks to all three, and speaks authoritatively. It also speaks authoritatively to economics, with which, obviously, civil government is intimately concerned. Study God's law. Meditate upon God's laws and how they apply to civil government, law, and public life. They do!

2. **Read books on how the Bible applies to civil government, law, and public life.**

Evaluate what each says in comparison with what the Bible says about the subject.

Read books about our Constitution, the Bill of Rights, and our Tenth Amendment: works which explain the intentions behind these things, not works which try to discount and discard the intentions of the men who gave us our Constitution, Bill of Rights, and Tenth Amendment. Compare what they say with what the Bible says on the subject.

Keep informed on the issues of the day. Read. Analyze and evaluate people's arguments on the basis of biblical standards of ethics.

3. **Think about how the Bible and God's law apply to the issues of civil government, law, public life, international relations, and liberty today. Encourage others to do so.**

4. **Pray without ceasing.**

Pray for our civil government officials at all levels; for our country; for Christians throughout the world, especially in countries where they are persecuted (persecution entails non-physical as well as physical persecution); for the re-Christianization of countries that used to be Christian; for the Christianization of countries that are not Christian; for godly civil governments and laws in all the nations of the world.

5. **Teach.**

As a minister of God, the Great Commission gives you a duty to help teach the nations all things that Christ has commanded us to do (Matthew 28:18-20). Since civil government is God's ministry and Christ is God, Christ's commands certainly apply authoritatively to civil government, law, and public policy.

Since all Scripture is inspired by God and is profitable for doctrine, correction, and instruction in righteousness that the man of God may be mature and thoroughly furnished for all good works (2 Timothy 3:16), the Bible applies authoritatively to civil government, law, public life, and all things pertaining thereto. Since Holy Scripture is a better standard than "nature," and since "nature" (the whole creation) is fallen and the nature of man is fallen in sin, in ethical rebellion against God, Scripture is certainly a better standard than "nature," "natural law," and the like. Since "conscience" (as the use of any concordance will show) is subject to various kinds of defects, Scripture is also a better standard than "conscience." So teach what the Bible has to say about the above, and how the Bible's teachings apply to civil government, law, public life, the issues of the day, the duty of civil government officials to obey their oaths to support our Constitution, and threats to our Tenth Amendment.

Now, our Constitution was not divinely inspired: it is not on the same level as Holy Scripture. It can and should be criticized according to biblical criteria. But if it should be changed to make it square more fully with biblical criteria, it should also be changed in a way which is consistent with biblical criteria: openly and honestly, by our Constitution's own Article V methods—not subtly and deceitfully, and not by means unauthorized by Article V. The same, of course, goes for our Tenth Amendment.

Make this teaching about what the Bible has to say about civil government and law a fundamental part of your ministry—including your youth ministry. Make sure that preaching and teaching on such things is a regular part of your yearly teaching and preaching. Preach special sermons or series of sermons on especially important issues as social and/or political circumstances demand.

Reach out to the church with this teaching: Talk with other pastors in your denomination. Talk with other pastors and elders in your local area, in your state, your region, your country, other countries. Write for your denomination's publications. Write for other publications. Write books. Create and maintain a website. Use the web site, at least in part, to teach about civil government and law; about our civil governments and the issues of the day; about the principles of our system of civil government, including federalism.

Reach out to the public with this teaching: Reach out through your regular preaching and teaching; through special sermons or lectures; through conferences. Reach out through writing, debating, etc.—in your local venues (newspaper, schools, colleges, etc.)—and through the Internet.

6. **Act to implement biblical principles and God's law in the various levels and kinds of civil government: local, state, and national. Influence others. Join with like-minded individuals and organizations.**

7. **Evaluate the Constitution, the Bill of Rights, the Tenth Amendment, and other amendments on the basis of bibli-**

cal criteria. Work to improve our Constitution according to biblical criteria.

8. **Study the arguments for and against the original intentions behind the Constitution, the Bill of Rights, and the Tenth Amendment.**

Evaluate these arguments biblically; teach all whom you can reach. Are the original intentions behind our Constitution, Bill of Rights, and Tenth Amendment more consistent with liberty in general, religious liberty, and Christian liberty than are the intentions of those who would give us centralized government, unlimited government, and arbitrary government?

9. **Act to influence the public and civil government officials to apply the principles of the Constitution (original intentions, not "evolving"/"living Constitution" pseudoprinciples), the Bill of Rights, and the Tenth Amendment to today's circumstances. Act to influence them to apply biblical principles to these things.**

10. **Act to influence your church's and/or denomination's young people (and other young people you can reach).**

Support Christian education—home-schooling, Christian schools, truly Christian colleges positively by word and deed. Support Christian education by working to protect it against secularists' and statists' attempts to nullify it by means of laws, bureaucratic regulations, and the like. Try to help all your church's or denomination's young people get a Christian education in a Christian school, home school, college, apprenticeship program, or vocational school. Try to make sure that that education includes good instruction on our Constitution, our Bill of Rights, and our Tenth Amendment.

11. Occupy 'til Christ Returns!

No matter what your eschatological views, like every Christian you have a duty to occupy—to do Christ the Lord's business—until He returns (Luke 19:13). Teaching about His ministry of civil government, and about how what He has commanded us to teach all nations to do, certainly qualifies as part of what we must do to "occupy" until He returns.

What Schools Can Do

1. If yours is a Christian school:

Teach an all-encompassing biblical world view: Apply the Bible's teaching to all areas of thought and life; to every subject in your curriculum; to everything within every subject.

Emphasize apologetics: explain and refute false world-views, false views of politics, government, and law; explain and refute false views of history and of our place and time.

Emphasize the Constitution: its historical context; its significance; the original intentions behind its design; the nature of our Constitution's design and intended functioning; the role of the states or state governments in our constitutional system; federalism; the original intentions behind our Bill of Rights; the Tenth Amendment and the original intentions behind it; our Constitution's importance today, including the importance and applicability of the Tenth Amendment today. Teach your students that these things are important: test your students on these things. Acquire and use books and other materials which give you and your students good information and analyses of these things; stock your school's library or libraries with these things; make sure your teachers use these things; do all you can to require your students to use these things.

Invite speakers who can speak about the importance of federalism and the Tenth Amendment. Work to get your teachers, staff, parents, and students politically knowledgeable and politically active.

2. If yours is a private school:

Do all of the above to the extent that they are compatible with your religious philosophy or view of the world and of life.

Whether or not Christianity is consistent with your view of the world and of life, treat the religious, moral, educational, and cultural background and context of our Constitution honestly: teach the truth about the influence of historic Christianity on early American culture, law, legal thought, legal education, political thought, politics, and government—including our War for Independence; our Declaration of Independence (and other governmental documents); our Articles of Confederation; our early state constitutions, declarations of rights or bills of rights; our Constitution, and our Bill of Rights.

Emphasize the importance of the Constitution, the Bill of Rights, and the Tenth Amendment; the rule of law (as opposed to the rule of men), of justice, and of liberty; the original intentions of the framers and ratifiers of our Constitution, Bill of Rights, and the Tenth Amendment.

3. If yours is a "public school":

Your hands will be "tied" much more than will those of a private or Christian school administrator or teacher. A lot depends on the views of the administrator of your school, your supervisor, and others who are or may be in a position to restrict your activity. **Do what you can within the limits of your situation.** You will probably have to buck the curriculum, the textbooks, and the school's emphasis on teaching to standardized tests upon which the school's and teachers' performances are rated. Do what you can.

Educate yourself in the areas noted above. Get and share good information. Try to get good books and publications into your school's library, then do what you can to make sure those resources are used. (Find out how long a book can stay on the library shelves without being checked out before it is discarded by the library, then make sure no good books on the subject meet that sad end.) If you can't get your school's librarian to add good books on the subjects mentioned above, accumulate your own library. Within the limits of your school's code of conduct, a better code of conduct, and a wise and careful approach to dealing with students, consider loaning out at least some of your books to students who are interested in these things and will read about them.

Talk with like-minded people in your school and school district. Share information, ideas, strategies, and tactics.

What Teachers Can Do

1. **Study! Master the subject and the topics that are related to it. Read.**

2. **Get good information and make it available to as many people as you can.**

Augment your own library, your church's library, your school's library, and your local public library. Find out how long a book is permitted to sit on the shelf not checked out before it is discarded, then take steps to prevent that from happening. Tell people who are interested or might become interested about the good resources on the subject(s) that are available. Make appropriate suggestions and assignments (requirements) to your students.

3. **Make Practical Applications.**

Create a unit or units within your curriculum and courses. Talk about these things at pertinent points in your courses. Show how the principles of our Constitution and our Tenth Amendment apply to today's conditions. Make appropriate assignments to your students. All too many students want to know only what they will be tested on: test them on our Constitution, our Bill of Rights, and our Tenth Amendment.

4. **Network: with other teachers, professors, political leaders, and knowledgeable people.**

What Organizations Can Do

1. **Study.**

2. **Teach.**

3. **Reach Out to the Public:**

Produce and distribute materials, or help those that do via funding, advice, and work.

Sponsor essay and oratory contests, video production contests, etc. with built-in or attached incentives.

Sponsor scholarships, and/or fellowships for study in History, Government/Political Science, Economics, and related "disciplines." Be selective with these: most colleges' and universities' (including nominally Christian ones) Liberal Arts faculties and Government or

Political Science faculties are largely staffed by "liberals" or Marxists, not by professors who understand or value our Constitution and our Tenth Amendment. Sponsor scholarships to colleges and universities which have "conservative" faculties, or at least some conservative professors who understand and value our Constitution and its Tenth Amendment. Do your research on this. Conservative think tanks like the Heritage Foundation should be helpful. But here too you need to be selective. There are a number of different kinds of "conservatism" and "conservatives." Make sure you are working with conservative professors who value both our Constitution **and federalism**. Build a list of contacts—conservative professors who value federalism—and keep that list updated so that you won't be funding students studying under hostile professors.

4. **Network.**

5. **Help Individuals and organizations:** like-minded professors, teachers, students, writers, producers of materials.

6. **Get involved in politics.**

Now that the U.S. Supreme Court has finally defended the First Amendment against McCain-Feingold it will be easier for organizations to get involved in politics. Still, check out the legalities of this before you get involved in politics, and be sure about the legality of whatever your organization does in the broadly defined realm of politics.

Getting involved in politics doesn't necessarily involve pushing a political party or endorsing candidates. You can educate your employees about the nature and importance of our Constitution, our Bill of Rights, and our Tenth Amendment without endorsing a political party or a candidate. You can inform them about how a particular law or legislative proposal—taxes, regulations, etc.—will affect them and their families: its economic impact on the American economy as a whole, on your state's economy, on your industry's conditions and prospects, on your (and their) business or organization. Discuss and/or provide information on long-run as well as short-run consequences, prospects, and the like.

7. **Educate your employees.**

Tell them what the schools, colleges, universities, and mainstream media didn't tell them. Teach them about our Constitution, the importance of constitutionalism, the rule of law, the predictability of law, the economic impact of government taxes, regulations, changing policies, federalism, etc. Give them information, or make it available to them: audios, videos, literature. Have guest speakers address these topics.

Educating your members or employees does not have to mean that you are urging them to join one party or another or to vote for one candidate or another. You can teach them that politics is important because its results—policies, laws, the direction and quality of leadership, etc.— have practical consequences on their lives and their families' lives and well being. You can teach them that it is important to know what is going on in politics, to register to vote, to vote, and perhaps to get actively involved in politics. Stress the practical aspects of taxes, regulations, federal mandates, and the like. Emphasize the certain and probable consequences for your organization's members and their families (and distinguish between the two). Emphasize and distinguish between the short-run and long-run consequences of these things. Show them where federalism is pertinent and how the consequences would be different if states were allowed to govern their own internal affairs in regard to these matters.

Keep them informed about what is going on in politics. Keep this information joined to analysis of its practical consequences—short-run and long-run—for Americans in general, for the people of your state and locality, and for them personally.

8. Engage in more narrowly "political" activities.

Advertise to teach certain moral or political principles, to advocate the right side of issues; to motivate people to think and act politically. **Publicize** for the same purposes. **Lobby** your local, state, and/or federal government officials. **Donate** to worthy organizations, causes, individuals, and/or political candidates. Urge your members or employees to **register to vote—and vote—**and to encourage others (who will probably vote for good candidates) to register to vote and vote.

What Local Government Officials Can Do

1. Study!

2. **Teach others about federalism's importance, relevance, practicality, and necessity today.** Inform local voters about current issues of central government-state government relationships, national government threats to states' rights, etc. Be ever-vigilant for threats to state and local governments.

3. **Support** state and national government candidates and officials who are **advocates of federalism and the Tenth Amendment**; oppose those who aren't.

4. **Support resolutions**—pass your own local ones—**favoring federalism** and opposing centralism and unconstitutional laws, policies, and programs emanating from our national government.

What State Government Officials Can Do

1. **Study.**

2. **Teach.**

Teach your family, your friends, your constituents and others, informally and formally.

3. **Maintain a "clean" way of life**.

Don't let yourself do anything which could compromise your example, message, and stands on the issues.

4. **Act.**

Influence others privately. Influence others publicly—via your speeches, writing, website, etc.

Work with like-minded officials at your level in other states' governments: governors and lieutenant-governors, judges, attorneys general, legislators, etc.

Analyze federal legislation, federal courts' decisions, etc. for constitutionality or unconstitutionality, impact on federalism and states' rights, economic impact, impact on freedom.

Formulate legal defenses and offensives against unconstitutional federal legislation, executive orders, judicial decisions, etc.

Network with like-minded citizens—in your locality, state, the nation (the "federal government"), and other countries. Network with like-minded public officials—in your locality, state, the nation (the "federal government"), and other countries.

Network with sympathetic local, state, national, and international news and communications media.

Formulate legislation and work for its enactment: resolutions, nullification laws, censures of your state's representatives in the U.S. House and Senate, the President and Vice-President, U.S. Supreme Court judges, federal judges, heads of agencies, etc. If you are an attorney, lend your knowledge and talents to legal efforts to protect our laws and liberty against American usurpers and tyrants.

Speak out on principles and issues. State public office may not be "a bully pulpit" like the presidency, but it is a "pulpit." Make good use of your means of communication.

Enact appropriate laws according to the Constitution's principles. Enact laws to defend your state and its civil government against unconstitutional federal government intervention/intrusion.

Formulate, enact, and promulgate *resolutions*. Positively: proclaim the principles of the Tenth Amendment—and keep teaching and reminding the public. Negatively: complain about violations of the Tenth Amendment; censure the offenders; confront the offenders. Speak out against the violators and the violations. Remind the public, the President, and Congress, and the Federal courts of their oaths and duty to uphold—and obey—the Constitution. Resolutions are not empty gestures. Resolutions have a teaching function. They teach the public. They provide opportunities for you to teach the public via the news media, debates, etc. They encourage and give ideas to like-minded people in your state and in other states (and nations). They create a document which can be published, republished, studied, and applied to existing situations. They teach your representatives in our national government that they can expect to suffer political consequences if they violate their oaths of office, cooperate in enacting or enforcing unconstitutional, state-authority and liberty-damaging laws, policies, decisions, and the like.

Enact nullification laws: laws rendering unconstitutional "federal" laws without authority and inoperative in your state. Nullification is a form of interposition—and therefore is a means of protecting the people of your state (and by extension, if other states are persuaded to join you, the people of the whole United States), their liberty and wellbeing against unjust and unconstitutional laws promulgated by the central government.

Nullification is constitutional. Remember: the Constitution does not state that the central government or any of its offices or institutions is the final interpreter of the constitutionality of any law. The Constitution does not state that **any** institution of our complex federal system is the final interpreter of constitutionality. Our Constitution gives every official in our governmental system the responsibility of interpreting the constitutionality of every law enacted and enforced by every governmental jurisdiction in our system. Not local governments and officials, nor state governments and officials, nor the national or central government and its officials are authorized by our Constitution to violate the Constitution. All and each of these officials must understand the meaning of our Constitution in order to distinguish between what is constitutional and what is not in order to uphold the Constitution which they swear or affirm they will do when they take their oath of office.

It is important to note also that our Constitution implies that "we the people of the United States"—who elect, directly or indirectly, all the officials who make, enforce, and/or adjudicate the laws of our various civil governments—have a duty to know the meaning of our Constitution and its various provisions. We do not have to take an oath (or make an affirmation) to do this, but the ultimate responsibility for the people whom we choose to run our civil governments is ours. They are all our representatives—at the local, state, or national level. If we do not understand our Constitution or care about it, we cannot realistically expect to elect representatives who will continue to honor and obey it. Though all of our elected representatives in civil government are responsible to uphold our Constitution, the ultimate responsibility for upholding our Constitution is ours.

The most important institution in the complex system of civil government bequeathed to us in our Constitution is the government of each state. Local governments are important because they are intended to handle most of the area of our lives which civil government is authorized to govern, they are the closest to us and so the easiest for us to influence, and they are training and proving grounds for higher office. The central or national government is, of course, important, largely for national security/defense reasons, and partly because it was designed with a system of separation of powers and accompanying checks and balances to protect liberty and justice by preventing any one branch of our national government from usurping and accumulating power at the expense of the other two branches of our central government. But, as Madison said so famously and well in Federalist No. 51, separation of powers in our national government is only half of the story of the design of our system of civil government for protecting justice and liberty. The state governments—or rather the system of separation of powers with accompanying checks and balances between our national or central government and our state governments—are the other half of the story of the design of our system of civil government for protecting justice and liberty. Federalism, said Madison in Federalist No. 51, provides "a double security to the rights of the people" by means of its system of separation of powers and checks and balances between our central government and our state governments.

The "Supremacy Clause" (Article VI, Paragraph 2) does not make any and every law enacted by Congress the supreme law of the land. It only makes laws made "in pursuance" of the Constitution the supreme law of the land. Laws not made in pursuance of the Constitution cannot be the supreme law of the land: so the states are not bound by any constitutional authority to obey such laws. Moreover, according to the plain meaning of the Supremacy Clause the states are certainly justified in opposing, resisting, and nullifying such unconstitutional laws. Without being authorized to take such actions, the states would be powerless to resist usurpation of their powers, centralization of power, and arbitrary rule by our central government, and, thus, our federalism would be the mere "paper barrier"—a totally ineffective device for securing liberty—which Madison complained against in Federalist No.

51.

Nullification, therefore, is obviously constitutional. If nullification were not constitutional, the Constitution would have created a centralized government, not a federal one, for the state governments would not be justified in doing anything to oppose unconstitutional "federal" laws except try to influence the elections of congressmen, senators, and presidents, and the appointment of federal and U.S. Supreme Court "justices."

Repeal the Seventeenth Amendment: The original intention of the framers and ratifiers of our Constitution was that the legislature of each state would elect the U.S. senators from that state. True, a state's legislature could provide that its U.S. senators would be selected in another manner, but until the adoption of the Seventeenth Amendment in 1913 U.S. senators were chosen by their state's legislature. This meant that senators were chosen by a body composed of people who are better judges of character and ability, more knowledgeable about politics, better informed about governmental and political issues than the average voter in their state. This gave each state's legislature a direct check against the central government by its choice of senators. State government officials' self-interest was supposed to motivate them to check against central government usurpations. Miseducation, the influence of modern leftist ideologies, and avarice (specifically the desire to live at other people's expense) have worked to lead many state government officials to actively promote, or at least acquiesce in, unconstitutional federal government laws, decisions, programs, and actions. Work to reverse these things!

What Federal Government Officials Can Do

1. **Study!**

2. **Teach.**

Teach individuals, groups, local citizens in general, your constituents, and all those whom your office enables you to influence. Your office is a "pulpit." Preach!

3. **Act.**

Master the rules of your institution. Master the workings of your institution. Master the workings of the federal government. Use this knowledge to defend and advance constitutionalism, federalism, and liberty.

Influence others as much as you can: privately and publicly.

Network: with like-minded citizens, like-minded intellectuals, like-minded public officials in your locality, state, nation, and other countries. Share information, ideas, strategies, and tactics. Work together; provide mutual support.

Formulate, enact, promulgate, and publicize resolutions.

Enact appropriate laws: Strict construction should be the rule. Otherwise we have at least "loose construction" and at most "non-interpretivism"—which means more or less rapid movement away from constitutionalism, limited government, federalism, and liberty.

Keep the "federal government" in its legitimate constitutional sphere: support the Enumerated Powers Act which Rep. John Shadegg (R., Arizona) has been introducing in the House each year for the past few years. This bill states that each bill introduced in Congress must specify in exactly what place the Constitution authorizes Congress to exercise the powers which the bill seeks to have Congress exercise. If Congress would stick to the enumerated powers of our Constitution— and make the President, the Supreme Court, and the Federal courts do so as well—we would have constitutional government and federalism and freedom would be protected. Question both potential and actual officeholders in the House of Representatives and the Senate about their knowledge of this bill and their support for it. Educate those who are ignorant of it. Support those who support it. Work against those who do not support it or who reject it.

Keeping the "federal government"in its legitimate constitutional sphere also requires **keeping the President in his constitutional sphere of authority**. The president has no legislative authority in our constitutional system of government. Congress needs to keep close tabs on presidents' executive orders—making sure that no president uses them to usurp the lawmaking power of Congress or of the state's legislatures. Nor should Congress permit the President to use executive orders to create "emergency" powers not authorized by our Constitution—particularly powers giving himself, or any official or combination of officials in the Executive branch the equivalent of dictatorial powers over Americans, or over sectors of American life such as the economy, or encroaching on the states' authority.

Keeping the President in his constitutional sphere of authority must also include preventing the President from using his power of appointment to set up the equivalent of a government within the government. Our current president has come close to doing this through his appointment of "czars" (Czars!) over all sorts of things. Presidential ambitions to the contrary not withstanding, our Constitution has no provision permitting the appointment of "czars" over anything. The fact that Ronald Reagan appointed a czar or two does not justify the appointment of any such officials. Regardless of the party or political philosophy of any president, none should be permitted to create such new offices unheard of in our Constitution. It should give us pause that a classic method of effecting a coup d'état involves the creation of a state within a state. Addition of an amendment to our Constitution to prevent this should not be needed, for our Constitution is and was intended to be an expressed-powers document. But given the perversity of human nature and the power of modern ideologies, an amendment is probably needed to make it explicitly and unmistakably clear that presidents may not invent new offices. At the very least, Congress, or the Senate, must not fail to exercise oversight regarding such offices and appointments—and the beliefs and character of the characters appointed to them. Work to make sure these things are done.

Reining in the "federal government" must also include, at a minimum, **reining in the federal bureaucracy**. All federal bureaucracies which are not authorized by our Constitution (not by the judicial chicanery of U.S. Supreme Court majorities!) should be abolished. Failing this, all federal bureaucracies (including those which are inconsistent with the original intentions of our Constitution and the amendments to it) should be required to function according to constitutional criteria— and so prohibited from legislating via bureaucratic regulations which have the force of law. Congress must exercise its responsibility to maintain oversight over the doings of federal bureaucracies and bureaucrats.

Rein in the Federal courts and the Supreme Court. Our Federal courts and Supreme Court have made themselves constitutional conventions in continuous session and judicial tyrants. Judges whose judicial philosophy is inconsistent with constitutionalism, the rule of law, and federalism should not be appointed in the first place, for their judicial philosophy requires them (or at least inclines them) to violate their oath of office and the provisions and intentions of our Constitution. Such a judicial or legal philosophy also threatens justice and our liberty. Judges and "justices" who act like tyrants deserve to be impeached and removed from office. Article III of our Constitution gives Congress authority over these courts. Use Article III—along with the power of the House to impeach and the Senate to remove from office—to rein in the federal courts and the Supreme Court.

Pay close attention to the legal philosophy, judicial philosophy, and honesty of presidential, senatorial, and congressional candidates as well as of nominees for Attorney General and judicial positions. Presidents appoint Federal judges and Supreme Court judges. Senators confirm them or reject them. Congressmen can help impeach Federal judges and other unsuitable Federal officials. Senators can help convict them and remove them from office. Legal philosophy and judicial philosophy matter! You have sworn to support our Constitution. You are not doing so if you acquiesce in the appointment or election of people whose legal philosophy and judicial philosophy are antagonistic to our Constitution, the rule of law, and our Tenth Amendment. And the rule of law is the rule of fixed, known principles of law; it is **not** the rule of laws merely enacted by those who are authorized to make laws—nor of those who falsely claim the authority to make laws. The rule of law is not a mere process: it has a content. Removal from office should be the rapid reward of all those who violate the rule of law, and in particular the rule of our fundamental law, our Constitution.

Conclusion

Our Tenth Amendment is, and was intended to be, a bulwark of our liberty. But a bulwark was not intended to function by itself nor does it function alone. A bulwark must be manned: it must be defended if what it is designed to protect is to be protected. Our Tenth Amendment was meant to protect federalism as a way of preserving and protecting state self-government, justice, and liberty. It must be understood, honored, and applied to current situations if we are to achieve its objectives.

All of our states' authority and legal rights have long been under attack. Today they are under assault as never before. The principle of federalism has been attacked in theory: it has been slandered, maligned, and misrepresented. It has been attacked in practice: it has not been taught; it has been propagandized against; it has been subverted by modern man-centered political ideologies; it has been assaulted by unconstitutional actions by presidents, unconstitutional laws enacted by Congress, and unconstitutional decisions by U.S. Supreme Court majorities. Those who ought to have been its defenders have been seduced by "Federal money," and the perquisites of "higher" office in our central government—all the temptations of power.

But through it all, our Tenth Amendment has remained there for all to see, for all to contemplate, for all to value. It remains the bulwark of our liberty. It remains a powerful means of defending our liberty. It remains to be manned, and to be used to defend our freedom.

I'm thankful there are defenders of liberty today who understand the importance of our Tenth Amendment and the federalism it protects to the recovery, protection, and future enjoyment of our liberty. Most of these are private citizens, but many are officials in our state and local governments, or candidates for office in these governments. Some of them are officials in, or candidates for office in our national government. They are manning the bulwark. If we love liberty and want to secure it for all Americans, we must join them.

Our Tenth Amendment is a gateway to liberty. A gateway provides access, but it is also a means of defense. A gateway, like a bulwark, must be well-designed and constructed with precision in order to be effective. It must also be well-maintained and vigilantly guarded against those who would assault it. Our Tenth Amendment is a key gateway to liberty because it is also a key means—a decisive constitutional power—for defending our freedom. It was well-designed and well-constructed by our earliest American statesmen, but it has not been well-maintained, and it has long been under attack. We need to wake up, arise, maintain it, defend it, and apply it!

Appendix

BOOK REVIEW:

33 Questions About American History You're Not Supposed to Ask

by Thomas E. Woods, Jr.

We have acquiesced to the subversion of our freedom largely because we have believed carefully fashioned myths about our history. Leftist historians, politicians, and publicists have fabricated such myths in order to exalt left-wing politicians, enshrine those politicians' pseudo-legal and institutional innovations, and advance the cause of statism, arbitrary government, and socialism. Thomas E. Woods, Jr. has devoted much of his academic life to discovering the truth about these myths, setting the record straight, and teaching us how the truth which these myths obscure speaks against interventionism and socialism and in defense of constitutional government and freedom.

In *33 Questions About American History You're Not Supposed to Ask*, Prof. Woods explodes a few conservative and many "liberal" and/ or "progressive" myths about our economic, social, legal, and constitutional (or, more accurately, unconstitutional) history. He gives us valuable lessons about American economic history which show the connection between theory and practice and the divergent practical consequences of bad and good economic theories. Interventionist, socialist, and Marxist economic theories undergird the popular lies/ myths about our economic history and provide arguments for unconstitutional, socialistic central government policies. Sound (Austrian, free market) economic thinking explains the economic realities and consequences which the myths hide, destroys the pseudo-historical arguments upon which the myths are based, and explains why limited, constitutional government is morally and practically far superior to the perversions of our Constitution done in the service of interventionism and socialism.

Perhaps the most important aspect of Dr. Woods's work—especially from the perspective of the importance of our Tenth Amendment—is his historical, moral, legal, and practical defense of the original intentions of our Constitution's framers and ratifiers. Those whose arguments he destroys are "living Constitution" propagandists and jurists, advocates of the "Imperial Presidency," such as Theodore Roosevelt, and the scholarly and judicial deceivers and "activists" who have perverted the Commerce Clause, the General Welfare Clause, and the Necessary and Proper Clause (the "Elastic Clause") to subvert and overturn those original intentions and the limited, constitutional, federal government, economic freedom, and liberty which the framers and ratifiers intended us to have and maintain.

Fundamental to our maintenance of that limited, constitutional government, economic freedom, and liberty is an understanding of the importance of the states' rights which Thomas Jefferson is most famous for espousing and which the Tenth Amendment was meant to protect. Our Constitution's principle of federalism and its corollary of states' rights, Woods notes, are basic to the Western tradition of liberty and the protection of liberty against centralism by means of a traditional multiplicity of institutions which stood between the individual and power-hungry (or power-mad) rulers of a central government. The idea of divided power (separation of powers) which opposes centralism and arbitrary government had its origin in medieval Europe. Prof. Woods rightly emphasizes the restatement of the principles of federalism, constitutionalism, and states' rights in "the Principles of '98" (1798), the great constitutional statements of the Virginia Resolves and the Kentucky Resolves, noting that these principles "raise timeless questions" about liberty (pp. 36-37). The so-called "Civil War," he notes, was fought because one side's political, legal, and constitutional philosophy championed the traditional multiplicity of institutions and the other side's philosophy championed centralism. It was precisely liberty which our Tenth Amendment was meant to protect and to enable us to preserve.

33 Questions is about more than American history, economics, constitutional interpretation, law, social policy, and foreign policy. It is about education, publishing, and the shaping of the public's mind. Its dominant themes are knowledge, truth, and freedom. We must have knowledge if we desire to destroy the craftily-fashioned myths which would enslave us to unlimited, arbitrary government or if we desire to comprehend the truth of our history and the principles of our constitutional system. Truth is necessary to justice, social harmony, economic liberty, and limited, constitutional government, which things are essential to freedom.

33 Questions gives us the answers we need to know to combat sloppy thinking, prolonged deceit, and the popular delusions which have been used to persuade us to discard our liberty for the false security which our central government claims to be able (and is all-too willing) to provide. It is an essential resource for students, teachers, writers, and all who would know the truth about our history. It is an important weapon for all who would work to defend and restore our freedom.

Selected Bibliography

Adams, Willi Paul. *The First American Constitutions: Republican Ideology and the Making of the State Constitutions in the Revolutionary Era* (Chapel Hill: University of North Carolina Press, 1980).

Berger, Raoul. *Federalism: The Founders' Design* (Norman and London: University of Oklahoma Press, 1987).

Bork, Robert H. *The Tempting of America: The Political Seduction of the Law* (New York: The Free Press, 1990).

Bradford, M.E. *A Better Guide Than Reason: Studies in the American Revolution* (LaSalle, Illinois: Sherwood Sugden and Co., 1979).

_____. *Original Intentions: On the Making and Ratification of the United States Constitution* (Athens and London: The University of Georgia Press, 1993).

_____. *The Reactionary Imperative; Essays Literary and Political* (Peru, Illinois: Sherwood Sugden and Co., 1979).

Dietze, Gottfried. *America's Political Dilemma: From Limited to Unlimited Democracy* (Baltimore: Johns Hopkins Press, 1968).

Dornan, Robert K. and Csaba Vedlik, Jr. *Judicial Supremacy: The Supreme Court on Trial* (Plymouth, Massachusetts: Plymouth Rock Foundation, [1980] 1986).

Eidelberg, Paul. *A Discourse on Statesmanship: The Design and Transformation of the American Polity* (Urbana: University of Illinois Press, 1974).

_____. *The Philosophy of the American Constitution; A Reinterpretation of the Intentions of the Founding Fathers* (New York: The Free Press, 1968).

Eidsmoe, John. *Christianity and the Constitution: The Faith of Our Founding Fathers* (Grand Rapids: Mott Media, 1987).

Elliot, Jonathan, ed. *The Debates in the Several State Conventions on the Adoption of the Federal Constitution*, 5 Vols. (Published in various editions; short title, *Elliot's Debates*.)

Evans, M. Stanton. "The States and the Constitution," *The Intercollegiate Review*, 2, Number 3 (November-December, 1965), 176-199.

273

Farrand, Max. *The Records of the Federal Convention of 1787* (New Haven and London: Yale University Press, [1911] 1966).

Goldwin, Robert A., ed. *A Nation of States; Essays on the American Federal System* (Chicago: Rand McNally and Co., 1963).

Hallowell, John H. *Main Currents in Modern Political Thought* (New York: Holt, Rinehart and Winston, [1950] 1963).

Hamilton, Alexander, James Madison, and John Jay. *The Federalist; A Commentary on the Constitution of the United States; Being a Collection of Essays Written in Support of the Constitution agreed upon September 17, 1787, by the Federal Convention* (in some editions this is titled *The Federalist Papers*).

Higgins, Thomas J., S.J. *Judicial Rreview Unmasked* (West Hanover, Massachusetts: The Christopher Publishing House, 1981).

Higgs, Robert. *Crisis and Leviathan; Critical Episodes in the Growth of American Government* New York and Oxford: Oxford University Press, 1987).

Jensen, Merrill. *The Articles of Confederation* (Madison: University of Wisconsin Press, 1940).

Jones, Archie P. *Christianity and Our State Constitutions, Declarations, and Bills of Rights, Parts I and II* (Marlborough, New Hampshire: Plymouth Rock Foundation, 1993).

Kenyon, Cecelia M., ed. *The Antifederalists* (Indianapolis: The Bobbs-Merrill Co., 1966).

Kirk, Russell. *The Roots of American Order* (La Salle, Illinois: Open Court, (1978).

McDowell, Gary L. *The Constitution and Contemporary Constitutional Theory* (Cumberland, Virginia: Center for Judicial Studies, 1985).

Miller, Perry. *The Life of the Mind in America; From the Revolution to the Civil War* (New York: Harcourt, Brace and World, 1965).

Morley, Felix. *Freedom and Federalism* (Chicago: Henry Regnery Company, 1959).

Morris, B. F. *The Christian Life and Character of the Civil Institutions of the United States* (Powder Springs, Georgia: American Vision, [1864] 2007).

Sandoz, Ellis. *A Government of Laws: Political Theory, Religion, and the American Founding* (Baton Rouge and London: Louisiana State University Press, 1990).

Singer, C. Gregg. *A Theological Interpretation of American History* (Philipsburg, New Jersey: Presbyterian and Reformed Publishing Co., [1964] 1982).

_____. *From Rationalism to Irrationality; The Decline of the Western Mind from the Renaissance to the Present* (Phillipsburg, New Jersey: Presbyterian and Reformed Publishing Co., 1979).

St. John, Jeffrey. *Forge of Union, Anvil of Liberty: A Correspondent's Report on the First Federal Elections, the First Federal Congress, and the Bill of Rights* (Ottawa, Illinois: Jameson Books Inc., 1992).

Storing, Herbert J., ed. *The Complete Anti-Federalist*, 7 Vols. (Chicago: University of Chicago Press, 1981).

Rossum, Ralph. *Congressional Control of the Judiciary: The Article III Option* (Cumberland, Virginia: Center for Judicial Studies, 1988).

Rutland, Robert Allen. *The Birth of the Bill of Rights 1776-1791* (New York: Collier Books, 1962).

Wines, E.C. *Commentaries on the Laws of the Ancient Hebrews; with an Introductory Essay on Civil Society and Government* (Powder Springs, Georgia: American Vision, [1853] 2009).

Woods, Thomas E., Jr. and Kevin R. C. Gutzman. *Who Killed the Constitution?: The Fate of American Liberty from World War I to George W. Bush* (New York: Crown Forum, 2008).

Woods, Thomas E., Jr. *33 Questions About American History You're Not Supposed to Ask* (New York, New York: Crown Forum, 2007).

Topical Index

A

B

C

D

E

F

G

H

I

J

K

L

M

R

W

Y